Multilingualism in the British Isles 2 Africa, the Middle East and Asia

edited by
Safder Alladina
Viv Edwards

LONGMAN
LONDON AND NEW YORK

Longman Group UK Limited,
Longman House, Burnt Mill, Harlow,
Essex CM20 2JE, England
and Associated Companies throughout the world.

Published in the United States of America
by Longman Inc., New York

© Longman Group UK Limited 1991

First published 1991

British Library Cataloguing in Publication Data
Multilingualism in the British Isles. – (Longman linguistics
Library).
2: Africa, Asia and the Middle East
1. Great Britain. Languages
I. Alladina, Safder II. Edwards, Viv
409′.41

ISBN 0-582-06366-3 CSD
ISBN 0-582-06365-5 PPR

Library of Congress Cataloging-in-Publication Data
Multilingualism in the British Isles/edited by Safder Alladina, Viv
Edwards.
p.   cm. – (Longman linguistics library)
Includes bibliographical references.
Contents: v. 1. The older mother tongues and Europe – v.
2. Africa, Asia, and the Middle East.
ISBN 0-582-01964-8 (v. 1). – ISBN 0-582-01963-X (pbk .: v. 1). –
ISBN 0-582-06366-3 (v. 2). – ISBN 0-582-06365-5 (pbk .: v. 2)
1. Multilingualism.   I. Alladina, Safder, 1943– .   II. Edwards,
Viv. III. Series.
P115.M8   1990
306.4′4′0941 – dc20   89–13672
CIP

Produced by Longman Singapore Publishers (Pte) Ltd.
Printed in Singapore

LONGMAN LINGUISTICS LIBRARY

MULTILINGUALISM IN THE BRITISH ISLES

Contents

Foreword

It was found in the Language Census of 1987 that there were 172 different languages spoken by children in Inner London Education Authority Schools. The reaction in many quarters was stunned disbelief. One British educationalist told me that England has become a third world country. After believing in the supremacy of English as the universal language, it was difficult to acknowledge that the UK was now one of the great immigrant nations of the modern world. It was also hard to see that the current plurality is based on a continuity of heritage.

The arrogance of colonialism led many to believe that English was the only language needed by the world and that all other languages were somehow inferior to it. This was a view reflected at home as well as abroad. Having denounced the three indigenous languages (Gaelic, Irish and Welsh) as less than equal, it is not at all surprising that the languages of the Blacks, Browns and Yellows would be considered deficient and unfit for educational attention.

The multicultural debate in the UK, unfortunately, has since then got bogged down in the spurious controversy between multicultural and antiracist education. Instead of discussing cultural variation and the cultural interaction between shared values and culture-specific values, this debate has been lost in the metalanguage of models and the muddles they have created.

The descriptions of different speech communities in this volume for the first time draws attention to the cultural renewals taking place within the value frame of each community. For the first time there is an indication of the formation of a cultural mosaic through structural incorporation of cultural elements from different ethnic groups. The cultural exchange across cultures can only lead to an overarching framework of values, which can give proper justification to a multilingual and pluricultural Britain.

This, however, has to be seen in the context of the prevailing monolingual view of the world in Britain. There is a curious contradiction in the approach to bilingualism. On the one hand, it is considered a quantum leap signifying acquisition of two languages. On the other it is seen as a threat to English. No wonder that the Swann Report 'Education for All' (1985) rejected the twin ideas of bilingual education and mother-tongue maintenance as a single educational aim. This ambivalence has resulted in favouring selective élite bilingualism, while resisting bilingualism for minority language speakers.

The most forceful monomodel is provided by the US, despite its cultural variation. Fishman characterises the US Bilingual Education Act as primarily an Act for Anglification of non-English speakers, an act against bilingualism.[1] The US provides for wholly inadequate bilingual education for speakers of Spanish and some other migrant language speakers without hiding its bias for Anglicization and the elimination of conditions favouring bilingualism. Britain, which closely follows the footsteps of the US in such matters, is also intolerant of minority languages and works towards deculturalisation of these groups and their eventual Anglicization.

Language use has serious educational consequences. There is evidence that a dominant language speaker studying through either a dominant or minority language medium does well in both. There is evidence too that wherever second or foreign language education is securely based on mother-tongue education the children do well in both. Substitution of the mother tongue for a second/foreign language is debilitating and creates *anomie*, alienation and frustration. In face of such evidence, usurpation of the language of minorities and migrants creates an unequal society. The British have traditionally been known for their policy of divide and rule. They have followed a policy of exclusion at home which does not embrace but rejects, plays one side against the other, group against group, region against region. The outsider, the immigrant and the oppressed have been perpetually marked and condemned, first for not learning English, second for not learning the right kind of English.

[1]Fishman, J. (1989) *Language and Ethnicity in Minority Socio-Linguistic Perspective*. Multilingual Matters, 405.

As the identity of the various oppressed groups is threatened, identity assertion movements ensue. These identities are built around languages, religions, ethnicities, regions and similar factors. When two or more such factors are combined, forming ethnolinguistic or ethnoreligious groups or regions, then sometimes these movements are directed towards recognition of specific regions or areas of such concentration, or consolidation of language leading to language maintenance. Hugo Baetens Beardsmore shows how a combination of political process, education and language has arrested massive language shift in Brussels.[2] In the UK itself the Irish ethnic movement thrives on a combination of nationalism, religion and language. Sometimes a home language is given up in order to maintain a distinctive identity. The Vietnamese Chinese in the UK giving up their language in favour of Cantonese is a case in point.

Identities are so apportioned between the majorities and minorities in the UK that the majority has no mother tongue. 'Mother tongue' refers to minority languages. The majority has no one ethnicity: ethnic language refers to minority and migrant languages. The majority is not a community: community language refers to minority and migrant languages. Ethnicity, which in the literature is variously expressed as an assertion of cultures, communal upsurges, revival of religions, voices and movements of marginalised peoples, regions and nationalities, hurts the power elites. It represents the affirmation of diversity, of indigenous identity, of organic as against televised or museumised cultures or classicised cultures as found in ancient texts. At a time when only the commercial value of language is emphasised it is no wonder that ethnicity should be condemned, its diverse facets appearing to be in opposition to one another.

In England none of the minority languages have the ethnolinguistic vitality to present a threat to the omnipotence of English. And yet English feels threatened and the managers of education lack the enthusiasm to provide educational support to these minority languages alongside English. As Smolicz rightly observes, 'frequently it is the country's dominant language which represents the majority's core, although its attempted imposition on others may be camouflaged under the guise of concern for the "life chances" of minority children, the need to preserve the

---

[2] Beardsmore, H. B. (1989, forthcoming) *The Evolution and current status of Brussels as a Bilingual City.*

cohesion of the State, conceived in a way which reflects the
majority's own cores and cultural predilections'.[3]
The minority's linguistic tenacity and the majority's tolerance
of linguistic pluralism determines the maintenance of minority
language and cultures. Britain is on the crossroads. It can take
an isolationist stance in relation to its internal cultural environment. It can create a resilient society by trusting its citizens to be
British not only in political but in cultural terms. The first road
will mean severing dialogue with the many heritages which have
made the country fertile. The second road would be working
together with cultural harmony for the betterment of the country.
Sharing and participation would ensure not only political but cultural democracy. The choice is between mediocrity and creativity.

DEBI PRASANNA PATTANAYAK

---

[3]Smolicz, J. J. (1989 forthcoming) *Language Core, values in Australia:
Some Polish, Welsh and Indian minority experiences.*

Acknowledgements

This book is the end point of a long and often very exciting process. In the attempt to chart the dimensions of linguistic diversity in the British Isles, we have often needed to look beyond the universities, polytechnics and colleges of higher education which are the normal locations for academic writers. One reason for extending the search is the racism which is an everyday reality for large numbers of British people. There is ample evidence, for instance, of the ways in which Black people are systematically denied access to employment in all sections of the job market and there is no evidence that higher education is an exception to this general rule. Another reason is the low priority which has been given in British universities to languages, in general, and non-European languages, in particular. We have therefore needed to cast our net much further afield to locate potential contributors to this volume. Our thanks are due to all those who have helped us in a fascinating exercise in networking.

We would also like to thank those who have offered information, helped us to develop our own thinking and commented on various aspects of the book. We are particularly grateful to Jagiro Goodwin, D. P. Pattanayak, Ryte Piskowyk, S. Thalib, Aleksas Vilkinskas and students past and present in the Department of Applied Linguistics at Birkbeck College, University of London.

Finally, we would like to acknowledge the following for permission to reproduce material: Colin Baker and Multilingual Matters Ltd for the map depicting the distribution of Welsh speakers in Volume 1, Chapter 6 from *Aspects of Bilingualism in Wales* (Multilingual Matters, 1985: 12); For Volume 2, figures 2.2 and 3.2, The Office of Population Censuses and Surveys for data from Table 51, *National Report (Part 2) Great Britain, Census*

1981 (HMSO, 1983); For the map in Volume 1, Chapter 4, Mouton de Gruyter for an adaptation of a map from Commins, P. (1988) 'Socioeconomic development and language maintenance in the Gaeltacht' *International Journal of the Sociology of Language*, 70; For a selection of Chinese characters (Volume 2, Figure 13.3), the selection is reprinted from *Speaking of Chinese* by Raymond Chang and Margaret Scrogin Chang, by permission of W.W. Norton & Company, Inc. Copyright © 1978 by W.W. Norton & Company, Inc.

The bringing together of thirty-one different writers to describe the thirty-three different communities covered in the two-volume sequence has been a highly complex task. It has sometimes involved extremely difficult editorial decisions. It has certainly required a great deal of patience, a spirit of compromise and considerable generosity on the part of all concerned. We hope that both the contributors and the wider readership for this volume and its companion will be satisfied with the end product.

Safder Alladina
Viv Edwards

Chapter 1

Many people, many tongues: Babel and beyond

It is a well-established tenet of folk linguistics that multilingualism is a bad thing and that for efficient human communication we need to work towards a monolingual norm. Yet this is contrary to what history tells us. For many centuries, extensive contact and co-operation between the speakers of different languages has been the norm. We know, for instance, of the interaction in various periods of world history between the Chinese, South Asian, Middle Eastern, African, Greek and Roman civilizations. Within South Asia, there is no shortage of evidence to show that the Gujjars from north India built temples in the south and that builders from south India helped to construct the Sun Temple at Konarka in the north (Pattanayak 1987). In a similar vein, the building of the Taj Mahal drew upon the skills of artisans from all over south Asia and beyond. In the European context, the Dark Ages can be equated with a period of introverted mono-lingualism and the Renaissance as a period of outward going and necessarily multilingual thirst for knowledge.

Developments in the last quarter of the twentieth century – the phenomenal leaps that have been made in world travel and com-munication, advances in print technology, translation and language generation – should lead us seriously to challenge monolingual prejudice. The legacy of negative attitudes towards multilingualism, however, lives on. Pattanayak (1985, 1987), for instance, analyses the attitudes of a range of modern scholars: recent work in this area has equated linguistic diversity with linguistic and economic backwardness; presented a causal relationship between multilingualism and low levels of Gross National Product (GNP) or economic underdevelopment; advo-cated that a common language would make for a more unified

and cohesive society; and asserted that monolingualism is a necessary precondition for modernism. It has also been claimed that
complete equality of status is possible only in countries that have
one or at the most three languages and that, in a modern society,
two languages are a nuisance, three languages are uneconomic
and many languages are absurd. In reply, Pattanayak (1987) argues that in the multilingual reality, many languages are a fact of
existence, any restriction in the choice of language is a nuisance,
and one language is not only uneconomic but absurd. For genuine
equality of opportunity and participation in democracies, people's
right to use and maintain their mother language is a prerequisite.

Thus the folk wisdom regarding multilingualism has established
itself in the edifices of academe in spite of the fact that, in this
era of technology, many modern and 'economically advanced'
societies like the Netherlands, Norway, Sweden and Japan
operate very successfully using an international language like
English while continuing to use their mother tongue. It would
seem that mother tongue maintenance only becomes an issue
when language groups that do not hold political and economic
power are under discussion.

A history of intolerance

Bilingualism has been an important fact of life for many sections
of the population throughout the history of the British Isles. Successive movements of European peoples have contributed to the
development of British culture throughout the centuries, each
group interacting with the ones who went before and contributing
to the process of cultural and linguistic change. The English
language today is a living testimony to this process. The Angles,
the Saxons, the Vikings and the Normans all helped to shape its
development and continue to exert an influence on its present
form. It is possible to show, for instance, that the ancient
divisions of the Anglo-Saxon kingdoms correspond closely to the
regional dialects of twentieth-century English some 900 years
after the demise of the monarchies themselves.

The gradual imposition of English has been a story of power
struggles and resistance. Political and economic forces began to
make inroads on the Celtic languages as early as the eleventh
century, although nineteenth and twentieth-century phenomena
such as industrialization and economic restructuring have considerably accelerated the process. The fact that small but
significant minorities of Welsh and Scots and Irish Gaelic
speakers continue against all odds to assert their right to use their

mother tongues is a powerful reminder of the potent symbolism of language in ethnic identity. Within the education system, however, the policy has been to replace the language of the home with standard English. The 1847 Report of the Church Commissioners on schools in Wales, for instance, viciously attacked the Welsh language on the grounds that it isolated 'the masses' from the 'upper portions of society', denied its speakers access to the top of the social scale and kept them 'under the hatches'. In the classroom there were cruel attempts to humiliate Welsh speakers by making anyone heard using the language wear a wooden halter known as the 'Welsh not'. The humiliation of having to wear the halter was compounded by the pressure to 'grass' on classmates, since the last person wearing the not at the end of the day was subjected to corporal punishment.

However, the targets for the Establishment throughout this period were not simply bilingual speakers on the Celtic fringes but other linguistic varieties at odds with what was seen as the norm. Speakers of regional dialects were also subjected to a range of unpleasant tactics, the effect of which was to leave no doubt as to the desirability of standard English. As recently as 1920 there were reports of Lancashire teachers who were deliberately sent out into the school yard at playtime 'to detect lapses of speech among children when amusing themselves outside buildings' (Hollingworth 1977). The 1921 Newbolt Report on the teaching of English in England reflects this preoccupation with the unworthiness of dialect, heaping opprobrium on children whose speech is 'disfigured by vulgarisms'. Seventeen years later, the 1938 Spens Report talks in similar terms of the 'slovenly, ungrammatical and often incomprehensible' nature of the English 'of common usage'.

The work of the sociologist Basil Bernstein in the 1960s (see, for instance, Bernstein 1973) did much to perpetuate these longstanding prejudices. He postulated two polar codes – the elaborated code and the restricted code and argued that the different distribution of these codes might account for the evidence that working-class children tend to underperform at all stages of education. Although Bernstein has strenuously denied that this was ever his intention, his work was widely interpreted as suggesting that the standard language could be equated with the elaborated code and non-standard dialects with the restricted code.

Bernstein's work has been severely criticized on many different fronts. It has been suggested, for instance, that his theory of language codes is both untestable and unrelated to linguistic evidence. He has also been severely taken to task for failing to take situational factors into account. More recently evidence has emerged from the work of writers like Tizard and Hughes (1984) and Wells (1987) that the main differences in language use occur not between working and middle-class children but between school and home. None the less, the legacy of Bernstein lives on. The highly influential Bullock Report, published in 1975, advocates that health visitors should urge parents to 'bathe their children in language'. In 1980, a project launched in the Lady-wood area of Birmingham tried to put this policy into practice. Speech therapists, health visitors and social workers made contact with mothers in neighbourhood supermarkets and distributed their children with 'Mum talk to me' stickers (Edwards 1983.)

Since Bullock, notions of criticism and rejection have – on a policy level, at least – been replaced with the notion of appropriateness. The 1981 Rampton Report, for instance, argues that the imaginative and creative use of a child's home language helps in developing awareness of different forms of language including standard English – and their appropriateness for different situations. This theme is further developed in the Cox Report (DES and Welsh Office 1988). The extent to which official policy is actually implemented in many schools, however, remains an open question. Children's views on dialect collected as part of the Survey of British Dialect Grammar (Edwards and Cheshire 1989) included the following comment from a fourth-year secondary-school child in Rotherham:

> Teachers always correct the way I speak and also the way I write. They correct the way I write more than anything. When I write a story and include talking, I write it how I would speak. But sometimes teachers cross it out and put in how they would talk. I don't think they should do that. They should leave it as it is.

This comment underlines the naïvety of attempts to modify children's speech through formal education. It has been estimated that less than 10 per cent of the population speak standard English, and, of these, perhaps as few as 3 per cent speak standard English with the Received Pronunciation traditionally associated with the public schools or broadcasting (Hughes and Trudgill 1978). The considerable pressures for linguistic conformity exerted by schools and the job market beyond would therefore seem to be singularly unsuccessful in achieving their aim. The evidence points to little change between the numbers of speakers of non-standard dialects of English leaving school at the end of compulsory schooling and the numbers who embarked on the process some eleven years earlier. Those who wish to change children's speech, either by eradicating the non-standard dialect or by extending their repertoire to include standard English, have usually been guilty of underestimating the potency of language as a symbol of identity.

New horizons

Any attempt to understand reactions to bilingualism in recent years thus needs to take into account this history of linguistic intolerance towards both speakers of Celtic languages and, in a broader context, regional dialects of English. It is also important to take into account the ways in which intolerance of this kind has tended to make linguistic diversity of all kinds more or less invisible. To take an extreme example, most British people are completely ignorant of the nature of British Sign Language (BSL), the normal language of interaction of an important section of the deaf community in Britain. Linguists have now shown that BSL is as complex and flexible as any spoken language and that it fulfils all the communication needs of its speakers. Yet, it is often not recognized as a language in these respects at all and, for most of the last century, it has been outlawed from schools for the deaf in much the same way as Welsh or Gaelic or non-standard English. In the same way, most people are unaware that Gypsies speak an ethnolect completely unintelligible to *gaujos* or outsiders.

Even when children are recognized as speaking a *bona fide* language, the attitudes of both schools and wider society are often extremely ambivalent. Many people show a marked hierarchy of preferences in their attitudes towards other languages. Thus children who speak French, either because they have a French parent or because they have lived in France, are considered to be very fortunate and are encouraged to make efforts to maintain their fluency in the language. The same is true of other Western European languages such as German, Spanish and Italian. In contrast, the bilingualism of the Gujarati or Panjabi or Hakka-speaking child is often undervalued or ignored.

Bilingualism has traditionally been considered in negative terms in Britain and elsewhere. We have already discussed the ways in which educators tried to argue that the use of Welsh would hold its speakers back. Such views were by no means restricted to the Celtic fringe: it has been commonplace throughout the last thirty years for bilingual parents to be told that it is in their children's best interests only to hear English in the home. A large number of studies undertaken between 1920 and 1960, reporting that bilingual children tended to perform more poorly than their monolingual peers, added weight to arguments for the undesirability of bilingualism. There has been a gradual recognition, however, of the serious shortcomings of these studies (cf Peal and Lambert 1960). In some cases, working-class children from under-resourced schools in poor areas were compared with middle-class monolingual peers. Other studies failed to take account of the fact that one language is usually dominant in bilingual speakers and have compared verbal scores on tests of the children's weaker language with those of monolingual pupils.

The 1970s marked the first official recognition of the positive value of linguistic diversity. The Bullock Report (1975: 293–4) described bilingualism as 'an asset, as something to be nurtured, and one of the agencies which should nurture it is the school'. Developments in the decade which followed were often very exciting. Schools began to value the language skills which children brought to school and bilingualism, for the first time, was seen in a positive light. The work of various researchers on the cognitive and intellectual benefits of bilingualism (see, for instance, Cummins 1984; Swain and Cummins 1986) was widely disseminated and teachers began to think in terms of language transference skills rather than language interference. Local education authorities such as the Inner London Education Authority (ILEA), Brent and Leicester and individual schools and colleges started to collect information on the language repertoire of their pupils.

National and international developments have often acted as a catalyst or reinforced the interest of educators in this area. As early as 1976, a draft of an EC directive on the language education of the children of migrant workers was issued to interested parties throughout Europe (EC Commission 1976). It was proposed that member states should offer free tuition in the national languages of migrant workers as part of the curriculum for full-time education. By the time the directive was published in the following year, however, important modifications had been made: member states were required only to 'promote mother tongue teaching' .... 'in accordance with their national circumstances and legal systems' (Council of Europe 1977). Considerable scepticism has been expressed about government willingness or ability to achieve even the modest aims set out in the revised version of the directive (Bellin 1980). It has been pointed out by some that the *raison d'être* of the EC directive may be to facilitate the future repatriation of non-EC nationals to their countries of origin. None the less, the issue of linguistic minorities has been put very firmly on the political agenda. Developments in Europe need to be seen in a world-wide context. In the USA, the Bilingual Education Act, which entitled educational establishments to financial assistance for their language teaching programmes, was passed in 1968. Although the Act was essentially assimilationist in that its primary concern was with the acquisition of English, the *Lau* v. *Nichols* case of 1974 established the right of a non-English-speaking child (in this case, of Chinese origin) to a meaningful education which acknowledges the child's home language. The Black English trial in Ann Arbor represented another major achievement, when Black parents won their argument that, if their children were to have access to equality of educational opportunity, all teachers in the school system needed to learn about and respect the language background of the home (Labov 1982). These advances, however, were short-lived. The Bilingual Education Amendments Act of 1981 and the Bilingual Education Improvements Act of 1982 began to erode the achievements of the 1960s and 1970s. In 1988, the Heritage Foundation which advises the President on cultural issues recommended that English be declared the official language of the United States. This is a glaring example of a politically dominant group imposing its language on all members of society, disregarding the multilingual reality and denying equality of opportunity and outcome in the educational and political processes. Such a move is in marked contrast to the Declaration of Language Rights supported, among others, by the International Association of Applied Linguists (AILA) and the International Association for Crosscultural Communication (AIMAV), which reads as follows:

The XXII Seminar of AIMAV on Human Rights and Cultural Rights held at the School of Law at the Universidad Federal de Pernambuco (Recife, Brazil), October 7–9, 1987, chaired by Francisco Gomes de Matos,

Considering that the ideals and principles of equality, solidarity, freedom, justice, peace and understanding, which have inspired international legislation and instruments on human rights, share a crucial linguistic dimension,

Recognizing that the learning and use, maintenance and promotion of languages contribute significantly to the intellectual, educational, sociocultural, economic and political development of individuals, groups and states,

Noting that the Universal Declaration of Human Rights, the
International Covenants related to human rights and other
international universal instruments make provision for cultural
rights,

Mindful of the need to arouse and foster awareness, within and
across cultures, of the recognition and promotion of the linguistic
rights of individuals and groups,

Asserting that linguistic rights should be acknowledged,
promoted and observed nationally, so as to bring about and assure
the dignity and equity of all languages,

Aware of the need for legislation to eliminate linguistic
prejudice and discrimination, and all forms of linguistic
domination, injustice, and oppression, in such contexts as services
to the public, the place of work, the educational system, the
courtroom, and the mass media,

Stressing the need to sensitize individuals, groups and States to
linguistic rights, to promote positive societal attitudes towards
plurilingualism and to change societal structures toward equality
between users of different languages and varieties of languages,

Hence, conscious of the need for explicit legal guarantees of the
linguistic rights of individuals and groups to be provided by the
appropriate bodies of the member states of the United Nations,

Recommends that steps be taken by the United Nations to
adopt and implement a Universal Declaration of Linguistic Rights
which would require a reformulation of national, regional and
international language policies.

The pattern of developments in the United States has been mirrored, to some extent at least, in the UK. After a considerable
period of neglect and decline, leading in the case of Cornish and
Manx to actual language death, linguistic minorities have gradually begun to assert themselves. Irish has been enshrined as an
official language in the constitution of Eire; Welsh has achieved
official status in Wales; and bilingual education programmes have
been developed in Ireland, Wales and, to a lesser extent,
Scotland. With the drive to recruit labour from the New
Commonwealth and the arrival of political refugees from
countries such as Uganda, Vietnam and Iran, the mother tongue
issue has become part of a much wider political platform. Many
well-established communities, such as the Italians, Lithuanians
and Poles who had first settled in Britain at the start of the century, had been subject to considerable pressure to assimilate to
the English-speaking majority. However, the arrival of new

groups of migrants in the post-war period, and the new atmosphere of ethnic self-assertion, has seen the rekindling of interest in, and commitment to, the mother tongue.

In an atmosphere such as this, teachers began to feel the need for information on the linguistic backgrounds of their children. The languages of ethnic minority children had in fact received remarkably little attention until the 1980s, and, even at this stage, it is possible to argue that linguistic diversity remained an under-researched field. Trudgill's (1984) *Language in the British Isles*, for instance, a work which might reasonably have been expected to give extensive coverage of this area, devotes only five out of thirty-three chapters to non-indigenous languages. Some progress has none the less been made. Black British English has perhaps fared best with three books and one edited collection of papers (Edwards 1979, 1986; Sutcliffe 1982; Sutcliffe and Wong 1986), supported by a wide range of material published on Caribbean language (eg Bailey 1966; Cassidy and LePage 1966; Dalphinis 1985). The language of the Italian community forms the subject of Tosi (1983); Mobbs (1985) provides a brief overview of South Asian languages in Britain; and Taylor (1987) pays some attention to language issues in her review of research on the Chinese community in Britain. Various publications (eg Edwards 1983; Houlton and Willey 1983; Tansley, Navaz and Roussou 1985; Rosen and Burgess 1980) look specifically at the educational implications of linguistic diversity.

By far the most pertinent work for present purposes, however, is the Linguistic Minorities Project (LMP) (1985) *The Other Languages of England*. Although some attempts (eg Rosen and Burgess 1980; ILEA 1978, 1981, 1983) had previously been made to document the extent and nature of diversity, the publication of this work represented the first and most extensive account of this area in a British context. Its scope is impressive: it provides information on the background and history, patterns of language use and mother tongue teaching provision for some eleven different communities; it also discusses bilingualism and education, surveys of school language and sharing languages in the classroom.

A work so ambitious in its aims inevitably attracts both praise and criticism. The difficulties of locating and sampling adult members of linguistic minority communities, for instance, make it extremely difficult to make reliable generalizations (Smith 1984). Although the population census of Britain gives information on the place of birth of respondents, this information is not always useful in determining language background. In certain instances, such as Poland, speculation on the possible home language can be very near the mark. However, respondents born in Cyprus might speak Greek, Turkish, Armenian and/or English as their home language. Similarly those born in Kenya might speak a Bantu language such as Swahili, a Nilotic language such as Luo, one of the South Asian languages or English. Moreover, population censuses do not give information on children who were born in Britain but none the less use a language other than or in addition to English.

Another problem faced by the Linguistic Minorities Project (LMP) was the difficulty of formulating questions which were acceptable to both the teachers administering the survey instrument and the children who were completing it (LMP 1984). Other factors, too, threaten the validity of their findings. As Nicholas (1988) points out:

> In at least three respects, the classroom stands between the survey and the elicitation of responses from plurilingual respondents. There is pressure from peers – the fear of exhibiting 'alienness' . . . . There is the fact that the survey is conducted in 'the language of the classroom': in a constrained situation and discourse, and in English only. There is the problem of untrained and unsuitable elicitors, teachers co-opted as interviewers.

In spite of criticisms of this kind, *The Other Languages of England* remains the most extensive, sensitively designed survey of linguistic diversity in Britain to date, and it is the intention of this volume to build on these foundations. One of the ways in which we hope to achieve this end is by extending the number of communities under discussion from eleven to thirty-one. When one considers that the 1987 ILEA *Language Census* recorded a total of 172 different languages, our own attempt can be seen as the tip of the iceberg. Nevertheless it represents an important step forward in the documentation of diversity.

Another significant feature of the present volume is the attempt to break down the 'them and us' mentality. All of the writers are themselves bilingual and, in the vast majority of cases, they are describing their own speech communities. This is a radical departure. The overwhelming majority of books on linguistic diversity in Britain have, in fact, been produced by writers who are describing speech communities other than their own. The disadvantages of being an outsider in this situation, while not insurmountable, are very real. There is a danger, for instance, of defining research questions from the perspective of the dominant society, thereby overlooking issues which are felt to be important by minority communities themselves. It is also possible to interpret the findings of such research through one's own cultural matrix, thus distorting the information which has been gathered. There are political considerations, too. For as long as writers choose to work on and be recognized as experts on a community other than their own, they are effectively setting themselves up in competition with members of minority communities for extremely limited research funding; they may also inadvertently engage in academic paternalism in which the hidden message is 'We understand your situation much better than you do yourselves.'

In attempting to document the sociolinguistic situation of a wide range of speech communities, many of the contributors to these volumes have had to confront the problem of unevenness of information. At one end of the continuum, there is a considerable body of research on the various Celtic speech communities; at the other end of the continuum there is virtually no published work on British communities who speak European languages like Hungarian and Lithuanian; or South Asian languages like Tamil and Sinhala; or African languages like Hausa and Yoruba; or East Asian varieties like Singaporean and Malaysian English. The task facing writers attempting to describe these various speech communities is thus necessarily more introspective than would be the case for those dealing with well-documented languages. It is very much to their credit that some modest start has been made in this direction.

The structure of the book

There are various ways in which the book might be organized. It would be possible, for instance, to divide the various language groups, purely on the basis of the size, into major and minor speech communities. Such a classification, however, might have the effect of blurring points of similarity between the various different groups and of creating the impression that the situation of the larger communities is in some way more valid or more important than is the case for the smaller ones. It would also detract from one of the aims of the present volume which is to provide information on many of the smaller communities which, up until very recently, have failed to attract the attention of researchers.

Alternatively it might be possible to arrive at some kind of chronological classification: those languages which have been a

feature of the linguistic landscape of Britain for a century or
more; those which arrived before World War Two; those which
arrived in the period of economic expansion of the 1950s and
1960s; and those which have arrived with political refugees in the
1970s and 1980s. This approach, however, assumes a unitary pattern of settlement for the different groups. The reality is very
different. Most South Asians arrived in Britain in the post-war
period. They were, however, joining a migration 'chain' which
had been established at the beginning of the twentieth century by
sailors who were abandoned by the shipping companies and who
decided to remain in England (see Visram 1986). Similarly most
Eastern European migrants arrived in Britain in several quite distinct waves of population movement.

We finally decided to organize the book along geolinguistic
lines (See Fig. 1.1, Geolinguistic Areas). There are seven main sections: the older mother tongues – Welsh, Gaelic, Irish and British
Sign Language and Romanichal which have been established in
the British Isles for many centuries; the languages of Eastern
Europe – Hungarian, Lithuanian, Polish, Ukrainian, Yiddish; the
languages of the Mediterranean – Greek, Italian, Moroccan
Arabic, Spanish, Portuguese and Turkish; the languages of South
Asia – Panjabi, Urdu, Hindi, Bengali, Gujarati, Tamil, Sinhala;
the languages of West Africa and the Caribbean; the languages
of East Asia as spoken in Hong Kong, Japan, Singapore and
Malaysia, the Philippines and Vietnam; and the languages of the
Middle East – Hebrew and Farsi. The languages included in the
volumes are, of course, only a small sample of those spoken by
the various speech communities in the British Isles and their inclusion is as much a function of the availability of writers as any
other factor.

The decision to divide the book along geolinguistic lines is not
without problems of its own. It is not always clear to which area
a particular language should belong, nor where the boundaries
should be drawn. Where, for instance, do we place Romanichal,
a language with historical roots in South Asia but which has come
to the British Isles via Eastern Europe? This situation is complicated further by the fact that Romanichal has been established
here for a sufficiently long period for it to be considered as one
of the 'older mother tongues', alongside Welsh, Gaelic and
British Sign Language.

None the less a geolinguistic approach has several advantages.
It is politically neutral and does not in any way imply that some
language minority communities are more important than others.
It also allows us to identify the many broad trends which draw

East Asia

Chinese languages
Putong Hua
Japanese

Tagalog/Filipino

Singapore/Malaysian
English
Hakka   Hong Kong
Chinese
Vietnamese
Cantonese

South Asia

Kashmiri   Nepali
Urdu
Panjabi
Pashto   Braj   Bihari
Hindi   Awadhi
Baluchi   Rajasthani
Sindhi   Bengali
Gujarati   Sylheti
Kachchi
Marathi   Tamil
Konkani
Sinhala
Maldivian

East Europe

Lithuanian
Yiddish
Polish
Hungarian
Ukrainian

Middle East

Hebrew   Farsi
Arabic

The British Isles

Gaelic
Romany
Welsh
Irish
British Sign Language

Mediterranean

Portuguese
Greek
Turkish
Italian
Spanish
Maltese
Moroccan Arabic

West Africa

Yoruba

Krio

Twi Fante

Caribbean

Afro-English
Creole
Hindi   Bhojpuri
Kwéyòl
French

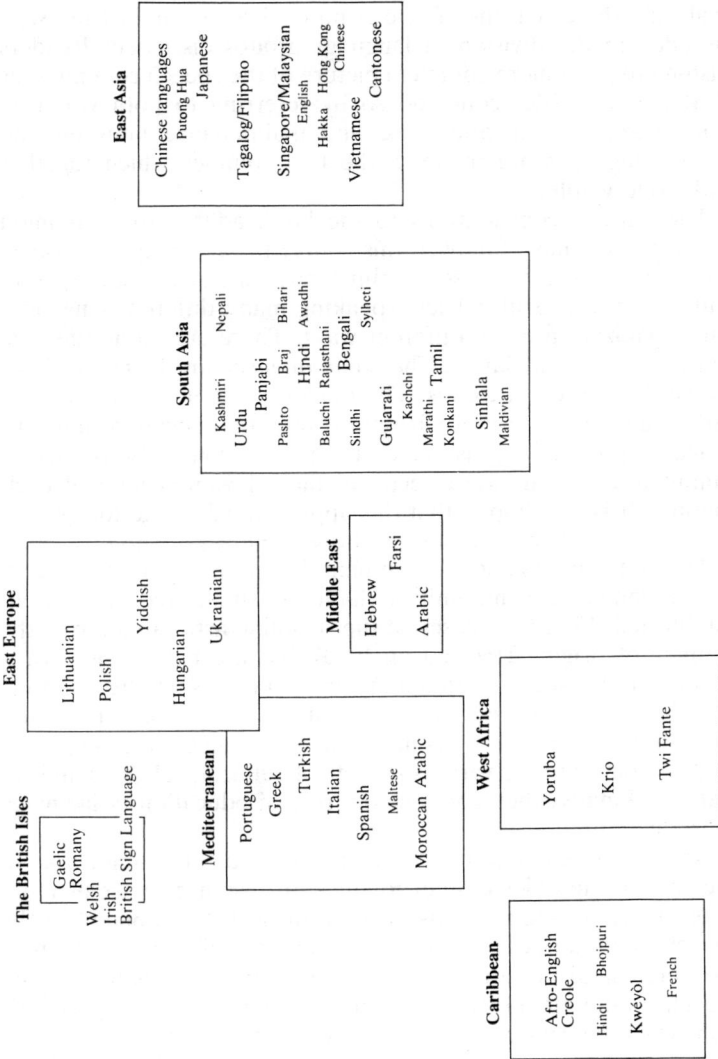

FIGURE 1.1 Geolinguistic Areas

together different speech communities since patterns of migration, as well as the sociolinguistic situation, tend to be broadly similar within a given geolinguistic area.

The book has been divided into two volumes purely for practical publishing reasons. There is no explicit or implicit message intended in the division of language groups discussed. Readers wishing to get a more complete picture of the speech communities of the British Isles could do so by referring to both volumes. Comparisons of histories, use and maintenance between and across languages are made in the two volumes which together make one whole.

The various contributions to the book adhere to a common structure. We have followed this course for a variety of reasons. We are dealing with some thirty-one different speech communities in the British Isles, speaking many different languages and organized in many different ways. There are, none the less, many points of similarity. The common structure helps highlight the various different trends. The reader concerned, for instance, with changing patterns of language use, or education and language reproduction, is able to make comparisons across communities by turning directly to the relevant section of each chapter. It is also hoped that this approach will make for greater consistency and cohesiveness in the volumes as a whole.

The contributors address five main issues which are of concern for all language communities, large or small, recent or well-established. First they describe the sociolinguistic situation in the country of origin. They go on to discuss the nature and distribution of the speech community in Britain. Next they address questions of language change and shift. This forms a backdrop for a discussion of the ways in which the languages are supported in the community by various aspects of cultural, religious and social life. Finally, they consider the role of education in language reproduction.

Not all speech communities fit neatly into this framework. In the case of the older mother tongues for instance, it seems more appropriate to talk in terms of the historical development of the speech communities and their geographical distribution than of the sociolinguistic situation in the country of origin and the speech community in Britain. Similar problems are posed for Yiddish which currently has no country of origin, and for Hebrew, whose roots lie well beyond the modern state of Israel. Some communities such as the Japanese are only temporary residents, for whom language maintenance and shift are not an issue. None the less, most contributions fit with relative ease into the scheme outlined above.

The sociolinguistic situation in the country of origin

Each contribution starts with a description of the sociolinguistic situation in the country of origin. For instance, which languages are spoken and what is their status? The fact that multilingualism is the norm in most societies becomes apparent from the various chapters. This multilingualism has been widely recognized in relation to Africa and South Asia, but it is possible to demonstrate a high degree of diversity even in countries which are usually perceived to be linguistically homogeneous. Thus Japan has significant populations of Korean speakers. And Spain has speakers of Catalan, Vasco and Gallego in addition to the various dialects of Spanish.

The standard language question is also of considerable importance. In Italy, for instance, the dialect of Florence forms the basis of a national literary language used in education and government. However, it is estimated that only 2.5 per cent of the population were able to use this variety on the unification of Italy in 1861 and highly divergent local dialects are still used very widely throughout the country. By the same token, most settlers from Bangladesh are speakers of Sylheti rather than standard Bengali, the national language; and most Urdu speakers in Britain speak Panjabi as the language of the home. In all these cases, however, the expectation is that children should be educated through the medium of the standard language. Information on the linguistic situation in the country of origin is of great relevance in a British context, because this same expectation applies to mother tongue teaching. Italian parents would expect mother tongue classes to focus on standard Italian rather than the southern dialect which many of them speak; Bangladeshi parents usually expect their children to learn Bengali, not the Sylheti spoken in the home; Panjabi Muslims associate Urdu, not Panjabi, with literacy and religious learning. Standard and non-standard varieties thus exist in a situation of diglossia in which the standard is reserved for formal domains such as education and literacy, while non-standard varieties are used in more intimate domains such as conversations with family and friends.

Traditions of literacy in the various countries of origin are also interesting and relevant for the description of language and maintenance of minority communities. Patterns and expectations are highly variable. At one end of the scale, countries like the Ukraine, Poland and Japan have almost universal literacy. At the other end of the scale are the pre-literate communities in parts of Africa whose small-scale, decentralized organization results in a greater dependence on the spoken than on the written

word. There are also different kinds of literacy: the rote learning
and calligraphic skills associated with Qura'ānic learning are very
different, for instance, from the recent development of creative
writing skills in many British schools.

Minority speech communities in the British Isles

Each contribution goes on to describe the history of the arrival
and settlement of the different speech communities. For instance,
the Poles and Ukrainians of the immediate post-war period, the
Hungarians in the 1950s, the Vietnamese refugees in the 1970s
and the Tamils in the 1980s, have sought asylum in Britain as
political refugees. In contrast, settlers from India, Pakistan,
Bangladesh and the Caribbean, have, in the main, come from
areas of high unemployment for economic reasons. It is not possible, of course, to make a simple split between political and
economic migrants since, even within the same group, motivation
differs through time. The Eastern Europeans who have arrived
in Britain since the Second World War have come for political
reasons; in many cases, however, they were joining earlier settlers
trying either to escape poverty in the home country or to better
their lot. Most Hong Kong Chinese came to Britain originally for
economic reasons but, with the transfer of Hong Kong to China
in 1997, the motivation is becoming increasingly political.

It is also possible to make a distinction between the long-
established communities such as the Italian, South Asian and
African which have maintained a presence — albeit numerically
small – for several hundred years and communities like the Vietnamese who have arrived more recently in Britain. A further
distinction can be made between these groups and the 'annual
migrant' Saudi Arabic speakers living in the more expensive areas
of London or the Japanese who are sent to work in Britain by
their companies for varying lengths of time.

Even within the longer-established groups there is significant
variation. Bangladeshis, for instance, differ in many important
ways from the other larger South Asian groups. They tended to
cling more tenaciously to the 'myth of return' and, although most
Bangladeshis arrived in Britain in the 1950s and 1960s, they sent
for their wives and children much later than other South Asians.
Because of increasingly stringent immigration legislation, there
have often been long delays in reuniting families. One of the consequences is that Bengali-speaking children form the most recent
and largest linguistic minority within the ILEA; and, because the
majority of children have been born in Bangladesh, they are in-

evitably in greatest need of language support within the schools. Remaining with South Asian communities, there are also important differences between those who have come direct from South Asia and those who have arrived via East Africa. Settlers from north India and Pakistan come from predominantly rural areas and have, in the main, received little formal education. In contrast, most of those who have lived in East Africa were traders, industrialists and middle-level professionals and artisans. In this respect East African Asians are closer to Sri Lankans – a highly educated élite who chose to stay in Britain after completing their higher education – than to their north Indian kinfolk.

A further important factor in the discussion of the various minority communities in Britain is the pattern of settlement. Some groups are concentrated into a relatively small geographical area which makes it possible to develop and maintain strong social networks; others are highly dispersed and consequently find it far more difficult to maintain a sense of community. Thus most Spaniards, Turks, Greeks and Vietnamese are to be found in London. Panjabis, Ukrainians, Poles, Tamils and Sinhala, however, are scattered throughout the country. In the case of Poles and Panjabis, the communities outside London are sufficiently large to be able to sustain an active community life; in the case of Ukrainians, Tamils and Sinhala the small numbers and the dispersed nature of the community make the task of forging a separate linguistic and cultural identity a great deal more difficult.

Groups who have little or no contact with the home country also face very real difficulties. Lithuanians, Latvians, Ukrainians and Estonians, for instance, cannot travel freely to the country of origin; they cannot receive visits from the families they left behind; nor is there the possibility of new immigration which would have the effect of revitalizing the community in Britain. None the less, those groups which find themselves isolated in this way have shown considerable resolve to maintain their ethnic identity, not only through community involvement in the UK, but by building links with similar groups in Europe and in the USA and Canada.

Changing patterns of language use

The inevitable consequence of settlement in Britain is a shift from the mother tongue to English. The extent of this shift will vary, of course, according to individual factors such as degree of identification with the mother tongue and culture; it will also depend on group factors such as the size of community, its degree of organization and the length of time it has been established in Britain. For more recently arrived communities such as the Bangladeshis and the Vietnamese, the acquisition of English is clearly more urgent a priority than the maintenance of the mother tongue. In the case of Eastern Europeans, however, where the present generation are the grandchildren of the original post-war settlers, the shift to English is such that mother tongue teaching is often an urgent community priority.

In the case of the first generation, language shift is evident in the adoption of a wide range of loan words for objects and concepts peculiar to the new country, though very often these words are used within the morpho-syntactic framework of the mother tongue (*cf* for instance, Muir on Polish (Ch. 9) and Cervi on Italian (Ch. 13) in volume one. In the case of the second and subsequent generations, there is a much wider range of adaptation: incidence of both code-mixing and code-switching is likely to increase and sometimes words from the mother tongue are inserted into an English syntactic structure rather than the reverse (*cf* Mahandru on Panjabi (Vol. 2, Ch. 8) and Estebanez on Spanish (Vol. 1, Ch. 15)); English variants are sometimes substituted for phonemes in the original language (*cf* Jenkala on Ukrainian (Vol. 1, Ch. 10)); children may aquire only a passive knowledge of the mother tongue, choosing to reply to their parents in English (*cf* de Zoysa on Sinhala (Vol. 2, Ch. 10) and Mehmet Ali on Turkish (Vol. 1, Ch. 12))

Several factors, however, can bring about language stability. The 'new ethnicity' which has been well documented in the USA and Canada, is beginning to make itself felt in a British setting, too. The realization that a language may be lost completely from the community can often greatly focus the mind: the astonishing cultural renaissance in Wales, Ireland and Scotland is no doubt largely a response to the very real threat of extinction for these indigenous minority languages. The rapid burgeoning of mother tongue classes in the 1970s suggests a similar reaction on the part of the indigenizing language communities. Many young adults are consciously seeking to learn or improve their skills in the mother tongue: Italian classes have recently been set up for the first time in Llanelli in Wales, for instance, where the Italian community has been settled since the early years of this century. In a similar vein, there are reports of British-born Ukrainians and Yiddish-speaking Jews who were brought up in predominantly English-speaking homes who are now striving to produce a Ukrainophone or Yiddiphone environment for their own children.

Language, culture and community

Most settler families in Britain have very strong links with the country of origin in the form of letters, visits and investment in land and property. The advent of the international telephone network, satellite television and the free availability of videos have also served to strengthen this ongoing contact. As we have already indicated, even in those cases where there is no access to the home country, strong links are cultivated with communities in exile in other parts of the world.

No individual, indeed no family, exists in a social vacuum and the role which the wider minority community plays in the maintenance of language and culture is clearly critical. The extent of community provision varies enormously. Later arrivals, such as the Portuguese, the Spanish, the Filipinos and the Maroccan Arabs, who work in jobs with long, antisocial hours in the hotel and catering industry very often have little time or energy to devote to community organization. Longer-established groups, however, often offer an impressive range of social, political, religious and cultural activities.

In many communities the church, mosque, *gurdwara* or temple plays a central part in the social life of the group, fulfilling an important welfare and cultural role as well as providing for spiritual needs. In some cases, life revolves around the family and the place of worship. Religious festivals such as 'Id, Christmas, Diwali and Vesak, and life-cycle celebrations, such as naming ceremonies, weddings and funerals, form an important focus for community life.

In most cases, however, there is also an extensive secular organizational network. Sometimes the focus is political, reflecting either political divisions within the country of origin (*cf* Mahandru on Panjabi (Vol 2, Ch. 8) and Mehmet Ali on Turkish (Vol. 1, Ch. 12)) or on issues such as anti-racism or housing which are of more immediate relevance for life in Britain (*cf* Husain on Bengali (Vol. 2, Ch. 5) and Nwenmely on Kwéyòl (Vol, 2, Ch. 4)) There is also a wide range of organizations, some religious, some secular, which focus on cultural activities such as music (eg Khan on Urdu (Vol. 2, Ch. 9); Papadaki d'Onofrio and Roussou on Greek (Vol. 1, Ch. 12)), dance (*eg* Dave on Gujarati (Vol. 2, Ch 6) and Perinpanayagam on Tamil (Vol. 2, Ch 10) drama (*eg* Nwenmely on Kweyol (Vol. 2, Ch. 4)) and art (*eg* Husain on Bengali (Vol. 2, Ch. 5)). A wide range of local, regional, national and international ethnic publications mirrors this cultural and political activity. Many communities also have extensive sporting networks, such as the eastern Caribbean cricket teams or the Turkish Cypriot football leagues.

Most communities have developed an extensive ethnic economy which services the needs of the community. In areas of important settlement, it is possible to find a wide range of cafés, restaurants, travel agents, food shops, clothing shops and video outlets run by and for a given minority community. In many of the larger minority communities, this ethnic economy provides employment for large numbers of workers and creates an environment in which it is often more natural to use the mother tongue than English. The workplace is thus an important factor in language maintenance.

Education and language reproduction

Formal language teaching is not always a community priority. Dalphinis (Ch. 2), for instance, talks of the ways in which many speakers of British Black English maintain distinctively Black speech patterns as a symbol of resistance to a racist White society, in spite of the fact that both parents and teachers have encouraged them to use British English. In a similar vein, Hancock (Vol. 1, Ch. 5) describes the strong ethnic identity which insulates Gypsies from the hostility of mainstream society and which ensures that Romanichal is transmitted with 100 per cent success to the youngest generation without recourse to any formal teaching. On the contrary, school represents a considerable threat by teaching values which are often directly contrary to those taught in a Gypsy home.

For most minority communities, however, it is possible to identify three main strands in language reproduction: family, community and school, and successful transmission from one generation to the next will usually depend on all three strands working in harmony. Responsibility for teaching minority languages in a British context began in the home. In the earlier days, before there were any well-developed community activities, parents took it upon themselves to maintain the language and culture within the family. Quite often this was because they felt that their stay in Britain would be temporary and many harboured the illusion that they would return to the homeland.

Parents were often anxious that their children were drifting away from traditional cultural and religious values. Sometimes there was a genuine breakdown of communication between grandparents and young children. Gradually, there was a realization that responsibility for language maintenance lay not only with the family but with the wider community and the first efforts to organize more formal mother tongue teaching were initiated. In some cases, the impetus and many of the resources came from the government of the group concerned. Thus mother tongue teaching in the Italian, Spanish, Portuguese, Greek and Turkish communities is supported in varying degrees by the Embassy or High Commission in London. In other cases, religious bodies have played an important role. Thus, historically, the Nonconformist Church has played a key role in the transmission of Welsh and the Catholic Church in the teaching of Polish, Ukrainian and Lithuanian; mosques have fulfilled a similar role in the transmission of Qur'ānic Arabic and Urdu, *gurdwaras* in the teaching of Panjabi and viharas in the teaching of Sinhala. Increasingly, however, the organization of mother tongue teaching is being taken on board by non-religious groups, especially parent associations.

In the early years, mother tongue classes were supported entirely by the community. As time went by, increasing numbers of LEAs began to recognize this provision, sometimes paying teachers' salaries, sometimes allowing rent-free accommodation, and occasionally providing both salaries and accommodation. The numbers of classes and of pupils involved in community language teaching are enormous. The LMP (1985) survey of mother tongue teaching provision in 1981–82, for instance, recorded 106 classes and 1,894 students in Coventry, 183 clases and 3,586 students in Bradford and 143 classes and 3,042 students in Haringey. These figures indicate that there is greater vitality in the area of language maintenance than is officially recognized.

The problems faced by those teaching the classes were not, of course restricted to finance. All have had to come to terms with the shortage of suitable materials for use with children in Britain. Very often the content of books and courses produced in the home country fail to speak to the interests and experience of British-born children and the linguistic level for a given age range is too advanced. Although some improvements are being made in this area (see, for instance, Dave (Vol. 2, Ch. 6) in relation to the examinations of the Gujarati Literary Academy and Cervi (Vol. 1, Ch. 13) in relation to new materials for overseas Italians), the only solution in most cases is for teachers to produce their own materials, an extremely time-consuming task.

Teaching methodology also offers many challenges. Staff who have been trained overseas often structure their teaching in a way which is markedly different from the relatively informal and child-centred approach of most primary classrooms, or indeed the communicative languange-teaching strategies which have recently gained ground in modern language teaching. In the case of teachers seconded by an overseas government, the lack of familiarity with the children's everyday experience in school can further exacerbate this problem. However, there are signs of progress. Many communities provide their own training programmes (see *eg* Jenkala on Ukrainian (Vol. 1, Ch. 10) and Dave on Gujarati (Vol. 2, Ch. 6)); many teachers make their own arrangements for professional training, seeking, for instance, places on Royal Society of Arts diploma courses on community languages (see for instance, Taheri White on Farsi (Vol. 2, Ch. 16); and increasing numbers already work within the state system as recognized teachers or as instructors.

The gulf between community and state provision has been the subject of a great deal of concern in recent years and there have been many attempts to bridge the gap between the two kinds of provision. This has been done in various different ways. In some cases, the community language has been introduced as a school subject. This initiative has much to recommend it. The exclusion of community languages from mainstream education can only have the effect of lowering their status in the eyes of Anglophone and minority-language-speaking children alike and recognition for the linguistic diversity within our midst is long overdue. However, the introduction of community languages has often been problematic. Sometimes they are taught at the same time as higher status subjects and the take-up rate is low. Sometimes they are offered as an option against the so-called 'low status' subjects on the school curriculum like art, craft or sport, or at lunch time or after school rather than being integrated into the timetable. This kind of organization reinforces the low status of the languages on offer in schools. Sometimes community languages *are* integrated into the timetable but are taught in the same way as modern languages. This approach fails to recognize that, while the children concerned may not have native speaker proficiency, their passive competence and productive abilities are well in advance of modern language students.

A broader concern about the introduction of community language teaching into state schools concerns the amount of control which is exercised over the content of teaching. For most communities, language teaching cannot take place in isolation but must address the history, culture and religion of the people (*cf* Muir on Polish (Vol. 1, Ch. 9) and Wong on Chinese (Vol. 2, Ch. 13 and 15)). There is thus, understandably, a fear that the teaching which takes place outside the community may not satisfy these needs.

There are political considerations, too. The growth in community language teaching has produced a demand for teachers which cannot be satisfied from the pool of currently qualified teachers. Yet there is no shortage of experienced teachers within the various minority communities. The problem lies on the one hand in the Department of Education and Science's reluctance to recognize overseas qualifications and, on the other hand, in their failure to provide sufficient places and funding for the further training which would make this recognition possible. As a result, very many people are currently working in schools as instructors. The low pay, low status and insecurity associated with the post of instructor is a source of widespread dissatisfaction for minority communities.

Community languages find their way into state schools in a variety of other ways. There have been moves, for instance, to acknowledge linguistic diversity in the hidden curriculum, by ensuring the availability of a wide range of books, posters and music; by writing children's names and captions on drawings in a variety of scripts; by inviting parents to tell stories in the mother tongue. Sometimes community languages feature as part of language awareness programmes which explore children's own language use and the language of the wider community. A growing number of schools now offer community languages as part of a 'carousel' or 'taster' programme of language teaching in the early years of secondary school, where children are exposed to a variety of languages for short periods of time. In many schools, bilingual language support teachers work alongside the classroom teacher in a team-teaching situation.

Some experimentation has taken place on the effectiveness of bilingual education. In an international context, of course, there is no shortage of evidence to support the use of the mother tongue as a medium as well as a subject of education for children from minority communities (cf Skutnabb-Kangas and Cummins 1988; Garcia and Otheguy 1987). The findings of British initiatives, in the form of the Bedfordshire Mother Tongue Project (Simons 1979) and Mother Tongue and English Teaching Project (Fitzpatrick 1987), also argue forcefully for the value of bilingual education. It would seem, however, that no progress will be made on this front in the foreseeable future. The Swann Report (1985), for instance, makes it clear that 'we cannot support the arguments put forward for the introduction of programmes of bilingual education in maintained schools in this country . . . we would regard mother tongue maintenance . . . as best achieved within the ethnic minority communities themselves'.

The unveiling of plans for the National Curriculum also indicates a waning of enthusiasm for minority languages. The only
minority language which is likely to benefit from the National
Curriculum is Welsh. However, even in this case, the benefits are
likely to be extremely limited. No reference was made to Welsh
in the earliest formulations of policy and even its current recognition is somewhat grudging:

> In some counties of Wales it would be appropriate – and in line
> with existing practice in schools – for Welsh to be made a
> foundation subject. But the linguistic pattern in Wales is varied,
> and in some areas the Secretary of State would expect that it
> would not at present be appropriate to require the study of Welsh
> throughout the period of compulsory education for pupils who
> study through the medium of English. At the least, the legislation
> will provide for attainment targets, programmes of study and
> assessment arrangements for Welsh wherever it is taught. DES
> (1987: 9):

More cynical observers might thus be tempted to interpret the
writing in of Welsh into the National Curriculum as an after-
thought, as a recognition of the present situation rather than a
serious attempt to promote the language.

Equally pertinent for the present discussion, the National Curriculum has precisely nothing to say about community languages
or bilingualism outside the Welsh context. It allows for 10 per
cent of curriculum time to be spent on modern foreign languages
at secondary level, but there is no mention of the potential role
of community languages in the cursory references to language
teaching. It would seem that this is yet another case of an opportunity missed. It might also be argued that the government has
failed to recognize the inherent dangers of an Anglocentric approach for large numbers of bilingual pupils.

The key feature of the National Curriculum is in fact the way
in which testing and assessment procedures are such an integral
feature of the package. The government very clearly lays out its
intention to set objectives to be reached by the ages of 7, 11, 14
and 16 and can only leave us to conclude that its aim is to cen-
tralize control not only of the curriculum but also of teaching.
The likely consequences of developments in this direction are a
limiting of the teachers' ability to exercise their judgement in responding to children's needs and a narrow, Eurocentric
curriculum. More worrying still is the possibility that any group
which does not conform to the norms against which the test is
referenced will suffer discrimination. We may well be on target
for a return to the pathological model of language where any

speaker – working class Black, or bilingual – who departs from the norm is labelled as deficient.

Bilingual children, however, may well be doubly disadvantaged. First, English may not be their dominant language but there is only provision for testing in English. Second, in order to meet the requirements of the test, teachers may decide that it is in children's best short-term interests to be taught using structural rather than communicative teaching techniques. This would inevitably have the effect of making access to the curriculum more difficult still for bilingual children.

The preoccupation with testing and objectives is likely to involve us in a downward spiral: bilingual children who are not fully fluent in English are likely to underachieve; their underachievement is likely to have an adverse effect on teacher expectations; this in turn, will lead to further depressed performance and so on. The repetition of the situation in the 1960s and 1970s where ethnic minority children were seriously over-represented in ESN schools and low-ability groups is almost inevitable: any system which relies heavily on assessment procedures of the kind proposed is likely to result in bilingual children being wrongly assessed and wrongly placed.

The pressing issues for minority language communities are thus not limited to timetabling, resources and pedagogy. They extend to the legitimate needs of large numbers of bilingual children to be recognized in the formulation of educational policy. Any commitment to equality of opportunity in education must go beyond mere lip service to involve genuine community consultation, and a willingness to resource the implications of linguistic diversity.

Postscript

The failure of central government to take on board the needs of bilingual children is certainly a subject of concern. It is unlikely, however, that insensitivity of this kind will blunt the grassroots enthusiasm for the positive aspects of bilingualism on the part of either educators or minority language communities themselves. There are other developments, too, which may well foster more positive attitudes towards linguistic diversity; 1992, the Year of Europe, may well mark the dawning of a new era in this respect. The process of European integration has extremely important implications for minority languages and the central role which these languages play in the cultural identity of communities and individuals. As we move towards a wider multinational, multi-linguistic and single Europe, many people are becoming aware of the new contexts and wider contacts which are opening up for speakers of lesser-used languages. The European Centre for Traditional and Regional Cultures (ECTARC) (1988), for instance, points out that: 'A notable feature of recent European development has been the revitalization of the regional concept and this will surely have a stimulating effect upon the promotion of lesser used languages. Will these languages, then, be the vital elements of, and the means towards intercultural and interpersonal understanding in the future?' While the ECTARC comments are focused more specifically on indigenous minority languages such as Welsh, Frisian and Catalan, the impact of a single Europe without boundaries will clearly be no less significant for the more recent indigenizing minority languages throughout the European Community.

If we are to judge by the experience of other multilingual areas of the world, the solution will lie not in the imposition of any one natural or synthetic language but in the recognition of multilingual reality. Modern history is replete with tales of linguistic repression and resistance: the repression of Welsh in Wales and the legal – and illegal – action taken to counter it; language martyrdom in Bangladesh by Bengali speakers desperate to maintain the place of their mother tongue rather than the Urdu language imposed upon them by West Pakistan after partition from India; language riots in Belgium provoked by the perceived injustices of Flamand speakers in relation to the Walloon majority; cries of 'Vive le Québec libre!' and, by implication, 'Vive la langue française!' uttered by Charles de Gaulle on a state visit to Canada. In these, and many similar cases, social order and a sense of justice have depended on the recognition of the rights of linguistic minorities rather than the imposition of the language of the dominant group. If we wish to bring about equality of opportunity, access and outcomes, we need to create conditions which will support and encourage multiliterate and multilingual development.

This book is an attempt to bring to the attention of readers the wealth and history of languages in the British Isles today. It is just a beginning. The users and speakers of the languages themselves are identifying areas for further research and issues which deserve the urgent attention of teachers, administrators and educational policy-makers. It is hoped that those with the power to make decisions will listen. It is also hoped that the various speech communities will learn from the experience and efforts of others in the area of language maintenance. And most of all, it is hoped that the British people of the twenty-first century will recognize and value the heritage of a multilingual Britain.

References

BAILEY, B. (1966) *A Transformational Grammar of Jamaican Creole.* Cambridge: Cambridge University Press.

BELLIN, W. (1980) 'The EEC Directive on the Education of the Children of Migrant Workers: a comparison of the Commission's proposed directive and the Council directive together with a parallel text', *Polyglot* 2, fiche 3.

BERNSTEIN, B. (1973) *Class, Codes and Control,* vol. 1. London: Routledge & Kegan Paul.

BULLOCK, SIR A. (1975) *A Language for Life.* London: HMSO.

CASSIDY, F. and LE PAGE, R. B. (1966) *Dictionary of Jamaican English.* Cambridge: Cambridge University Press.

Council of Europe (1977) *Council Directive on the Education of the Children of Migrant Workers* (77/48b/EEC). 25 July.

CUMMINS, J. (1984) *Bilingualism and Special Education: Issues in Assessment and Pedagogy.* Clevedon, Avon: Multilingual Matters.

DALPHINIS, M. (1985) *Caribbean and African Languages.* London: Karia Press.

Department of Education and Science (DES) and Welsh Office (1988) *English for Ages 5–11*: Proposals of the Secretary of State for Education and Science and the Secretary for Wales. London: HMSO.

Department of Education and Science (DES) [and the] Welsh Office (1987) *National Curriculum 5–16: a consultative document.* London: HMSO.

EDWARDS, V. (1979) *The West Indian Language Issue in British Schools.* London: Routledge & Kegan Paul.

EDWARDS, V. (1983) *Language in Multicultural Classrooms.* London: Batsford.

EDWARDS, V. (1986) *Language in a Black Community.* Clevedon, Avon: Mutilingual Matters.

EDWARDS, V. and CHESHIRE, J. (1989) 'A Survey of British Dialect Grammer'. In J. Cheshire, V. Edwards, H. Münstermann and B. Weltens (eds.) *Dialect and Education: Some European Perspectives,* Clevedon, Avon: Multilingual Matters, pp. 200–18.

The European Centre for Traditional and Regional Cultures (ECTARC) (1988) Literature for Conference on *'Lesser-Used Languages in a Europe without Boundaries'*, 25–27 November. Llangollen: ECTARC.

European Communities Commission (1976) *An Education Policy for the Community. Resolution of the Council and of the Ministers of Education. Meeting within the Council of 9 February 1976.* Background note published 26 March 1976.

FITZPATRICK, B. (1987) *The Open Door.* Clevedon, Avon: Multilingual Matters.

GARCIA, O. and OTHEGUY, R. (1987) 'The bilingual education of Cuban–American children in Dade County's ethnic schools', *Language and Education* 1 (2): 83–96.

HOLLINGWORTH, B. (1977) 'Dialect in school: an historical note', *Durham and Newcastle Research Review* 8: 15–20 .

HOULTON, D. and WILLEY, R. (1983) *Supporting Children's* Bilingualism. York: Longman for the Schools Council.

HUGHES, A. and TRUDGILL, P. (1978) *English Accents and Dialects. An Introduction to Social and Regional Varieties of British English.* London: Edward Arnold.

Inner London Education Authority (ILEA) (1978, 1981, 1983, 1985, 1987) *Language Census.* London: ILEA Research and Statistics.

LABOV, W. (1982) 'Objectivity and commitment in linguistic science: the case of the Black English trial in Ann Arbor', *Language and Society* 11: 165–201.

Linguistics Minorities Project (LMP) (1985) *The Other Languages of England.* London: Routledge & Kegan Paul.

Linguistic Minorities Project (LMP) (1985) *Schools Language Survey: Manual of Use.* University of London Institute of Education.

MOBBS, M. (1985) *Britain's South Asian Languages.* London: Centre for Information on Language Teaching and Research.

NEWBOLT, H. (1921) *The Teaching of English in England.* London: HMSO.

NICHOLAS, J. (1988) 'British Language Diversity Surveys (1977–1987): a critical examination', *Language and Education* 2(1): 15–33.

PATTANAYAK, D. P. (1985) *Language and Power.* Conference Report, London: North London Community Group.

PATTANAYAK, D. P. (1987) *Multilingualism and Multiculturalism: Britain and India.* Occasional Paper No. 1, International Association for Intercultural Education, University of London Institute of Education.

PEAL, E. and LAMBERT, W. (1960) 'The relation of bilingualism to intelligence', *Psychological Monographs* 76: 546

RAMPTON, A. (1981) *West Indian Children in our Schools* (Interim report of the Committee of Inquiry into the Education of Children from Ethnic Minority Groups). London: HMSO.

ROSEN, H. and BURGESS, H. (1980) *The Languages and Dialects of London Schoolchildren.* London: Ward Lock Educational.

SIMONS, H. (1979) *Mother Tongue and Culture in Bedfordshire.* EC Pilot Project, First External Evaluation Report, Cambridge: University of Cambridge Institute of Education.

SKUTNABB-KANGAS, T. and CUMMINS, J. (eds) (1988) *Minority Education: From Shame to Struggle.* Clevedon, Avon: Multilingual Matters.

SMITH, G. (1984) *Sampling Linguistic Minorities: A Technical Report on the Adult Language Use Survey.* LMP/CLE/LINC Working Paper No. 4, London: University of London Institute of Education.

SPENS, W. (1938) *Report of the Consultative Committee on Secondary Education with Special Reference to Grammar Schools and Technical High Schools.* London: HMSO.

SUTCLIFFE, D. (1982) *British Black English.* Oxford: Basil Blackwell.

SUTCLIFFE, D. and WONG, A. (1986) *The Language of the Black Experience.* Oxford: Basil Blackwell.

SWAIN, M. and CUMMINS, M. (1986) *Bilingualism and Education.* London: Longman.

SWANN, LORD (1985) *Education for All.* London: HMSO.

TANSLEY, P., NAVAZ, H. and ROUSSOU, M. (1985) *Working with Many Languages: A Handbook for Community Language Teachers.* London: School Curriculum Development Committee.

TAYLOR, M. (1987) *Chinese Pupils in Britain: A Review of Research into the Education of Pupils of Chinese Origin.* Windsor: National Foundation for Educational Research/Nelson.

TIZARD, B. and HUGHES, M. (1984) *Young Children Learning.* London: Fontana.

TOSI, A. (1983) *Immigration and Bilingual Education.* Oxford: Pergamon.

TRUDGILL, P. (ed.) (1984) *Language in the British Isles.* Cambridge: Cambridge University Press.

VISRAM, R. (1986) *Ayahs, Princes and Lascars.* London: Pluto.

WELLS, G. (1987) *The Meaning Makers: Children Learning Language and Using Language to Learn.* London: Hodder & Stoughton.

Part one

West Africa and the Caribbean

Morgan Dalphinis
Hubisi Nwenmely

West Africans and their Caribbean descendants share a common historical and linguistic heritage. This is by no means a recent realization. For example, Orlando Equiano refers to the process of being captured as a slave in the West African hinterland, followed by successive marches to the coast, during which he could recognize a number of similarities between his language and the successive ethnolinguistic groups among whom he and his captors stopped for brief periods during the march (Holm 1979). It is exactly the types of similarity recognized by Equiano, ranging from the extremely general to the profound, which have characterized a common West African heritage now being perpetuated within the Caribbean context. For example, a number of grammatical features have been found to be common to both Caribbean creoles and African languages, including the use of serial verbs:

Sant Lucian Kwéyòl:

i	*pwan*	*liv*	*la*	*bat*	*yo*
(s)he	take	book	the	beat	them

Jamaican Creole:

im	*tek*	*buk*	*biit*	*dem*
(S)he	take	book	beat	them

Wolof:

dafa		*jèl*	*tère*	*dor*	*len*
(s) he (stabilizer)		take	book	beat	them

Twi:

ò	*fa*	*buku*	*nò*	*dibu*	*wòn*
(s)he	take	book	the	beat	them

all of which mean, 'He/she took the book and beat them' (see Dalphinis 1981, for further discussion of structural similarities of this kind).

In this part of the book we will be looking at three different speech communities. The first consists of the Nigerian, Ghanaian, Sierra Leonean and other speakers of African languages who make up the various West African speech communities in the UK. Next we will focus on the Afro-Caribbean communities of creole speakers who originated in islands such as Jamaica, Barbados, Trinidad, St Vincent and Antigua which were colonized by English speakers. Here the dominant vocabulary base is English, although the underlying grammatical structure, as we have already seen, bears a striking resemblance to the African languages of the first speakers. Finally we will turn our attention to the communities of creole speakers from St Lucia and Dominica. Although these eastern Caribbean islands were under British control for most of the nineteenth and twentieth centuries, they had previously been subject to extended periods of French colonial rule. As a result, the vocabulary base for the creole which developed there is predominantly French. Although there are many differences between the sociolinguistic situations in these various speech communities, we will also be concerned to describe the points of similarity which unite British speakers of African languages and Afro-Caribbean creoles.

References

DALPHINIS, M. (1981) 'African influences in creoles lexically based on Portuguese, English and French, with special reference to Casamance Kriul, Gambia Krio and St Lucian Patwa'. Unpublished Ph.D. thesis, SOAS, University of London.

HOLM, J. (1979) 'The creole English of Nicaragua's Miskito Coast: its sociolinguistic history and a comparative study of its lexicon and syntax'. Unpublished Ph.D. thesis, University of London.

Chapter 2

The West African speech communities

Morgan Dalphinis

Magana jari ce – speech is wealth
(HAUSA PROVERB)

No doubt because the West African speech communities are much smaller numerically than their Afro-Caribbean counterparts, their presence in the UK is often overlooked. In doing so we fail to recognize a rich source of cultural and linguistic diversity. Equally important, we fail to make important links between West African and Afro-Caribbean communities which help to explain a wide range of linguistic, social and historical parallels between these groups in relation to the dominant White society.

The total number of African languages is estimated at 1,250–2,100 languages (Dalby 1978:6). The main African languages are Swahili (approximately 49 million speakers), spoken in East Africa Hausa (approximately 45 million speakers) and Pula/Fula (approximately 15 million speakers), spoken in West Africa, and Arabic (approximately 175 million speakers), spoken throughout Islamicized areas of the continent (Gunnemark and Kenrick 1985). West African languages belong to the Niger–Kordofanian family which can be divided into the main branches (Dalphinis 1985: 5–6) shown in Fig. 2.1.

NIGER–KORDOFANIAN

MANDE	WEST ATLANTIC	ADAMAWA -EASTERN	GUR	KRU	KWA	BENUE -CONGO	KORDOFANIAN
Bambara (Mandinka)	Wolof Pula	Sango	Mossi	Efik	Yoruba Ibo Ewe Akan	Swahili Lingala Kikongo	Koalib

FIGURE 2.1 The Niger-Kordofanian language family

Despite this evident great variety of West African languages, the close structural interrelationship between them has been noted since at least 1700, by writers such as Labat (1728) and, more recently, by many other scholars, including Dalby (1970) and Dalphinis (1981). Indeed their structural similarities, in contrast with their dissimilarities in vocabulary, point to ways of classifying language/dialect differences other than those based on differences in sounds and vocabulary, which are more dominant as traditions in distinguishing between European languages. Compare, for example the Akan/Ghanaian view that one language is so many days, in learning time, away from the language that the speaker uses as a mother tongue, *eg* that Twi is a one-day language from Fante, but that Ewe is more days distant from either (Hockett 1958: 326–7). The differences in the languages concerned are often those of vocabulary rather than structure.

Since European invasion and conquest of West Africa, in the seventeenth century, West African languages have been used in a diglossic situation, within which European languages have high status and African languages low status relative to them. However, some West African regional/second languages enjoy a middle-status position between other West African languages and the relevant European language, in a situation described, for East Africa, as triglossia (Abdulaziz Mkilifi 1972: 197–213). Some varieties of West African languages are also viewed as higher status than the European language in specific domains. For instance, Katsina varieties of Hausa are viewed as higher status in Hausa songs, while Arabic is considered a superior language of the faith of West African and other Muslims. All African languages enjoy higher covert prestige (Labov 1966) in family and personal domains, than their European languages of contact.

With anti-colonial movements and the independence of many West African countries, West African languages have been caught between the political forces of pragmatism and nationalism. Pragmatism suggests that, if technological and educational advancements are at present situated in the Western world, then African governments can better serve their peoples by promoting the use of the European language of their former conqueror. Thus, in Senegal, French was actively promoted under the former president, Senghor. This strategy is independent of the capitalist/socialist divide, as most African Marxist-influenced governments actively promote European languages as part of the process of changing the material conditions of their peoples. Mozambique, for instance, promotes Portuguese. The nationalist view that West Africa should be charting its own independent course, has led to the use of a number of West African languages as national/regional languages, alongside the European language, *eg* Wolof, Serer and Pula are three of the African national languages used in Senegal.

European languages, wherever adopted in West Africa, have generally been the language of a minority – an urban and relatively small African élite. They have been restricted to the written domain, and, often, contrast with or complement the relevant African language which dominates in the more prominent oral domains.

West African languages have often influenced the adopted European language, giving rise to expansions of the European language, *eg* 'They have travelled' in Nigerian English is closer in its meaning to Hausa *Sun yi yawo* (They have gone wandering), than to the English meaning of the sentence. Sometimes such influences are seen as part of the inevitable and necessary domestication of the European language for African purposes. On other occasions, they are seen in terms of a lack of purity in the use of languages which should be kept separate, in the acquisition of true multilingualism.' Thus Senghor, in relation to French and African languages in Senegal, advocates an avoidance of creolisms (Dumont 1983: 31).

However, such attempts at language purity also need to bear in mind the historical facts: West African creole languages[1] of both Portuguese and English vocabulary and African grammatical structure, date from the seventeenth century, and are also indicative of some of the present-day African-language influences on European languages. The African oral tradition also has an important effect on the written tradition in both European and African languages. Oral genres from the epic to the proverb and praise epithet are apparent, for example, in the writings of Islamicized West Africans like the Kanuri, Fula and Hausa as well as in the English and French writings of both Christianized and non-Christianized groups like the Igbo and the Wolof. As Achebe (1980) comments in *Things Fall Apart*, 'The art of conversation is regarded very highly and proverbs are the palm-oil with which words are eaten'. The importance of oral culture is evident even in the English writing of African authors.[2]

The West African sociolinguistic context is, thus, one of a mainly rural population who speak African languages, contrasted with an urban setting, within which a minority speak a European language. The setting is, however, fundamentally a multilingual one, in which West Africans are, traditionally, speakers of two or three languages, often including the mother tongue, the dominant regional language and the dominant national language.

The West African speech communities in the United Kingdom

The first Africans arrived in Britain in Elizabethan times (*cf* Walvin 1970), although for many years this presence was limited to small numbers of individuals. With the coming of the slave trade and, later, the establishment of colonial links with Africa, these numbers gradually increased, only to reduce to a trickle by the late nineteenth century. Soon, however, substantial numbers of African sailors began to put down roots in the major ports of Cardiff, Liverpool and London. Africans also fought in both the First and Second World Wars and by 1947 some 2,000 former servicemen had returned to Britain to pursue their studies in London which rapidly became a base for post-war African nationalism (Walvin 1984).

Britain has continued to be a favoured destination for many West African students from former British colonies and also a centre for African nationalist and pan-African activities. An estimated 52,656 of a total African population in Britain of 267,252 came from West Africa according to the Official Census of 1981 (OPCS 1983). The larger East African group, however, is likely to have consisted mainly of British citizens from Kenya, Uganda and Malawi of South Asian descent who chose to come to the UK for political and economic reasons (see Fig. 2.2).

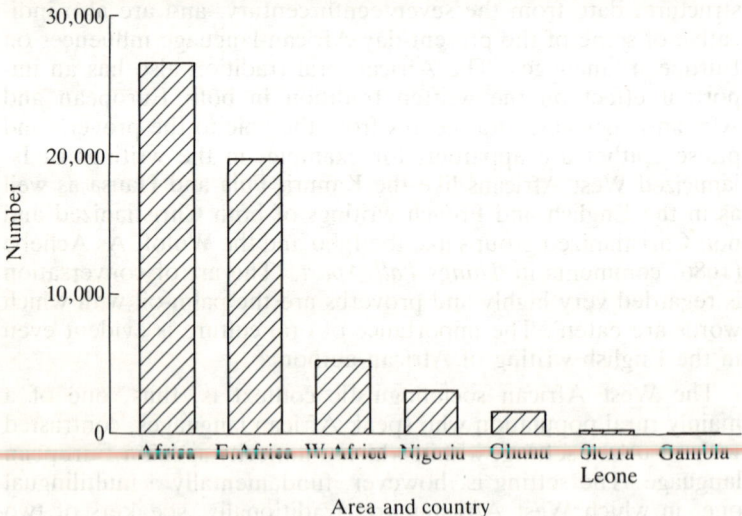

FIGURE 2.2 Africans resident in Britain, 1981

TABLE 2.1   Speakers of West African languages reported in the ILEA
Language Census, 1981–87

	1981	1983	1985	1987
Yoruba	757	683	1,120	2,031
Twi	288	446	724	947
Ibo	525	514	646	755
Ga	55	229	287	347
Fante	150	146	199	273

The highest numbers of Africans resident in Britain live in and around London. Of the West African group, the majority come from Nigeria and consist mainly of Yoruba, Twi and Ibo. This may be due to longer and closer contacts between these groups and Britain during the colonial period. The ILEA *Language Census* for 1987, for instance, shows some 5 African languages with over 100 speakers, all of which are West African languages (Table 2.1). Particularly noteworthy is the 167 per cent increase between 1981 and 1987 in the numbers of Yoruba speakers who currently constitute 3.13 per cent of bilingual pupils within the ILEA. They include a high proportion of students and professionals, whose stay in Britain is usually temporary. Only 40 per cent of the West African population in the UK is female. This low percentage reflects the strong African tradition of women in domestic roles, for instance as mothers and workers for the extended family, irrespective of their level of Western education. These roles tend to make West African women extremely focused on the family and decrease their motivation for travel outside their village, town or ethnolinguistic group, let alone their country.

Changing patterns of language use

A few of the older generation may use the mother tongue only. However, as English is the official language in the home countries of West Africans in Britain, most of the older generation will have a basic understanding of English, especially if they are from the former British West African coastal regions. Where there is no knowledge of English, most will have some grasp of English pidgin, which is widely used as a language of inter-ethnic communication, especially for the purposes of trade. For instance, Ibo traders in northern Nigeria would generally use Nigerian pidgin to sell their goods to non-English-speaking Hausa customers.

Code-switching between languages, involving the use of a European, or indeed any other language, for a defined purpose is almost second nature to West Africans in Britain as in Africa. Thus, a discussion about education could begin in English, with the basic concepts being firstly described in English; the discussion could then be elaborated in an important regional language such as Wolof and finally, personal opinions could be expressed in the mother tongue of the speakers, say Diola. Code-switching in West African languages is often affected by the expectations of tradition. For instance, it is generally expected that polite language, possibly full of honorifics, would be used by younger people when talking to older people and *Baba* (Grandfather) would be said to any older Hausa person, whether they were really related or not.

This multilingual tradition makes West Africans quite open to the promotion of many language varieties simultaneously. However, economic and political factors such as the potential use of the language concerned for trading purposes, would play an important part in influencing the choice of languages to be learned for the West African. Consequently, all West Africans wish to promote their own mother tongue, as well as any other languages with an evident utilitarian purpose.

Most of the older generation prefer to use their mother tongue to each other. Where the younger generation live with the older generation, the mother tongue is passed on through oral use in the household. Where, more frequently, the older generation is in the home country and the parents of the third generation are busy working long hours, the mother tongue is also passed on orally, but not with the same degree of competence and exposure, to the third generation. Reactions to this difference of exposure may range from acceptance of the limited use of the mother tongue as inevitable, to sending their children back to West Africa in order that they learn the mother tongue and its related culture(s) in greater depth.

Language, culture and community

With the exception of the Alladura Christians, who at times make use of Yoruba in their worship, the majority of West African languages are mainly supported through their greater use at ceremonies associated with rites of passage, such as naming ceremonies, weddings and funerals. Only cultural/political groups with an African nationalist perspective, such as the Hackney Black Peoples' Organization, the Hackney African Organization and the Africa Centre, provide any other support for African languages in Britain. The Africa Centre, for example, holds regular evening classes in conjunction with the ILEA in Arabic, Swahili, Hausa and other African languages, as well as on various aspects of African life including art, literature, politics and development studies. All three groups provide a focal point for participation in African cultural life through various regular activities, which may include conferences, exhibitions, films and videos, traditional dances, lunchtime meetings, poetry readings, talks and discussions, theatre, national evenings, music, book launchings, dances and African food and drink.

Contact with the home country has, for West Africans, traditionally meant contact with their families through meeting (extended) family obligations, *eg* sending money home for a relative or a relative being sent to stay with them in England, in order that the relative can pursue their studies, while being maintained by those in England. Such obligations are reinforced by visits home. These visits are, however, often less frequent than desired, as the expectation of relatives for a present often has to be saved for in addition to the fare home. Messages are also brought orally by those travelling in either direction, *eg* 'Morgan sends his greetings, and wants you to know that he and his family are well.' Written messages, too, are sent by letter, at times delivered by hand, by travellers who know the family both in England and at home. Telephone calls, where available, are also used.

There are no major publications, in an African language, being circulated in Britain. However, the magazine, *West Africa*, published in English, is an important and widely read written source of information on West Africa for West Africans, including languages and culture.

Education and language reproduction

Utilitarian attitudes towards language have no doubt combined with the African oral tradition of language learning to make the organization of mother tongue classes a low priority in the West African community, though some provision does exist. For instance, six classes were offered in the London borough of Hackney in 1986 teaching Swahili, Hausa, Twi and Somali. Such classes were often run as part of a wider dissemination of Pan-Africanist values, for example, at the classes of the Hackney African Organization.

As the pupils learning their mother tongue in Britain are out of direct contact with their countries of origin, culture and

religion are an important part of the 'language' classes, particularly as many of the classes are also simultaneously attended by
pupils of Afro-Caribbean origins who want to make a tangible
link with their African roots through learning an African language. For such pupils, the African cultural context is an essential
part of the 'language' learning.

There are few written materials available for mother tongue
teaching. Those available are often imported from West Africa
and often suffer from a highly academic perspective. However,
teachers often make use of the rich African oral tradition of
language drawing on participation in games, proverbs, songs,
poetry, and story-telling. For example, the learning of the following word game in Hausa, in which children repeat key phrases
one by one, emphasizes important differences between the
variants of the consonant phoneme /k/ which include [kw] and
[k'] (see Dalphinis 1985, 1990):

kwad'o	*a*	*koko*	*a*	*kwanche*
frog	at	cocoa	at	lyingdown

The languages are not usually taught in mainstream schools, but
are offered at a few universities in Britain, for example, the
School of Oriental and African Languages of the University of
London, where the teaching of African languages was originally
provided as part of the training of British colonial officers serving
in colonial West Africa. West African languages also sometimes
feature in non-statutory provision in adult education institutes and
cultural and political organizations run by Africans and/or
Caribbeans.

The rich oral tradition on which West African speakers draw
deserves much wider recognition. The primacy given in the
Western world to the written word has often resulted in an under-
valuing of oral culture. Yet the considerable prestige attached to
skilful speakers in African society is hardly consistent with the
picture of verbal deprivation which has often been painted by
literate outsiders. It is also interesting to note that the African
approaches to language learning, such as the word games
described above, are beginning to figure more prominently in
mainstream language teaching which has traditionally relied on
more literate approaches to language learning. As we begin to
realize the importance of creating real communication situations
for effective language learning, teachers will hopefully reassess
the African perspective.

Notes

1. See p. 42–3 for a discussion of pidginization and creolization.
2. See John (1979, 1984) for a discussion of the role of the oral tradition, from the point of view of research and practice of librarians.

References

ABDULAZIZ MKILIFI, M. H. (1972) 'Triglossia and Swahili–English bilingualism in Tanzania', *Language and Society* **1**: 197–213.
ACHEBE, C. (1980) *Things Fall Apart*. London: Heinemann.
DALBY, D. (1970) *Black Through White: Patterns of Communication*. Bloomington, USA: Indiana University.
DALBY, D. (1978) *The Language Map of Africa*. London: International African Institute.
DALPHINIS, M. (1981) 'African influences in creoles lexically based on Portuguese, English and French, with special reference to Casamance Kriul, Gambian Krio and St Lucian Patwa.' Unpublished Ph.D. thesis, SOAS, University of London.
DALPHINIS, M. (1985) *Caribbean and African Languages*. London: Karia Press.
DALPHINIS, M. (1990) *Hausa Game-Songs and Education*. London: Karia Press.
DUMONT, P. (1983) *Le Français et les Langues Africaines au Sénégal*. Paris: ACCT/Karthala.
GUNNEMARK, E. and KENRICK, D. (1985) *A Geolinguistic Handbook*. Kungalv, Sweden: printed by Goterna.
HOCKETT, C. F. (1958) *Course in Modern Linguistics*. London: Macmillan.
JOHN, M. (1979) 'Libraries in oral-traditional societies', *International Library Review* **11**: 321–39
JOHN, M. 1984 'The role of libraries in oral-traditional societies', *International Library Review* **16**, 393–406
LABAT, J. B. (1728) *Nouvelle Relation de l'Afrique Occidentale Contenant une Description Exacte de Sénégal*, Paris.
LABOV, W. (1966) *The Social Stratification of English in New York City*. Washington DC: Center for Applied Linguistics.
Office of Population, Census and Surveys (OPCS) (1983) *Census 1981: National Report Great Britain*. London: HMSO.
WALVIN, J. (1970) *Black and White. The Negro and English Society 1555–1945*, London: Allen Lane.
WALVIN, J. (1984) *Passage to Britain*. Harmondsworth: Pelican.

Chapter 3

The Afro-English creole speech community

Morgan Dalphinis

> *Kau neva no di yus of im tel til di butcha kot it of*
> The cow didn't know what use her tail was until the butcher cut it off
>
> JAMAICAN PROVERB

The Caribbean, like Africa, was subjected to various colonial powers: the Dutch in Surinam; the Spanish in Cuba; the French in Guadeloupe; the British in Barbados. Many West Indian territories, such as St Lucia and Trinidad, have been successively colonized by various European governments. In spite of these various national influences, the political and economic conditions experienced throughout the Caribbean ensured a unity of response. Consequently, much of what is said about the British-dominated territories is also valid throughout the Caribbean. The present chapter, however, will deal only with those where the main political influence was British, namely Jamaica, Trinidad and Tobago, Barbados, Guyana, Nevis, Antigua, Anguilla, St Vincent, Montserrat and St Kitts.

The language varieties spoken in the Caribbean today grew out of a situation of multilingual contact. The Africans initially transported to the West Indies came mainly from the coast but were later followed by Africans from the interior, as the European enslavers came to know more and more of the continent. Africans who spoke the same language(s) were deliberately separated as a means of ensuring maximum control. It became a matter of urgency, therefore, to develop a form of communication between the Africans themselves. When people from different language backgrounds are thrown together, there is a struggle to find the lowest common denominator: vocabulary is reduced: grammar is simplified and the process of pidginization gets under way. Pidgins were not, of course, a new phenomenon in the Caribbean. When such pidgins became the mother tongues of subsequent generations in the Caribbean in the period between 1600 and 1800, the simplified pidgins were rapidly expanded into creole languages which fulfilled all the communication needs of their speakers. Although the European impact upon the Caribbean has been well documented, the impact of Africans on the Caribbean has received relatively less attention. This is particularly true from the point of view of African languages in the Caribbean, where relatively few texts, especially by European publishers, highlight the common African-language origins of the Caribbean creole languages.

The Caribbean creoles are believed to have developed, at least partly, through the remoulding of European vocabulary according to the semantic, syntactic and phonological patterns of African languages (Comhaire-Sylvain 1936). Both political and linguistic factors impinge upon the question of which language family or families the Caribbean creoles form a part. From the point of view of their vocabularies, they could be said to belong to the Romance language family if their vocabulary is French, and to the Germanic family if their vocabulary is English. From the point of view of their grammatical structure, however, both groups of creoles could be said to belong to the Niger–Kordofanian family, as shown in Fig. 3.1.

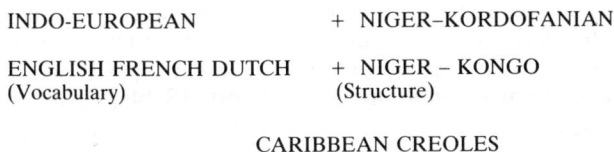

INDO-EUROPEAN	+ NIGER–KORDOFANIAN
ENGLISH FRENCH DUTCH (Vocabulary)	+ NIGER – KONGO (Structure)

CARIBBEAN CREOLES

FIGURE 3.1 Language family affiliations of Caribbean creoles

These mixed origins have had political and practical consequences. First, the European languages which provided their vocabulary base were also the languages of the slavemasters who brought the original Africans to the Caribbean. This association was no doubt responsible for hostile views and theories about the genetic inferiority of Africans. Second, historical linguistics, as a discipline, was founded on the study of European languages and was based, therefore, on similarities in sounds and in the vocabulary of these languages. This emphasis resulted in scholars overlooking the ways in which the grammatical similarities and differences which we were discussed above (see p. 34) were more important to African languages.

European languages are recognized as the national languages of most Caribbean territories, although creoles are much more widely spoken. It would be wrong, however, to think of the linguistic situation in the Caribbean in terms of two distinct, polar varieties. The broad creole – or Patwa – described by writers like Bailey (1966) is undoubtedly a psychological reality for Caribbean speakers; so, too, are the local standard varieties which differ in a small number of areas from British standard English in ways similar to American or Australian standard English (*cf* Trudgill and Hannah 1985). In actual speech situations, however, speakers will range between the Patwa and standard ends of the continuum. Older, rural, poorly educated speakers will use more Patwa features than younger, urban, well-educated speakers; but all speakers will use more Patwa features in informal conversation with family and friends than in more formal domains such as commerce, government and education.

The difficulties of describing this speech community have attracted the attention of many linguists including De Camp (1971), Bailey (1971) and Bickerton (1981) who have advocated the idea of intermediate varieties between Patwa and standard varieties within a continuum. Other linguists have emphasized a range of other solutions including code-switching between a distinct Patwa and a distinct Caribbean variety of English (Lawton 1980); acts of psychological identity in which speakers make attempts to use either the Patwa or the standard variety, but may never realize that aim due to limited competence in the variety with which they may wish, at any given moment, to identify (Sebba 1989; Le Page and Tabouret-Keller 1985); and the use of creoles as part of the symbolic resistance of Afro-Caribbean youth to the oppression of English (Brandt 1988).

Variation in Patwa speech can be exemplified as follows:

i	de	nyam	tanya
i	de	it	yam
he	de	it	yam
he	does	it	yam
he	eat		yam

all of which means 'He/she eats yam'.

It is possible to describe this fluid situation in terms of transitional bilingualism, a condition which has prevailed throughout the language history of Caribbean creoles, which started off as pidgins, before the transition to creoles. In some cases, such as Barbados, where there is a tradition of assimilation towards metropolitan cultural norms, English creoles seem again to be on a transitional road to reabsorption by their European languages of origin, while, in other cases, such as Jamaica, where there is a tradition of independent and different cultural norms, they appear to retain their permanence as separate languages (*cf* Valdman 1978; Dalphinis 1981 who point to similar differences among the French creoles).

The situation in the Caribbean can therefore be described in terms of a diglossic situation, with the creoles being used as low-status spoken languages reserved for domains such as family and home and the European languages being used as high-status written languages in commerce, government and education. This situation has particularly evident educational and administrative problems, in territories where literacy is low but there is a wish to promote literacy, not in the mother tongue – creole – but in the official language.

While European languages have a written tradition, Caribbean creoles and their African antecedents have a well-established oral tradition evident in the form of songs, riddles, proverbs, prose narratives, poetry and tongue twisters. This rich and lively Afro-Caribbean oral culture is evident, for instance, in speech-making (Abrahams 1972), story-telling (Crowley 1966) and the toasting, rapping and dubbing of the younger generation of Afro-Caribbean performers (Dalphinis 1981; Bones 1986; Berry 1986). Because English is the language of education, the vast majority of Caribbean literature and reading materials are written in English. None the less, there is a growing tradition of authors such as Louise Bennett who either write their poetry and narrative entirely in Patwa or, like Naipaul and Callender, make extensive use of Patwa in their dialogue. These new 'superliterates' (*cf* Acton and Dalphinis 1990) are also literate in the European language of their country, and contrast with the creole non-literates, who are neither literate in creole, nor in the relevant European language.

Afro-Caribbean communities in Britain

The history of the Afro-Caribbean community in Britain is very similar to that of the West African speech communities. Africans first came via the West Indies to Britain as a result of the slave trade and colonial interests in the Caribbean. West Indians came as sailors in the late nineteenth and early twentieth centuries, settling in the major ports. They also fought in both World Wars, though most later returned home.

The most significant migration from the West Indies, however, took place in the 1950s. The post-war economic boom had created serious labour shortages, especially in jobs which were low-paid and demanded antisocial hours, and employers such as the National Health Service and London Transport launched recruiting drives in various areas of the New Commonwealth, including the West Indies. Unemployment in the Caribbean was high and North America, the traditional destination for emigration, had been cut off by legislation enacted in the early 1950s. The opportunities opening up in the UK made this a logical new destination.

Some 200,000 West Indians arrived in Britain between 1955 and 1961. This rapid flow had begun to slow down when progressively more stringent immigration legislation had the effect of increasing the rate of immigration in an attempt to beat the new laws. By 1971, some 543,000 West Indians had settled in the UK. The size of the various communities, according to the 1981 Census (OPCS 1983) is as shown in Fig. 3.2.

London is the most important Afro-Caribbean settlement with important centres in Brixton and Haringey. However, West Indians have also settled in industrial centres all over the country. The initial pattern of settlement was often affected by the island of origin of the original settlers, who would often try to settle close to each other, as well as encouraging more of their friends and relatives to come and join them in England. Thus, Slough has a high Anguillan population, High Wycombe a large Vincentian population, while the Caribbeans in Reading are predominantly Barbadian (Edwards 1986). To this island solidarity was added the racialized context of physical attacks on Caribbeans, which further solidified these island-based patterns of settlement.

The employment made available to West Indians was mainly menial and often of lower status than the jobs they had left behind in the West Indies. Extensive racism, in employment and in housing, was, and continues to be, practised against Afro-Caribbeans. For instance, in the 1980s one and a half times as many Blacks as Whites have been registered as unemployed and, for males over the age of 35 who live outside Inner London,

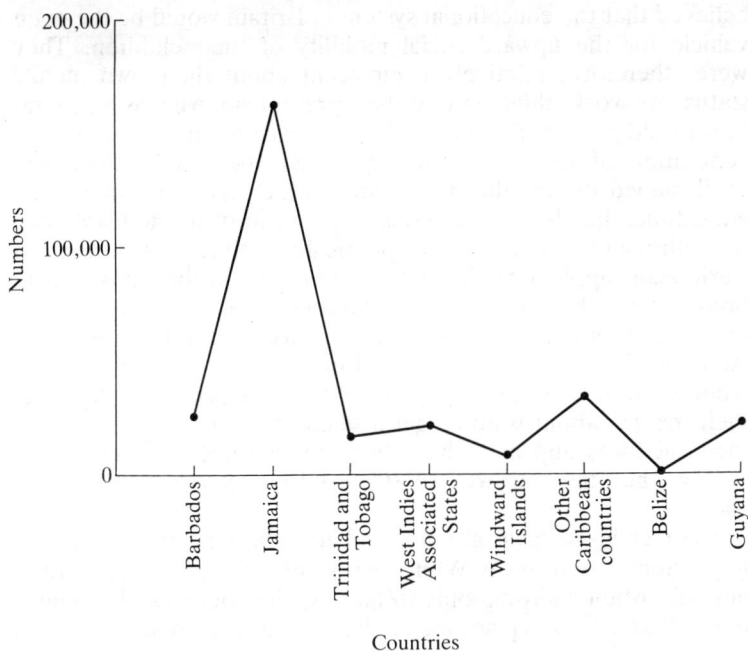

FIGURE 3.2 Caribbeans resident in Britain, 1981

Birmingham and Manchester, the rate of unemployment is twice as high as for the White population (Brown 1984). Such racism, extended into the educational context, has resulted in Afro-Caribbean children being unable to perform at their full potential in educational tests (Coard 1971; Townsend 1971; Milner 1983; Rampton 1981). Writers such as Eysenck (1971) have used this underachievement as data to justify racist educational ideas which suggest that, basically, Africans and their Afro-Caribbean descendants are a genetically inferior species of *homo sapiens*. Some of this ideology is reflected in the massive educational under-achievement of Black children in British schools whereby a disproportionately large number of children have found their way into lower streams, non-examination classes and schools for the educationally subnormal (Coard 1971; Townsend 1971). Institutionalized racism is now widely recognized as the major factor in the underperformance (Rampton 1981).

On initial settlement in Britain, many Caribbean parents

believed that the educational system in Britain would be the main vehicle for the upward social mobility of their children. They were, therefore, relatively complacent about their own menial status and work, thinking that their present suffering as a generation would provide the foothold for their children. However, this generation of settlers in the 1950s and 1960s were extremely disillusioned by an education system which failed to meet their educational needs. As a response, some return to the Caribbean on retirement, some become politically active, others work in Caribbean supplementary schools and other Caribbean organizations. Many, however, have withdrawn into themselves in the face of discrimination and its consequences (with its roots in the Atlantic slave trade): their children may be unemployed, in schools for the educationally subnormal, in prison or asylums; their menial labour is no longer a selling point in the job-market; their sacrifices appear to have been for nothing and, almost invisibly, they have grown old (Coard 1971; Smith 1976; Brown 1984).

Their children have also reacted to racism in many different ways. Some try to be as White as possible in mental and cultural outlook, often choosing only to have White friends and to marry only Whites. Others place an emphasis on directly opposite beliefs and practices which emphasize Blackness rather than rejecting it. Thus, Rastafarianism, Black Pentecostalism and Black political movements, such as the Black Power movement of the 1960s, all stress an acceptance of positive pride in the African heritage, as well as a need for activities which promote spiritual, economic and political freedom among peoples of African descent. Both schools of thought lead to different political objectives and carry the historical division between house slaves in the Caribbean (pro-European) and field slaves (pro-African) into present-day Britain.

Changing patterns of language use

There have been many important changes in the use of Patwa in the Afro-Caribbean speech communities in Britain since the early 1970s. Until this point, there was a continuing source of new arrivals from the West Indies whose linguistic behaviour would, initially at least, have been very similar to the patterns described above for the Caribbean. From 1975 onwards, however, almost all Afro-Caribbean children starting school in the UK have been born in Britain.

Creole is spoken by the older generation, among themselves and is also used to the younger generation. However, there is an expectation that younger people should use English and not Patwa to their parents. This non-reciprocal pattern of usage is closely linked with expectations that the younger person should not be held back as they make their way through an English-speaking educational system by an overfamiliarity with Patwa. The context for the learning of Patwa thus lies as much outside the home in the peer group as it does in the family.

Various differences have been noted between the Patwa of British Blacks and that of their Caribbean-born parents and grandparents. There is evidence, for instance, of extensive code-switching between English and Patwa (Sutcliffe 1982). And in a study of British-born children of Jamaican parents in the West Midlands, Edwards (1986) has shown that actual competence in Patwa, the frequency of usage of Patwa features and patterns of language use are related to social networks in such a way that the more integrated into the Black community, the more frequent and widespread the use of Patwa features, the greater the competence of the speaker.

The use of Patwa for British Blacks can thus be seen very clearly as an identity issue. The choice of distinctively Black features in young people's speech is a positive assertion of their Black identity and a rejection of the low status accorded to Black people and their speech by mainstream White society. It is also interesting in this respect to note reports of Patwa usage among White youths who closely identify with Black culture and wish to become a part of it (Hewitt 1986; Edwards 1986).

Language, culture and community

Contact between Britain and the Caribbean is extensive and growing. Many people travel home, especially on festive occasions, such as carnival and Christmas. Given that there are virtually no new arrivals from the Caribbean today, such links remain a sign of strong solidarity for Caribbean families living on both sides of the Atlantic. An increasing number of older people are retiring to the Caribbean and many more Caribbeans are now able to afford to visit their relatives in Britain. It is becoming much more common for British-born children to spend a few months or even years with their grandparents in the Caribbean in order that their parents in Britain may take advantage of the extended family to help with child rearing. A small number of

British-educated and professionally qualified young people are also returning to work in the Caribbean where, often in contrast to their experience of racism in Britain, they have found it easy to find work.

In addition to the island solidarity already mentioned, the realities of the housing market and racism have led many Black people to live in predominantly Black areas, where friends, neighbours and family are close by. Thus community solidarity is high, although housing conditions are generally bad and a vicious cycle of poverty is cemented with low expectations of Black children in British schools.

Older and younger Black people meet in supplementary schools, theatre groups, social clubs, youth clubs, cafés, Pentecostal churches, political groups, sports teams, local carnivals and any other settings which favour the natural gregariousness of Afro-Caribbean peoples and which stress externalization and, above all, the high verbal skills of an oral tradition. Although language behaviour in these situations will vary enormously according to the subject of conversation, the individuals concerned, and the identity which they want to project, a great deal of creole usage is likely to be heard in these settings, particularly between peers. Such settings are the natural context for Afro-Caribbean culture: speakers generally feel less inhibited by the negative image of their culture which emanates from White people and are more comfortable in externalizing their true Caribbean selves through creole.

Music remains the most widespread and dynamic medium through which the mother tongue is perpetuated. The African tradition of using oral culture as a vehicle of social criticism is enhanced by music, which often acts as an aid to memorization. Calypso is the most evident example. The great Trinidadian performer, 'Sparrow', for instance, in 'Bill and Zaina', sees the departure of American soldiers from their bases in the Caribbean at the end of the Second World War as an opportunity for the local men to reassert their control because 'Yankee gone, Sparrow take over now'. Historically, calypso was followed by ska, reggae and dub or toasting, all forms of this same tradition. Of the latter, reggae is the best known. The late Bob Marley, widely regarded as one of reggae's most important singers, continued the tradition of creole social criticism, highlighting racism as a cause of war:

> Until the philosophy which holds one race superior
> And another inferior is finally and permanently

Destroyed and abandoned, everywhere is war
Is a war . . . .

Dub or toasting emerged as an art form with the development of
sound system or mobile discotheques. Disc jockeys, partly in
order to enhance audience participation in the music, sing their
own personal verbal elaborations over the record they are playing. The lyrics of toasts, like those of reggae, not strongly
influenced by creole. Take, for instance, the work of the Jamaican-
born and British-educated poet and musician Lynton Kwesi
Johnson (1981) in *Inglan is a Bitch*:

wel mi dhu day wok and mi dhu night wok
mi dhu clean wok an ' mi dhu dutty wok
dem seh dat black man is very lazy
but if you si how mi wok y'u woulda sey mi crazy

Inglan is a bitch
dere's no escapin' it
Inglan is a bitch
y'u better face up to it

dem have a likkle facktri up inna Brackley
inna disya facktri all dem dhu is pack crackry
fi di laas fifteen years dem get mi laybah
now awftah fifteen years me fall out a fayvah

Inglan is a bitch
dere's no escapin' it
Inglan is a bitch
dere's no runnin' whey fram it

mi know dem have work, work in abundant
yet still, dem make mi redundant
now, at fifty-five mi gettin' quite ol'
yet still, dem sen' mi fi goh draw dole

Inglan is a bitch
dere's no escapin' it
Inglan is a bitch
is whey wi a go dhu 'bout it?

Creole also emerges as a major medium of artistic creativity in
the writing of British Black writers such as James Berry, Samuel
Selvon, Linton Kwesi Johnson and Jennifer Johnson and Desmond Johnson. Take, for instance, the linguistic self-exploration
in Desmond Johnson's 'Yard Talk' (1984):

YARD TALK

no-no
  b
    r
      o
        k
          e
            n
inglish
mi a knuckle up buckle up an chuckle up
mi words
like the stammer of sentences in de bottom
of some people's throat
yardtalkinglishintosubmission
till mi pat-wa bus tru an conquer. . . .

Thus Black writing is an extension of an Afro-Caribbean cultural continuity in creole. This is in itself a continuity of the African oral tradition, in which the responsibility of oral artists includes criticism of the social contexts in which they find themselves.

Education and language reproduction

Because English is the medium of instruction in the Caribbean, there was never any expectation on the part of West Indian parents that creole should become part of the curriculum in a British context. Indeed creole was always seen by them as a hindrance to their own upward social mobility and progress was always measured in terms of ability in English. In a Caribbean context, power, resources and social comforts have historically fallen within the ambit of English-speaking and mulatto peoples. It is therefore not surprising that many present-day Caribbeans should feel that it is the language of these groups, rather than their political power, which will lead to their own emancipation and, where this is clearly not possible, to that of their own children.

By the same token, not only was there no attempt to introduce creole into the curriculum in the early years but teachers demonstrated varying degrees of ignorance and antipathy towards it. For example, the National Association of Schoolmasters is on record as saying that 'The West Indian child usually arrives speaking a kind of "plantation English" which is socially unacceptable and inadequate for education' (NAS 1969:5). Similarly a report published by the Birmingham branch of the Association of Teachers of English to Pupils from Overseas (1970) refers to West Indian language as 'very relaxed like the way they walk'. Teachers in the early 1970s, on assessing recurrent differences between Caribbean creolized speech and standard English (eg 'He going home' versus English 'He is going home'), concluded that these differences were due to the cognitive/genetic inferiority of Africans and Afro-Caribbeans (Edwards 1979). Some attempt was finally made to address these problems with the publication of the Schools Council Concept 7–9 materials, but these, too, were couched within the pathological framework which characterized much thinking on non-standard language at the time. This situation was summed up by CRE (1976:5) in the following terms:

> It is ironical that at a time when Creole dialect did cause problems of communication and comprehension in schools, the question was largely ignored. However, by the time Creole had been identified as an educational issue, the majority of West Indian children were no longer speaking it in schools. It is often pointed out to us that some time during the early years at secondary school many West Indian pupils who up till then have used the language of the neighbourhood, begin to use Creole dialect. But its use is a deliberately social and psychological protest, an assertion of identity, not a language teaching problem.

More recently, greater recognition of linguistic diversity as a resource rather than a problem has led to the efforts of some teachers to introduce Patwa into the curriculum. Such efforts, however, have been met with considerable suspicion, both from teachers (eg the headteacher who said he would introduce Patwa only 'over his dead body', see Edwards 1979) and from parents who wonder if this is yet another attempt to hold our children back. Caribbean parents have been instead more supportive of the formation of supplementary schools which give emphasis to traditional skills rather than any notion of promoting creole. The subconscious aim of many parents may well be to reproduce in Britain a version of the Caribbean educational system which also emphasized mathematics, English, reading and writing.

Some Caribbean groups who have a high awareness of education, such as the Caribbean Communications Project, do support the promotion of the mother tongue. However, many Black radicals and educationalists have pointed to the dangers inherent in introducing Patwa into the curriculum. Stone (1981), for instance, has argued that the introduction of Patwa into schools is simply an attempt to defend the 'legitimate' culture of the school against the 'heretical' culture of Black people, and suggests that if teachers 'legitimize' the use of Patwa this will lead to the development of new varieties of Patwa which serve the same function of resistance as the present forms. Others argue that the presence or absence of creole in the curriculum is not related to the level of political resistance of Caribbean pupils and cite the case of many English-speaking Black Americans whose resistance has not diminished with their own loss of creole (Dalphinis 1985).

Carby (1980) points out that familiarity with Patwa on the part of teachers will by no means remove racist attitudes within schools which are by far the most serious obstacles to social equality for Black people. However, the focus of Carribean people in Britain has often been the extension of their educational opportunities and improvement in their material conditions. The eradication of racism in White teachers has therefore been seen as an obstacle to those goals rather than an end in itself. Consequently, where parents have any desire to promote creole, they are concerned with preserving their cultural heritage for their children and not for White teachers.

None the less, there are many teachers and educators, both Black and White, who argue that the recognition of Patwa, possibly in the form of language awareness programmes which draw on all the languages and dialects of teachers and children in the school has much to recommend it. The underlying rationale for this approach is that it is more realistic to value and build on the linguistic resources which children bring with them to school, than to criticize, ignore or reject their language skills. This may be particularly important in the case of Caribbean pupils. The languages of many other minority groups are increasingly accepted in the mainstream curriculum as community or heritage languages and children are offered English-language support. The long neglect of the linguistic situation of Caribbean pupils may well have contributed to the high incidence of suspensions, mental health problems and underachievement.

While it could be totally inappropriate to teach Patwa as a subject, there are thus strong grounds for recognizing its validity in various parts of the curriculum, such as in the teaching of literature and discussions on linguistic diversity (Dabydeen 1988; Kingman 1988). Some very powerful creole writing has emerged from British Black schoolchildren, much of which is used as a regular classroom resource, eg Paul George's Memories and Chelsea Herbert's Melting Pot, produced by the ILEA Learning

Resources. The Manchester Caribbean Project also works in the same mould of using students' writing in creole as a resource, in this case in an adult education setting.

References

ABRAHAMS, R. (1972) 'The training of the man of words in talking sweet'. *Language in Society* 1 (1) pp. 15–30.

ACTON, T. and DALPHINIS, M. (eds) (1990) *Superliterates and the Struggle for Multilingualism*. London: Karia Press.

Association of Teachers of English to Pupils from Overseas (ATEPO) (Birmingham branch) (1970) *Work Group on West Indian Pupils Report*.

BAILEY, B. L. (1966) *A Transformational Grammar of Jamaican Creole Syntax*. Cambridge: Cambridge University Press.

BAILEY, B. L. (1971) 'Can dialect boundaries be defined?' In D. Hymes (ed.) *Pidginization and Creolization*, Cambridge: Cambridge University Press, pp 341–8.

BERRY, J. (1986) 'The literature of the Black experience'. In D. Sutcliffe and A. Wong (eds) *The Language of the Black Experience*, Oxford: Basil Blackwell, pp 69–106.

BICKERTON, D. (1981) *Roots of Language*. Ann Arbor: Karoma Press.

BONES, J. (1986) 'Reggae dee jaying and Jamaican Afro-lingua'. In D. Sutcliffe and A. Wong (eds) *The Language of the Black Experience*, Oxford: Basil Blackwell, pp 52–68.

BRANDT, G. (1990) 'British youth Caribbean creole – the politics of resistance'. In Action and Dalphinis, op. cit.

BROWN, C. (1984) *Black and White Britain*. London: Policy Studies Institute.

CARBY, H. (1980) 'Multicultural fictions'. Occasional Stencilled Paper No. 58, Centre for Contemporary Cultural Studies, University of Birmingham.

COARD, B. (1971) *How the West Indian Child is Made Educationally Sub-Normal in the British School System*. London: New Beacon Books.

COMHAIRE-SYLVAIN, S. (1936) *Le Créole Haitien: Morphologie et Syntaxe*. Port au Prince, Haiti.

Commission for Racial Equality (CRE) (1976) *The Select Committee on Race Relations and Immigration Enquiry on the West Indian Community. Evidence on Education from the Community Relations Commission*. London: CRE.

CROWLEY, D. (1966) *I Could Talk Old-Story Good: Creativity in Bahamian Folklore*. Berkeley and Los Angeles: University of California Press.

DABYDEEN, D. (1988) *A Handbook for Teaching Caribbean Literature* London: Heinemann.

DALPHINIS, M. (1981) 'African influences in Creoles lexically based on Portuguese, English and French, with special reference to Casamance

Kriul, Gambian Krio and St Lucian Patwa'. Unpublished Ph.D. thesis, SOAS, University of London.

DALPHINIS, M. (1985) *Caribbean and African Languages*. London: Karia Press.

DE CAMP, D. (1971) 'Towards a generative analysis of a post-Creole continuum'. In D. Hymes (ed.) *Pidginization and Creolization*, Cambridge: Cambridge University Press, pp. 349–70.

EDWARDS, V. (1979) *The West Indian language Issue in British Schools*. London: Routledge & Kegan Paul.

EDWARDS, V. (1986) *Language in a Black Community*. Clevedon, Avon: Multilingual Matters.

EYSENCK, H. J. (1971) *Race, Intelligence and Education*. London: M. T. Smith.

HEWITT, R. (1986) *Black Talk, White Talk*. Cambridge: Cambridge University Press

JOHNSON, DESMOND (1984) *Deadly Ending Season*. London: Akira Press.

JOHNSON, L. K. (1981) *Inglan is a Bitch*. London: Race Today Publications.

KINGMAN, J. (1988) *Report of the Committee of Inquiry into the Teaching of English Language*. London: HMSO.

LAWTON, D. (1980) 'Language attitude, discreteness and code-shifting in Jamaican creole', *Language in Society* 7: 171–82.

LE PAGE, R. B. and TABOURET-KELLER, A. (1985) *Acts of Identity*. Cambridge: Cambridge University Press

National Association of Schoolmasters (NAS) (1969) *Education and the Immigrants*. Hemel Hempstead, Herts: Educare.

Office of Population, Census and Surveys (OPCS) (1983) *Census 1981: National Report Great Britain*. London: HMSO.

RAMPTON, A. (1981) *West Indian Children in Our Schools* (Interim Report of the Committee of Inquiry into the Education of Children from Ethnic Minority Groups). London: HMSO.

SEBBA, M. (1989) 'What is mother tongue? Some problems posed by London Jamaican'. In Acton and Dalphinis, op. cit.

SMITH, D. (1976) *The Facts of Racial Disadvantage*. London: Political and Economic Planning.

STONE, M. (1981) *The Education of the Black Child in Britain: The Myth of Multicultural Education*. London: Fontana.

SUTCLIFFE, D. (1982) *British Black English*. Oxford: Basil Blackwell.

TOWNSEND, H. E. R. (1971) *Immigrants in School: The LEA Response*. Slough: National Foundation for Educational Research.

TRUDGILL, P. and HANNAH, J. (1985) *International English: A Guide to Varieties of Standard English*. London: Edward Arnold.

VALDMAN, A. (1978) *Le Créole: Structure, Statut et Origine*. Paris: Editions Klincksieck.

Chapter 4

The Kwéyòl speech community

Hubisi Nwenmely

Kwéyòl-la sé yón bèl kado
The kwéyòl language is a wonderful gift
(LOUISY and TURMEL-JOHN 1983)

Kwéyòl is like a ship ready to go on a voyage and calling
everyone aboard.
If you do not come, you'll be left behind.

(CONSTANCE 1988)

French creoles are spoken in many different parts of the world:
Mauritius, Réunion, the Seychelles and Rodrigues in the Indian
Ocean; Louisiana in the USA; Cayenne in South America; and
Haiti, Martinique, Guadeloupe, St Lucia, Dominica, Grenada,
Cariacou and the Grenadines, Trinidad and Tobago, Désirade,
Marie Galante, St Martin, Les Saintes and St Barthélemy in the
Caribbean. In the same way that English creoles have often followed in the wake of English colonialism, French creoles have
often developed in French-dominated territories. The same linguistic processes operate in all these situations: when people from
many different language backgrounds come into contact, they
need to find a common means of communication. In the first instance, a simple pidgin arises with a very basic vocabulary and an
extremely reduced grammar (see Ch. 3 for a discussion of the
same process in an Afro-English context). Later, however, when
the pidgin becomes the first language of subsequent generations,
it undergoes a process of elaboration and expansion. The creole
language which results fulfils all the communication needs of its
speakers but, while the vocabulary is drawn from the dominant
language, the structures which it uses are often very different,
and often originate from the dominated languages.

The precise circumstances surrounding the development of the various French creoles vary a great deal. In Mauritius, for example, there are large Indian and Chinese communities, whereas in the Caribbean the majority of the population was originally transported as slaves from different parts of West Africa. None the less, the similarities between French creoles are far more striking than the differences. Take the following examples:

	I went	you're going	he/she/it'll go	they had gone
Haiti:	*mwen alé*	*u ap alé*	*il va alé*	*yo té alé*
St Lucia:	*mwen alé*	*ou ka alé*	*i ké alé*	*zòt té alé*
Dominica:	*mwen alé*	*ou ka alé*	*i ké alé*	*zòt té alé*
French				
Guiana:	*mo alé*	*u ka alé*	*li wa alé*	*uè tè alè*
Réunion:	*mi parti*	*u lapré parti*	*li sa parti*	*zòt tei parti*
Lousiana:	*mo kuri*	*vu ap kuri*	*li va kuri*	*yé té kuri*
Mauritius:	*mo alé*	*u pé alé*	*li va alé*	*zòt ti alé*

Although there are small Seychellois and Mauritian communities in the UK, by far the largest French creole-speaking population comes from the eastern Caribbean. French creoles are spoken by small numbers of older speakers in Grenada, Trinidad and the Grenadines. In St Lucia and Dominica, however, the majority of the population speak French creoles as their mother tongue and the main focus for this section will therefore be on these two islands.

The French West Indian Company first established St Lucia as a French colony in 1642. In the next 150 years the island changed hands between the French and the British some fourteen times, but remained under British control from 1803 until independence in 1979. Dominica has had a similarly chequered history. It was French between 1632 and 1732 and again between 1778 and 1783 when it finally passed to the British. These extended periods of contact with French at a critical period in the history of the Caribbean have had a lasting effect on the linguistic situation in both islands.

The transfer to British colonial power in the nineteenth century has complicated this situation still further. During the time that the French were in power, French and Afro-French creole would have existed in a diglossic situation. French being reserved for the so-called 'high' domains such as education and administration and the creole coming into its own in 'low' domains, such as informal conversation with family and friends. The arrival of the British meant that English now replaced French in the high domains. Thus, while the French creole continued to thrive in informal contexts, there was an inevitable shift to English in more formal settings, and inevitably St Lucian and Dominican creoles make some use of English loan words as a result. Dalphinis (1986) points to the process of relexification in which English gradually replaces French vocabulary in an otherwise French creole structure. Take the transition from the broad French creole *gason-an ka manjé piman* to the standard English '*the boy eats pepper*'.

gason-an	ka	manjé	piman
boy-la	ka	manjé	piman
boy-la	ka	it	pepa
boy-la	does	it	pepa
the boy		eats	pepper

Social class has been one of the dominant factors in the relexification process. The middle-class well-educated speaker will often use a higher proportion of English words. However, all sections of the population are more likely to use English vocabulary in formal than in informal situations. Individual speakers' level of attachment and identification with a distinctively Afro-French – rather than French – language and culture also plays a part in the pattern of language choice in these communities. Not surprisingly, the least Anglicized eastern Caribbeans show the greatest interest in learning to read and write the Afro-French creole.

Considerable progress has been made in recent years in moving away from the exclusively Anglophone model for education and literacy. Various individuals and bodies, including researchers from the University of the West Indies and the Université Antilles-Guyane, the Creole Committees of St Lucia and Dominica and the Groupe d'Étude et de Recherche en Espace Créolophone, have collaborated in the development of a creole orthography culminating in 1982 with the publication of a standardized orthography by the Standing Committee for Creole Studies. Work is in progress towards a Kwéyòl dictionary (see Fontaine 1988) and various descriptions of Kwéyòl grammar (*eg* Dalphinis 1985, 1986; Carrington 1984) have been published. Groups and institutions, such as the Folk Research Centre in St Lucia, and Mouvman Kwéyòl Sent Lisi and the Komité pou Etid Kwéyòl in Dominica, are also playing a key role in promoting the language by publishing material or organizing classes in Kwéyòl.

The widespread popular support for Kwéyòl has not escaped the notice of the political parties. It is not uncommon, for instance, for politicians to deliver election speeches in Kwéyòl or to be heard using it in public settings such as church services. Official recognition of the centrality of Kwéyòl for eastern Caribbean society is also growing. In both Dominica and St Lucia October 26th is celebrated as *Jounen Kwéyòl* (Kwéyòl Day). In Dominica, *Jounen Kwéyòl* is part of the much larger *Simenn Kwéyòl* (Kwéyòl Week) festivities and the Komité pou Etid Kwéyòl (Committee for the Study of Kwéyòl) operates as a semi-autonomous body recognized by the central government.

Acceptance of a distinctive eastern Caribbean Afro-French identity is becoming increasingly widespread in the Caribbean and is illustrated, for instance, by a change in terminology. St Lucians and Dominicans have traditionally referred to their language as Patwa whereas people from Martinique and Guadeloupe call it Kwéyòl. When the Standing Committee for Creole Studies standardized the orthography in 1982, it was agreed to call the language Kwéyòl, thus bringing it into line with Banzil Kwéyòl – the international Kwéyòl movement.

The Kwéyòl speech community in Britain

Emigration from the Caribbean to Britain took place mainly between the mid-1950s and 1970. People from the eastern Caribbean islands of St Lucia and Dominica formed only a very small proportion of the overall West Indian migration to the UK. In the period between 1955 and 1961, for instance, of the 227,040 West Indians who entered the country, only 7,291 came from St Lucia and 7,663 from Dominica. The effect of this numerically small migration on the eastern Caribbean, however, was profound. It has been estimated that some 10 per cent of the population of St Lucia left the island, and an even higher proportion of the population of Dominica.

Kwéyòl speakers decided to emigrate for the same reasons as for other West Indians: unemployment was very high; the racist practices of McCarthyism had closed the doors to the USA, the traditional destination for emigration; and the UK was actively seeking cheap labour in the New Commonwealth to meet the demands of the post-war boom economy. Eastern Caribbean people had long been associated with the UK, having served on British soil during the war and having settled in ports like London, Liverpool and Cardiff well before this time. It was only during the 1950s and 1960s, however, that more substantial migration took place. Outside the capital, eastern Caribbean communities are to be found in Birmingham, Bradford, Huddersfield,

TABLE 4.1 Numbers of French speakers reported in the ILEA
Language Census, 1981–87

Year	Number
1981	2,808
1983	2,167
1985	2,030
1987	2,357

Liverpool, Luton, Manchester, Milton Keynes and Preston. However, London was the main destination. Eastern Caribbeans are scattered throughout the capital but have particularly strong community bases in Paddington, Forest Gate in Newham, East Dulwich and Peckham in Southwark, Hackney, Haringey and Tower Hamlets. It is interesting in this respect to consider the ILEA *Language Census* returns for speakers of French in its schools set out in Table 4.1. Comparisons with numbers of speakers of languages such as German, Dutch and Danish spoken in other European Community countries with no established pattern of settlement in the UK, would suggest that the French speakers reported in the ILEA *Language Census* are not the children of Eurocrats (Alladina 1986). The most likely explanation is that they are, in the main, speakers of French and Afro-French creoles from the eastern Caribbean and Mauritius.

The Caribbean writer Andrew Salkey reflects in his novel *The Adventures of Catullus Kelly*, 'The blanket term West Indian doesn't exist in the West Indies; it does in London, has to for protection's sake.' This reflection has particular poignancy in the case of Kwéyòl speakers: our Afro-French language and culture in many ways set us apart from the Afro-English Caribbean. British people, however, saw us simply as West Indian and remained, for a very long time, oblivious of our separate identity. Subject to the same kind of racial inequalities in education, housing and employment as Jamaicans, Barbadians or Trinidadians, our common Afro-Caribbean heritage became more important 'for protection's sake' than any differences which exist.

Changing patterns of language use

When the vast majority of St Lucians and Dominicans arrived in the UK, Kwéyòl was the language of the home. With the passing of time, however, there have been important changes. As children went to British schools and English became the language of choice – in conversation with the peer group at least – the linguistic balance in most families began to swing from Kwéyòl to English. First-generation St Lucians and Dominicans still make extensive use of Kwéyòl in conversation with people of their own age and Kwéyòl remains the only acceptable language for important social and family functions. British-born children are thus likely to have a good receptive knowledge of Kwéyòl, but in most cases, their productive competence is extremely limited. The fact that the eastern Caribbeans form a small and relatively dispersed community within the UK makes the task of language maintenance particularly difficult.

In the early years of immigration Kwéyòl was also the language of solidarity for the Caribbean-born children who were making their way through the British school system, serving to isolate them both from the racist comments of British children and teachers and, to some extent, from derogatory remarks offered by other Afro-Caribbeans about their speech. It is noteworthy, though, that over the years, British Black English has gradually taken over this function from Kwéyòl. The tendency of British people to perceive – and treat – all Afro-Caribbeans in the same way has inevitably led large numbers of second-generation St Lucians and Dominicans to see themselves primarily as part of a larger British Black grouping and British Black English rather than Kwéyòl as the language of wider currency. Its use is an assertion of a positive Black identity and a symbol of resistance (*cf* Dalphinis 1986; Edwards 1986).

Language, culture and community

Kwéyòl is a language of solidarity which figures prominently in social and cultural events within the community. Most community associations organize a wide range of social events, often centred around fund-raising. Music plays an important part in gatherings of this kind and Kadans music, traditionally associated with older members of the community, is becoming increasingly popular with young people within the community and beyond. Kadans has its roots in French-speaking African countries like Togo and Zaire, but is also sung throughout the Caribbean and other creolophone regions where the French lyrics are replaced by Kwéyòl. Some community associations, such as Yaa Asantewa and the Claudia Jones Organization promote a wide range of cultural activities. There is also a St Lucian Housing Association and eastern Caribbean cricket teams.

Most eastern Caribbeans are Roman Catholics, although there

is also a small number of Seventh Day Adventists. In both cases, the church is an important focus for community life in areas of Kwéyòl settlement. Although the services in the UK are conducted in English, social exchanges before and after worship usually take place in Kwéyòl. The same is true of the various church groups and activities. Markets in areas of important eastern Caribbean settlement, such as the Ridley Road Market in Hackney, the Burdett Road Market in Tower Hamlets, sometimes reverberate to the sound of Kwéyòl, as do certain public houses in these same areas.

One of the most culturally active Kwéyòl groups within the UK has grown out of the East London Patwa/Kwéyòl Project (see also section on Education and language reproduction, below). So far the project has published a newsheet, *Patwa Primer* and *Kalalou Kwéyòl*, a collection of short stories, poems and other works in Kwéyòl and English. In addition, members have written and videoed two short plays and performed two full-length plays. One act of the first full-length production, *Papa Montenez*, was performed at the Tower Hamlets Adult Education Institute 'Open Curtain' Festival in 1985. This was the first time that a Kwéyòl play had been performed in the UK and proved very popular with the audience. The second play, *Volè an laplas-la*, was performed at the GLC-sponsored Caribbean Focus in 1986 to an equally enthusiastic reception. More recently, extracts from *Kalalou Kwéyòl* were performed at the East London Festival of Languages.

Members of the project continue to produce a wide range of material which is now starting to be more widely circulated, enjoyed and often used as part of adult literacy work. Take, for instance, 'Sent Lisi' by Cindy Marie Augustin which appears in *Kalalou Kwéyòl:*

Sent Lisi

Sòlèy-la ka bat asou do mwen,
Mé mwen kontan, mwen wivé,
Sent Lisi, mi mwen, mwen viwé.
Sé pa dé zan dépi mwen té kité,
Mé apwézan mwen *vini* pou wèsté.
Fwédi-a anlè-a té twò mové
Mwen vini pou pwan chalè sòlèy-la.
Glo-a anba-a té tèlman fwèt,
Mwen vini pou gouté lanmè salè.
Sé fèy-la la-ba-a té twò sèk,
Mwen vini pou touché zèb séwen.
Magwé mwen ja maché otan chimen,
Mwen épi Sent Lisi pa sa sépawé.

Saint Lucia

The sun beats down on my back,
But I am glad I am here,
Saint Lucia, here I am, I have returned.
It is not two years since I have been away,
But this time around, I am here to stay.
Thé cold above was just too much,
I have come back to taste the sun,
The water below was much too cold,
I have come back to taste the sea.
The leaves beyond were just too dry,
I have returned to touch the moist grass.
Although I have walked many a street,
Saint Lucia and I could never part.

A recent development is the formation of the Mouvman Kwéyòl: London, a body with a wide-ranging agenda. The movement sees the Kwéyòl language and literacy as a tool for cultural maintenance and enhancement within the UK. Although Kwéyòl literacy activities were initiated by English speakers, it is felt that the time has now come for Kwéyòl speakers to play a central role in this process as tutors. The movement also aims to link into the world-wide Kwéyòl network through organizations like Banzil Kwéyòl in the Seychelles and the Eastern Caribbean Standing Committee for Creole Studies which encourage the use of Kwéyòl as a spoken and written language. It plans to build up an archive of history, music, folk culture and contemporary issues in Kwéyòl for use as resource and research material.

Education and language reproduction

The low status of Kwéyòl in the Caribbean has meant that, until recently, it has received little attention from educators: English is the medium of education; Kwéyòl is the language of the home. In Britain, most people assumed that, because English was the official language of the eastern Caribbean, St Lucian and Dominican children would naturally speak English. The low status of Kwéyòl also meant that people from the eastern Caribbean were slow to volunteer information on their linguistic background. In the course of their own education they would have received severe reprimands and, in some cases, beatings from parents for engaging in what was commonly called 'yard talk' or 'that bad language'. For many years following their arrival in

Britain, they, too, discouraged their children from talking Kwéyòl. For these reasons, teachers and others often came to learn only by accident that Kwéyòl was a fundamental part of the linguistic repertoire of this area of the Caribbean and, indeed, the mother tongue of the majority.

The reactions of teachers and students in one east London adult education institute (AEI) in the mid-1970s were typical in this respect (Nwenmely and Morris 1986). A national adult literacy campaign had been launched in the UK in 1975 to establish classes for people who had difficulty in reading and writing. By 1976 many Dominican and St Lucian people had enrolled in the ILEA Bethnal Green AEI scheme and were coming into classes to improve their literacy skills, but tutors soon became concerned that they were not meeting the needs of these eastern Caribbean students. The following conversation took place one day over lunch:

Course organizer:	Excuse me, but do you speak another language?
Dominican student:	Patwa! No, it's not a language, it's just what we speak among ourselves.
St Lucian student:	It's broken French, you can't write it down. No, it's not another language.

After a number of similar conversations, Carol Morris, the course organizer, looked for help and advice concerning a written form of Kwéyòl. These searches led her to visit St Lucia in 1980. She found the teaching tapes prepared by a Trinidadian linguist, Lawrence Carrington, which were used for instructing US Peace Corps Volunteers working on the island. She found a number of people involved in the Creole Standing Committee and that, despite what many people had said to the contrary, the population of St Lucia spoke Kwéyòl, known locally as Patwa. This initial contact was the first of many contacts culminating in 1983 with a four-month working visit.

In the meantime a number of seminars were organized in east London to discuss Kwéyòl language issues and sound out the views of the local eastern Caribbean community regarding a Kwéyòl literacy scheme. The Kwéyòl issue can sometimes be a very sensitive one. It is a language of social solidarity and, as such, suggestions that it should be used in domains which are normally reserved for English, can provoke very defensive reactions. Constance (1988), for instance, records the following comments on the subject of learning to read and write Kwéyòl:

Kwéyòl is our culture and we have to keep what is left of our culture to ourselves.

If you want white people to know your business, that is up to you. But let me say it is trouble that you will get. When the same man you have taught goes and teaches the police all that he knows, on that day we are all in trouble.

Do you think I would let these people influence how my language should be spoken? Never!

Am I stupid or a mad man? Can't I and the other people see what the government is up to? After all these years they have been saying that Kwéyòl is not a language, now they've changed their minds and want to write it. When they write it they will rename it and call it theirs.

While many people remain defensive about Kwéyòl, there is none the less a growing feeling that the Kwéyòl community in Britain should keep pace with what was happening in the Caribbean; and a great many people see the advantages of being able to read and write the mother tongue. One incident in particular brought home the value of being able to write Kwéyòl in a British context. The nephew of a member of the seminar group was at the centre of a heart-rending situation. His school were asking all parents to write stories in their own language so that these could be produced in the mother tongue and English, with illustrations by the children, and used as bilingual readers in the classroom. What could the Kwéyòl-speaking parent do when there was no written form of the language? The interim solution was to transcribe the St Lucian folk-tale 'Pyé Papay-la' using English orthography before translating it into English. This book took its place in the school's set of bilingual readers and also became a popular addition to the material used in the local adult literacy schemes. Later, the Kwéyòl was written in standard orthography by Perlette Louisy, the Chair of the Creole Standing Committee and one of the foremost scholars and promoters of Kwéyòl in the eastern Caribbean. This book is very popular with children and adults alike.

The Patwa Project was formally launched in 1984, with Kwéyòl classes running alongside a Black Studies course at the Tower Hamlets AEI. Resources have always been a headache and at the start of the project the only teaching material available was *A Handbook for Writing Creole* (Louisy and Turmel-John 1983). The classes have therefore always been run on a workshop basis: the experts are the Dominican and St Lucian Kwéyòl speakers, and the tutors guide the workshops by structuring the approach to spelling and grammar and working with students to produce teaching and reading materials. Some additional materials are now available from St Lucia and Dominica to supplement our efforts. *L'Ékòl Kwéyòl* (Fontaine 1988) for example, is an extremely well-produced and structured introductory book with tape developed in Dominica, while groups in St Lucia have produced a number of useful readers. The Folk Research Centre in St Lucia has also co-ordinated the production of a Kwéyòl newssheet, *Balata*.

Another focus for the project is to make Kwéyòl language classes available as part of the adult education programme in the same way, for instance, as Spanish, French, Urdu and Hindi. These classes appeal to young people whose parents are Kwéyòl speakers and who want to be able to use the language for social and cultural heritage reasons, especially when they visit the Caribbean and want to be able to talk with their friends and families. The Mouvman Kwéyòl (see section on language, culture and community, above), an offshoot of the Patwa Project, also aims to work towards the possibility of Kwéyòl as a GCSE subject. However, classes are also of interest to people who are going to visit the eastern Caribbean either on holidays or for work. The aim is thus to provide two tiers of language provision: Kwéyòl for cultural and heritage purposes targeted at the children of Kwéyòl speakers and Kwéyòl as a foreign language.

In addition to the initial base at Tower Hamlets AEI, classes are also held at The Book Place in Peckham and at the Claudia Jones Organization. Funding is currently being sought for the training of new tutors and the development of materials. A particular interest is to explore the use of Kwéyòl literacy in supporting the acquisition of language skills *per se* and especially in the acquisition of English to the level of proficiency required by each individual.

Although activities in the areas of Kwéyòl literacy and language teaching are recent, the signs are that they have been built on a solid foundation. It is important to understand, for instance, that any developments in the UK are not taking place in isolation. The growing recognition of Kwéyòl in the eastern Caribbean inevitably reinforces the efforts of Kwéyòl speakers in Britain; so, too, does the awareness of belonging to a world-wide Kwéyòl-speaking community. The present situation can perhaps be summed up with a Kwéyòl proverb: 'Sé pou'w mantjé néyé pou ou apwann najé (In order to learn to swim, you must survive drowning). The shift from Kwéyòl to English is such that the mother tongue in Britain is in danger of drowning. However, initiatives such as the Patwa Project and the Mouvman Kwéyòl mean that, for the present at least, a growing number of people are swimming irrespective of the tide.

References

ALLADINA, S. (1986) 'Black people's languages in Britain – a historical and contemporary perspective'. *Journal of Multilingual and Multicultural Development* 7 (5): 349–60.

CARRINGTON, L. (1984) *St. Lucia Creole: A Descriptive Analysis of its Phonology and Morpho-syntax*. Hamburg: Helmut Buske Verlag.

CONSTANCE, E. (1988) 'Pros and cons of learning Kwéyòl'. In John-Rose, John-Rose and Nwenmely, op. cit., *pp* 2–6.

DALPHINIS, M. (1985) *Caribbean and African Languages*. London: Karia Press.

DALPHINIS, M. (1986) 'French Creoles in the Caribbean and Britain'. In D. Sutcliffe and A. Wong (eds) *The Language of the Black Experience*, Oxford: Basil Blackwell, *pp* 168–91.

EDWARDS, V. (1986) *Language in a Black Community*. Clevedon, Avon: Multilingual Matters.

FONTAINE, DJAMALA M. (1988) L'Ékol Kwéyòl. Grand Bay. Dominica: the author. Available from the Patwa/Kwéyòl Project, Tower Hamlets AEI, The Mile End Centre, English Street, Bow, London E3.

Inner London Education Authority (ILEA) (1981, 1983, 1985, 1987) *Language Census*. London: ILEA Research and Statistics.

JOHN-ROSE, J., JOHN-ROSE, S. and NWENMELY, H. (1988) (eds) *Kalalou Kwéyòl*. London: Mouvman Kwéyòl.

LOUISY, P. and TURMEL-JOHN, P. (1983) *A Handbook for Writing Creole*. Castries, St Lucia: Research St Lucia Publications.

NWENMELY, H. and MORRIS, C. (1986) 'The Kwéyòl language: the language of millions yet denied to millions'. Mimeo, The Patwa Project, Tower Hamlets AEI, The Mile End Centre, English Street, Bow, London E3.

Part two

South Asia

The South Asian area, and India in particular, has been described as a 'sociolinguistic giant' (Srivastava 1984). The wealth of languages contained within this area is immense. This linguistic richness is also reflected in Britain where people originating from this geolinguistic area have made their home. In this part, seven major languages of South Asia – Bengali, Gujarati, Hindi, Panjabi, Sinhala, Tamil and Urdu – are discussed in detail, though reference is also made to over thirty languages which coexist with or are related to the seven.

Of these, Tamil is a south Indian language of the Dravidian family. Sinhala, although located in south India, originated in the north. The north Indian languages have their roots in Sanskrit which over the course of time interacted with local languages giving rise to what is commonly called the Prakrit languages. This process of Prakritization is reminiscent of a similar process in Europe, where the interpenetration of Latin and the local languages gave birth to modern varieties like French, Spanish, Italian and Portuguese. Of the north Indian languages, Urdu, although a sister language to Hindi, which is of Prakrit origin, further interacted with Classical Farsi giving it its modern and distinctive form. In addition, Urdu is written in the Perso-Arabic script which also adds to its distinctiveness among the languages of South Asia. The other languages in this area, though they may have different linguistic roots, all derive their writing systems from the ancient Brahmi script.

Although there are known to be sizeable numbers of other South Asian speech communities, including Baluchi, Konkani, Marathi, Nepali, Pashto, Sindhi and Burmese, only a passing reference can be made to these languages in a book of this kind.

Quite often speakers of these languages will also speak other major languages of South Asia and their numbers get subsumed into the larger language group. For example, Sindhi, Pashto or Baluchi speakers of Pakistani origin may also be speakers of Urdu and declare this as their home language. Similarly a Konkani speaker may also be a speaker of Marathi or Portuguese and Nepali and Sindhi speakers of Indian origin may declare Hindi as their home language.

The languages touched on in discussions of South Asia are necessarily abundant. Rather than present the traditional 'family tree of languages' to show origin and relations, Fig. P2.1 sets out the complex interrelationships between the languages of South Asia referred to in this part.

A great deal more work remains to be done in the charting and description of South Asian languages and patterns of language use in Britain. As was noted in Chapter 1, there is no comprehensive survey of languages and those sources of information which do exist (population census data; LMP 1985; Rosen and Burgess (1980); the ILEA Language Census, 1981–87; and schools language surveys conducted by various LEAs) can only be regarded as linguistic snapshots of what is taking place.

Because these surveys have sometimes been designed from a monolingual perspective which underestimates the complexity of multilingualism, the reliability of data is sometimes open to question. Although some twenty South Asian languages are named in the ILEA census, there are reports of only thirteen Marathi speakers and one speaker each of Telegu or Kannada. Such small numbers seem suspiciously low and may well be a function of the fact that children have reported the major South Asian language which they speak instead of, rather than in addition to, their main home language (cf Alladina 1985).

Another difficulty is that surveys often fail to address a wide range of important issues. There is no information, for instance, in most schools language surveys on children's ability to speak more than one language, nor on levels of literacy in the home languages. Thus, for example, there is no way of knowing whether the sole Assamese child identified in the 1987 ILEA Language Census also speaks, reads or writes Bengali or Hindi. Yet it is not an unreasonable assumption that this should be the case. As Pattanayak (1985) points out, multilingualism is the norm for people of South Asian origin. The need for information of this kind remains an urgent one.

Diversity within South Asia is not, of course, restricted to the level of language. There is also a diversity of religions – Hindus,

Sarhad Languages   **North Indian Languages**   **East Indian Languages**

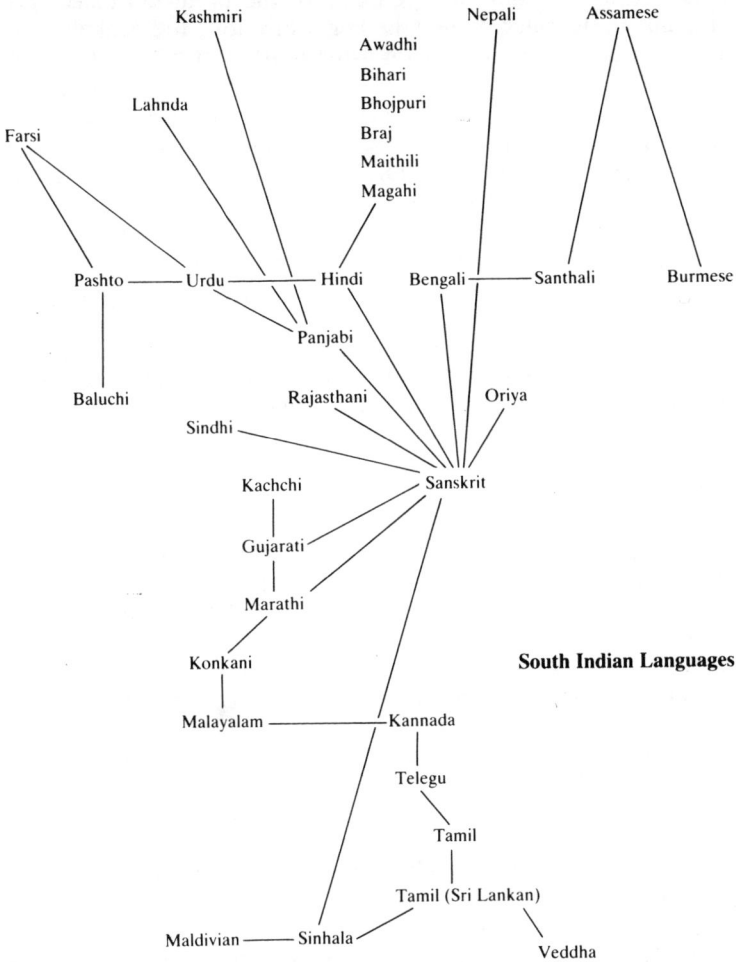

FIGURE P2.1   Languages of South Asia referred to in this part

Muslims, Sikhs and Buddhists; and a diversity of literary and cultural traditions. The history of migration from various parts of India, Pakistan and Bangladesh also contributes to the range of different South Asian peoples who have made their home in Britain. During the nineteenth and twentieth centuries, the major group to travel overseas were the Hindi speakers; today, how-

ever, Hindi speakers in Britain are very much a minority and are
composed almost entirely of a middle-class and highly educated
élite. Because Britain has been one of the preferred places for
Sri Lankans to pursue their higher education, the Sinhala and
Tamil speakers who stayed on after finishing their studies also
form an educated élite, though the background of the refugees
who have arrived since the recent political troubles is a good deal
less homogeneous. In contrast, settlers from Panjab, Bangladesh
and, to a lesser extent, Gujarat, come from a rural background
and are, in the main farmers with little formal education. Their
compatriots who arrived in Britain via East Africa and Fiji and
Mauritius form another distinct group: they are well educated and
come from a background as traders and entrepreneurs.

The priorities and preferences in the area of mother tongue
maintenance for these various different groups will inevitably
vary. A recurring issue is the question of which variety should be
supported. For Panjabi Muslims, the language of literacy is Urdu;
for Panjabi Sikhs it is Panjabi; for Panjabi Hindus it is Hindi.
Most Bangladeshis in Britain are speakers of Sylheti, yet the expectation is, in most cases, that their children will learn Bengali.
Many Kachchi parents elect for their children to learn Gujarati
as the language of the wider community. Muslims from many different backgrounds may choose to learn Urdu in addition to
their mother tongue. Similarly children from a wide range of language backgrounds may want to study Hindi as the national
language of India and the language of Hinduism.

There can be no question, however, of the degree of community support for mother tongue teaching, whether in the
voluntary sector or in mainstream education. Although the
material support offered to the voluntary sector by some LEAs
has greatly increased in recent years, there is still a great deal of
room for improvement. The question of community language
teaching as part of the mainstream curriculum also remains to be
resolved. Many problems as yet have no satisfactory solution, including the status accorded to community languages and
community language teachers within the school, the availability
of materials and the suitability of examination syllabuses. The
lack of official commitment to mother tongue maintenance is sad
indeed when contrasted with the official and academic support
these languages enjoyed in the heyday of the British Empire
(Alladina 1986).

References

ALLADINA, S. (1985) 'Research methodology for language use surveys in Britain – a critical review'. In P. Nelde (ed.) *Methods in Contact Linguistic Research*, Bonn: Dümmler, pp. 233–40.

ALLADINA, S. (1986) 'Black people's language in Britain – a historical and contemporary perspective', *Journal of Multilingual and Multicultural Development* 7(5): 349–60.

Inner London Education Authority (ILEA) (1981–87) *Language Census*. London: ILEA Research and Statistics.

Linguistic Minorities Project (LMP) (1985) *The Other Languages of England*. London: Routledge & Kegan Paul.

PATTANAYAK, D. P. (1985) *Language and Power*. Conference Report. London: North London Community Group.

ROSEN, H. and BURGESS, T. (1980) *Languages and Dialects of London School Children*. London: Ward Lock Educational.

SRIVASTAVA, R. N. (1984) 'Linguistic Minorities and National Languages.' In F. Coulmas (ed.) *Linguistic Minorities and Literacy*, The Hague: Monton, pp. 29–37.

Chapter 5

The Bengali speech community

Jyoti Husain

নানান দেশে   নানান ভাষা
বিনা স্বদেশী ভাষা
মিটেকি আশা ।

Nānān   dēshē   nānān   bhāshā   binā   shodeshi   bhāshā
mitēki   āshā
One can use the languages of other countries, but one can only get
fulfilment in the mother tongue.

RAMNIDHI GHUPTA

When India was divided into separate Hindu and Muslim states
in 1947, predominantly Hindu West Bengal remained a part of
India while Muslim East Bengal became East Pakistan, separated
from West Pakistan by some 1,500 kilometres. In 1970, after a
bitter civil war, the people of East Pakistan demanded independence and the state of Bangladesh came into being the
following year. The Bengali speech community in Britain thus
consists of two different groups – a small, predominantly Hindu,
community from Indian West Bengal and a much larger Muslim
community from Bangladesh, the majority of whom have their
roots in the rural region of Sylhet. It is the larger Bangladeshi
community which will form the focus for the present chapter.

Bengalis from West Bengal, and also those from the privileged classes of Bangladesh, speak varieties close to standard Bengali or Bangla as their home language. By far the largest proportion of Bengalis from Sylhet, however, speak Sylheti as their home language, but receive their schooling in standard Bengali. Some may also learn English as a foreign language and Arabic for religious reasons. A small number of people have a knowledge of Urdu or Hindi.

Bengali is the official state language of Indian West Bengal; it is also widely spoken in Assam, Bihar and Orissa. In fact, it is considered by some (see, for instance, Chatterji 1986) to be the most important language in India after Hindi. The pre-eminence of Bengali in Bangladesh, however, has not always gone unchallenged. It had originally been proposed that Urdu would be the official language of both West and East Pakistan. This suggestion was not universally welcomed in West Pakistan (see Ch. 9) but met with overwhelming opposition in East Pakistan where no section of the population spoke Urdu as their mother tongue, and where very few people had a working knowledge of the language (cf Tamaddum Mazlis 1947).

After partition, concern over the economic and cultural exploitation of Bengalis by the West Pakistan government led to the Bengali nationalist movements of the 1950s and 1960s in which language played a large part (Chakravarty and Narain 1986). A number of attempts to impose Urdu and the Perso-Arabic script resulted in acts of martyrdom for the mother tongue and 21st February is still observed in Bangladesh as *Bhasha Dibosh* (Language Day) in memory of those who gave their lives. The formation of the Central Board for the Development of Bengali in the same year gave a practical expression to the aspirations of the language movement and led, among other things, to the production of the Bengali typewriter. However, it was not until cessation from Pakistan in 1971 that Bengali was accepted as the official language.

Bengali is a member of the Indic branch of the Indo-Iranian subgroup of Indo-European language family. Its roots lie in Prakrit, the modern variety of the classical language Sanskrit, but it has existed as an autonomous language for at least ten centuries (Hudson 1985; Mobbs 1985; Chatterji 1986). Various languages have exerted an influence on Bengali over the years. For instance, as a result of Moghul rule in the thirteenth century (see also Ch. 8), Persian, Turkish and Arabic influences can be seen in the Bengali language, particularly on the level of vocabulary (cf Persian *Miyan* (Mister); Arabic *tabla* (drum) and *chakmoki* (bright) from Turkish *caqmaq*). The more recent influence of English can be seen in words like *table* and *school*. There are a number of dialects of Bengali closely related to one another. Two notable examples are Chalit Bhasa and Sadhu Bhasa, Chalit Bhasa forms a dialect continuum along the Hugli river and includes speakers from Calcutta. Calcutta is generally recognized as the intellectual centre by educated Bengalis and the variety spoken here is, therefore, recognized as the spoken standard. Sadhu Bhasa, in contrast, is used for literary and cultural purposes and for very formal discourse. It is a more conservative dialect, more highly inflected and adhering more closely to its Sanskrit roots.

Bengali is written from left to right and the words are hung on the lines. The alphabet is based on the ancient Indian system called Brahmi which developed from the Gupta script of AD 400–500. Each word has a line drawn above it and this is an important component of the word. The Bengali language uses *Samyukta Barnas* or conjunct letters which often look very different from the original components.

In Britain, the vast majority of Bangladeshis come from the rural region of Sylhet. Although they receive their schooling in standard Bengali, most speak Sylheti and not standard Bengali as their mother tongue. Sylheti is closely related to Bengali and it is in fact a controversial issue whether it should be considered a language in its own right or a dialect of Bengali. Grierson (1903) and Risvi (1974), for instance, highlight the various phonological differences between the two varieties, while Shivprshanna Lahiri (1961) points to the many lexical, morphological and structural differences. This has led writers such as Smith (1985) to suggest that the grounds for classifying Sylheti as a dialect rather than as an autonomous language are socio-political rather than linguistic. Chatterji (1986) argues from a similar position, pointing out that there are more differences between Sylheti and Bengali than between Assamese and Bengali, but whereas Assam is recognized as a separate state with a well-established literary tradition, Sylhet is not and, therefore, Sylheti is not accorded language status in Bangladesh.

Bengali speakers in Britain

There is strong evidence to suggest that there may well have been a Bengali-speaking community in the East End of London as early as 1873 (Watson 1977). Certainly, there was a well-established, mainly male, community in Britain in the 1920s and

1930s (Adams 1987). Most of the early arrivals came to Britain from Sylhet and, to a lesser extent, Chittagong, as migrant seamen, having worked as cooks and galleymen. Many were stranded in England and settled in centres such as Bradford, Cardiff, South Shields, Sunderland and the Stepney area of east London.

However, the vast majority of Bengalis arrived during the 1950s and 1960s. Various factors predisposed Bengalis to migrate to Britain at this time. The political instability which followed partition, together with the various natural calamities which have befallen Bangladesh in the second half of the twentieth century, placed an enormous burden on a once thriving economy (Learmonth and Rolt 1981). High unemployment led to emigration to various parts of the world including Burma, Hong Kong, Singapore, the USA and, more recently, the Middle East. However, Britain was a logical destination in the early post-war period, partly because of its boom economy and consequent labour shortages and also partly because of the long-standing ties between Sylhet and Britain through the jute, tea and shipping industries.

The actual number of Bengalis in the UK is difficult to estimate. Numbers vary from 48,517 (OPCS 1983) to 100,000 (Home Affairs Committee 1986) while some community estimates are as high as 160,000. The Bengali community has been growing rapidly in the 1980s and is likely to continue to do so. The myth of return seems to have persisted much longer in the Bengali than in other South Asian communities and the early male settlers were much slower in sending for their wives and families to join them in Britain. In the interim, changes in immigration legislation made it increasingly difficult for families to be reunited. Pressure exerted by various community groups and immigrant organizations finally resolved anomalies in the law, making it possible for wives and dependants to enter the country after long delays.

The Bangladeshi community is dispersed throughout the UK. For instance, LMP (1985) reports that some 800 Bengali-speaking children took part in their Schools Language Survey in Coventry and 400 in Bradford. By far the largest number of Bengali speakers, however, is to be found in London. Of these, almost half are to be found in the borough of Tower Hamlets; the rest are distributed throughout the capital with the largest number in the borough of Camden (OPCS 1983).

Between 1981 and 1987, the ILEA *Language Census* records a very rapid increase in the number of Bengali speakers (Table 5.1).

TABLE 5.1 ILEA *Language Census* data on Bengali speakers, 1981–87

Year	Number	%PHLOE*
1981	5,377	12
1983	9,098	18.1
1985	12,627	22.3
1987	16,976	26.12

*PHLOE = Pupils with a home language other than or in addition to English.

Since 1981, the number of Bengali speakers within the ILEA has tripled. Bengali-speaking children now account for over 26 per cent of all pupils within the authority and are the largest linguistic minority in London.

The clothing industry has been a traditional source of employment for Bengalis, though this industry is now in decline due to competition from cheap imports from other countries. The 'Indian' restaurant businesses have been monopolized by Bengalis and have spread throughout London and the provinces. This was a natural development for seamen who had worked as cooks. More and more people are realizing the benefits of self-employment and are spreading into other businesses such as sari shops, grocery shops and travel agencies.

However, the job opportunities available to Bengalis tend to be very limited (Carey and Shakur 1985; Department of Employment 1985, 1987). The unemployment rate in Tower Hamlets where the bulk of the Bengali population live is one of the highest in the country. Most Bengalis tend to find employment through family or personal ties, thus weakening their ability to negotiate their pay and work conditions (Runnymede Trust 1987). In many cases, employment prospects do not match skills or qualifications. Often language difficulties have been put forward to explain this situation. However, for South Asians increased fluency has not improved the chances of economic and social advancement and the vast majority of Bengalis find employment in unskilled jobs and in the manufacturing industries (Jupp, Roberts and Cook-Gumperz 1985).

The employment situation has serious repercussions in the area of housing. Housing ownership among Sylhetis is a recent phenomenon and, although there are pockets of owner-occupied areas in Haringey and Brent, most still live in council housing or rented accommodation, often in very overcrowded and poor conditions. The extend of homelessness is also a matter for concern. Many people have been placed in 'bed and breakfast' accommodation by local authorities, sometimes for extended periods. There is a worrying number of families with small children in one-room accommodation. In Finsbury Park in north London in 1987, for instance, there were 600–700 children between the ages of 5 and 16 living in accommodation of this kind at any one time, the majority of whom were Bengali speaking (Finsbury Park Homeless Project 1987).

Unemployment and poor housing conditions have, in turn, serious educational consequences. In Tower Hamlets in 1988, as many as 400 children, mainly of Bangladeshi origin, could find no places in primary schools (ILEA 1988) and there is some evidence to suggest that girls over the age of 11 may be being kept away from school by their parents because of the shortage of places in single-sex schools. Homelessness and poor housing conditions often give rise to ill health which keeps children away from school. And all families are further stressed by the knowledge that racial attacks on their community are on the increase and that they cannot rely on the protection of the police (Carey and Shakur 1985).

Changing patterns of language use

According to LMP (1985), more than a third of the London Bangladeshis who took part in the Adult Language Use Survey (ALUS) worked in places where all of the work-force were Bangladeshi. Women are even less likely than men to be exposed to English, partly because they are unlikely to have received a formal education in Bangladesh and partly because most of their time is spent at home or in the homes of families and friends. The flow of new arrivals from Bangladesh has meant that, for many parts of the community, the issue has been the acquisition of English, as well as the maintenance of the mother tongue. Other data collected as part of the ALUS and reported in Table 5.2, also support this interpretation.

TABLE 5.2 Language data on the Bengali speech community, extrapolated from LMP (1985)

		Bengali	English
% of respondents who know language fairly well or very well	Coventry (N=79)	98	52
	London (N=185)	94	47
% of people in respondents' household who know language fairly well or very well	Coventry (N=308)	80	71
	London (N=802)	75	57

Almost all the adult respondents report a very high level of competence in Bengali and a much lower level of skill in English. The data on the language skills of all members of the household, which will include some British-born children, shows only very small changes in the relative competence in Bengali and English. The shift to English in Bengali children has, it would seem, come much later than for other linguistic minority groups. Only 16 per cent of the London respondents and 37 per cent of the Coventry respondents indicated that their children used mainly or only English between themselves. Further information is available in the form of ILEA *Language Census* data. The majority of Bengali-speaking children included in the 1987 ILEA *Language Census* (some 89.4 per cent) were not considered to be fluent English speakers and a large proportion (40 per cent) were reported as being first-stage learners.

There has therefore been no significant shift to English, though there are many clear signs of change. High unemployment has forced many Bengalis to move out of completely Bengali-speaking environments to seek work in English-speaking areas. Significant numbers of British-born Bengalis now have native-speaker fluency and are starting to find employment outside the immediate community, many in white-collar jobs and the professions. There are various initiatives, for instance, within Tower Hamlets to encourage Bengali speakers to become teachers, social workers and community workers. For the first time, women are considering work, although the majority of men prefer their wives and daughters to stay at home. It should also be recognized that girls identified as 'English as second-language learners' often have access to a limited curriculum and, thus, restricted job possibilities (Brah and Minas 1985). However, 'home working', especially, is on the increase; so, too, is work in crèches and offices.

All these changes will inevitably have consequences both for the level of fluency in English and for the language choices which will be made within the community. There is every reason to suppose that, while the linguistic profile of the Bangladeshi community is currently very distinctive, the pattern which will emerge over the next two decades will approximate more and more closely to that of other South Asian speech communities.

Language, culture and community

Various factors already discussed, including the myth of return and the close-knit nature of the community, ensure that the mother tongue permeates most aspects of life in Britain for the majority of the Bangladeshi community. Informal social occasions

TABLE 5.3 Language use in a range of settings, extrapolated from LMP (1985)

% of respondents speaking only Bengali with the first person mentioned as someone they spent free time with	Coventry London	57 80
% of respondents who said most or all of their neighbours could speak Bengali	Coventry London	5 49
% of respondents who said they had seen a video in Bengali in the last 4 weeks	Coventry London	35 74
% of respondents who said they sometimes visited a shop where Bengali was spoken by the shopkeeper or assistants	Coventry London	82 86
% of respondents who had a Bengali doctor	Coventry London	17 50

Coventry: N=79
London: N=185

and cultural and musical evenings, birthdays and weddings are extremely important in the maintenance of language and culture. For the men, the local cafés, tea shops and street corners are an important part of the social scene, while women's social life revolves around visiting friends and relatives and watching videos at home.

The ALUS conducted by LMP (1985) points to the wide range of ways in which the community supports the use of the mother tongue, set out in Table 5.3. Although there are important differences between the relatively small Bengali-speaking community in Coventry and the much larger and more cohesive community in London, it is clear that most aspects of daily life can be conducted in both settings through Bengali without ever needing to resort to English.

Although high rates of unemployment mean that many Bangladeshis are now moving outside the immediate community to find work, the fact that many of those who are employed work as part of an ethnic economy has wide-ranging consequences, both for the continuing use of the mother tongue and for the very limited opportunities for the acquisition of English. The ALUS conducted by LMP (1985), for instance, would suggest that Bengali is used extensively in the workplace in London, though to a lesser extent in Coventry (Table 5.4).

TABLE 5.4 Bengali in the workplace, extrapolated from LMP (1985)

% of working respondents where at least one fellow worker speaks Bengali	Coventry:	34
	London:	79
% of working respondents where all fellow workers speak Bengali	Coventry:	18
	London:	39
% of respondents (who work for someone else) where the boss speaks Bengali	Coventry:	20
	London:	32
% of respondents who use only or mostly English with workmates	Coventry:	53
	London:	18

Coventry: $N=38$
London: $N=87$

Families keep in close contact with Bangladesh through regular visits and writing letters. Help is given to relatives who wish to join them in Britain and to those who remain in Bangladesh through regular remittances. Most Bangladeshis have also invested their earnings in the home country and therefore have an active interest in the political situation there. There are various groups supporting the political parties of Bangladesh such as the National Awami League, the centre-right Bangladesh Nationalist Party and the more religious Muslim League. There have also been active Maoist and Marxist factions in the past. Most political activity, however, is centred on the welfare of the Bangladeshi community in Britain. The younger generation, particularly the males, is more concerned with pressing issues such as racist attacks and has formed its own groups such as The Youth Approach and The Youth Movement for Equal Rights.

A wide range of religious, social and political events help to promote Bengali language and culture. There are frequent book displays in local libraries in Tower Hamlets, Islington and Haringey and in resource centres such as the Tagore Centre in Haringey, the Resources Centre for Asian studies in Stepney and the ILEA Learning Resources Centre.

There are various Bengali publications including *Samachar*, (News), *Surma* (River Surma), *Bangladesh Weekly* and *Janomat* (Public Opinion). *Surma*, in particular, has given prominence to the Sylheti issue. There is also a women's newspaper, *Nari Sangram* (Women's Struggle). Local English newspapers such as the *Spitalfields News* cater for the local Bangladeshi community with advertisements, articles and announcements in Bengali. A wide range of bilingual circulars, leaflets and magazines on issues of health, education and anti-racism printed by local government agencies is also available.

Education and language reproduction

Mother tongue teaching is a highly sensitive and important issue for the Bengali community. One of the key questions for this, as for many other linguistic minorities, is the variety which should be taught. There is a widespread expectation that children in Britain, as in Bangladesh, should be taught standard Bengali. However, many Bangladeshis argue that greater recognition should also be given to Sylheti both as a medium of instruction in Bengali classes and for the language support of bilingual learners in the mainstream curriculum.

As was the case for most language minority communities, Bengali classes were first organized by community organizations in churches, community centres and school buildings. Because of the patterns of immigration already described, the setting up of mother tongue classes was a much later development in Bengali than in most other linguistic minority communities. For instance, classes were only established in Haringey in 1980 and in Bradford in 1981 (LMP 1985).

Community groups tend to use traditional methods of teaching with a definite cultural and religious basis. Standards of teaching, learning and organization vary widely. At one extreme, one class inspected in Tower Hamlets in 1984, for instance, was described as 'simply an opportunity to provide children with space and activities to play outside their crowded homes'; at the other extreme was the show-piece East End community school where inspectors found 'an atmosphere of motivation and discipline' (ILEA 1985). Community classes accept children from a wide age range – usually between 5 and 15 years. They take place in the evenings or at weekends and vary in length between 3 and 10 hours a week. Many children also attend Arabic classes for religious purposes. Pressures of time can be enormous.

Support from LEAs for community classes varies a great deal. In Bradford and Haringey, for instance, the LEA provides either the teachers' salaries or accommodation. In Tower Hamlets, teachers are employed by the adult education institute on the same terms and conditions as other part-time teachers, though the Language Department receives more requests for community languages classes than it is able to sponsor. There is currently a complex pattern of voluntary, adult education and Youth Service involvement in community language teaching and it is freely admitted that it is not clear how this provision 'interrelates in either educational or geographical terms or how parents and children are informed and admitted to groups' (ILEA 1985).

The teaching of Bengali in community classes can also have a marginalizing effect and there have been a number of attempts to raise the status of Bengali by introducing it into mainstream schooling. There has been a marked increase in the number of bilingual teachers working in a team-teaching situation with classroom teachers to offer language support to Bengali and other children who speak minority languages through the use of the mother tongue. Various aspects of this provision, however, including the shortage and status of suitably qualified teachers, have given rise to a great deal of concern (see Ch. 1). In the context of the Bangladeshi community, there is the additional question of which language variety should be used for bilingual support – Bengali or Sylheti?

Some work has also been done in the area of curriculum development for Bengali speakers. The World in a City materials (Wright 1982) consists of forty cards in Bengali and other languages aimed at children within the ILEA who are already literate in their own language. Bengali speakers were also targeted in the joint EC, ILEA and Schools Council Mother Tongue Project which set out to produce materials which would help children in the 7–11 age range to develop literacy skills in the mother tongue alongside English and to encourage monolingual English teachers to help make use of their full linguistic repertoire (see Tansley, Nowaz and Roussou 1985, for details of the materials produced as part of this project).

A number of secondary schools, mainly in Tower Hamlets, offer the London University Board GCSE in Bengali. There are also Mode 3 examinations set by the Joint Matriculation Board. There is unease in many quarters, however, at the problems caused by treating Bengali as a modern rather than a community language and many people feel that the present curriculum, and examinations do not best serve the needs of the Bangladeshi community (see also Vol. 1, Ch. 13 for discussion of the EC Project on Community Languages in the Secondary Curriculum).

No doubt because they are not constrained by examination syllabuses, greater flexibility and imagination have been shown in adult and further education than in mainstream schooling. Adult education institutes, especially in Tower Hamlets, have played a key role in promoting the mother tongue by setting up integrated classes for families, by teaching English through the mother tongue and by offering some mainstream classes in areas such as child care, dressmaking and typing in Bengali. Some further education colleges in the borough are also employing bilingual counsellors and advisers and exploring ways of using Bengali as a medium of instruction.

References

ADAMS, C. (1987) *Across Seven Seas and Thirteen Rivers*. London: THAP Books.

BRAH, A. and MINES, R. (1985) 'Structural racism or cultural difference: schooling for Asian girls'. In C. Weiner (ed.) *Just a Bunch of Girls*, Milton Keynes: Open University Press. pp. 15–25.

CAREY, S. and SHAKUR, A. (1985) 'A profile of the Bangladeshi community in East London.' *New Community* **12**(3): 405–17.

CHAKRAVARTY, S. R. and NARAIN, Y. (eds) (1986) *Bangladesh*, Vol. 1: *History and Culture*. New Delhi: South Asian Publishers.

CHATTERJI, S. K. (1986) *The Origin and Development of the Bengali Language*, Vol 1–3. Calcutta, Allahabad, Bombay and New Delhi: Rupa & Co.

Department of Employment (1985) 'Ethnic origin and economic status', *Employment Gazette*: 467–77.

Department of Employment (1987) 'Ethnic origin and economic status', *Employment Gazette*: 18–29.

Finsbury Park Homeless Project (1987) *Report*. London: Finsbury Park Homeless Project.

GRIERSON, G. A. (1903) *The Linguistic Survey of India*, Vol. 5, Part 1. Calcutta: Government of India.

Home Affairs Committee (1986) *Bangladeshis in Britain*, Vol. 1. London: HMSO.

HUDSON, D. F. (1985) *Teach Yourself Bengali*. London: The English Universities Press.

Inner London Education Authority (ILEA) (1981, 1983, 1985, 1987) *Language Census*. London: ILEA Research and Statistics.

Inner London Education Authority (ILEA) (1985) *Tower Hamlets Institute of Adult Education, Report of Inspection*. Further and Higher Education Sub-Committee. London: ILEA.

Inner London Education Authority (ILEA) (1988) 'Moves to meet shortfall', *ILEA News*, 28 January.

JUPP, T. C., ROBERTS, C. and COOK-GUMPERZ, J. (1985) 'Language and disadvantage: the hidden process'. In J. J. Gumperz (ed.) *Language and Social Identity*, Cambridge: Cambridge University Press. pp. 232–256.

LEARMONTH, T. and ROLT, F. (1981) *Underdeveloping Bangladesh*. London: War on Want.

Linguistic Minorities Project (1985) *The Other Languages of England*. London: Routledge & Kegan Paul.

MOBBS, M. (1985) *Britain's South Asian Languages*. London: Centre for Information on Language Teaching and Research.

Office of Population, Census and Surveys (OPCS) (1983) *Census 1981: National Report Great Britain*. London: HMSO.

Runnymede Trust (1987) 'Bangladeshis in Britain – government response', *Bulletin* **207** (September): 3.

RISVI, S. N. H. (ed.) (1974) *Bangladesh District Gazeteers: Sylhet*. Dhaka: Government of the People's Republic of Bangladesh Press.

SHIVPRSHANNA LAHIRI (1961) *Sylheti Bhasa Totter Bhumika* (Introduction of Sylhetti Language). Dhaka: Bangla Academy.

SMITH, G. (1985) *Language, Ethnicity, Employment, Education and Research: The Struggle of Sylheti-Speaking People in London*. CLE/LMP Working Paper No. 13, University of London Institute of Education.

TAMADDUM MAZLIS (1947) *Pakistaner Rashtra Bhasha, Bangla na Urdu* (Pakistan's National Language: Bengali or Urdu?). Dhaka: Tamaddum Mazlis.

TANSLEY, P., NOWAZ, H. and ROUSSOU, M. (1985) *Working with Many Languages: A Handbook for Community Language Teachers*. London: School Curriculum Development Committee.

WATSON, J. (ed.) (1977) *Between Two Cultures*. Oxford: Basil Blackwell.

WRIGHT J. (1982) *The World in a City: Bilingual Learning Materials*. London: ILEA Learning Materials Service.

Chapter 6

The Gujarati speech community

Jagdish Dave

જયાં જયાં વસે એક ગુજરાતી ત્યાં ત્યાં સદાકાળ ગુજરાત

Jyan jyan vase ek Gujarati, tyan tyan sada jal Gujarat
Wherever a single Gujarati resides, Gujarat is ever there

A. K. KHABARDAR (1881–1953)

The Gujarati community in Britain is extremely heterogeneous.
It consists of two main groups – those who have come direct from
India and those who have come via East Africa. Each of these
groups can be further divided into two main religious groups –
the Hindus and the Muslims; Hindus can be subdivided still further on the grounds of caste and Muslims on the basis of the sect
to which they belong. This chapter will aim to present a sociolinguistic picture of Gujaratis in Britain by tracing the historical,
social and linguistic roots of these diverse communities, tied by
the bond of language.

The sociolinguistic situation of Gujarati in Gujarat

The state of Gujarat is situated in the north-west of India. It has
an area of almost 2,000 square kilometres and a population of
some 25 million people. Gujarati is the official language of the
state, though several other languages are also spoken, including
Hindi, the national language (see Ch. 7) which most Gujaratis
can understand and speak and Urdu which is widely studied by
Muslims. In addition, Rajasthani, Sindhi, Marathi, Bengali and
various southern Indian languages can be heard in urban areas
among speakers who have come to settle in Gujarat, and students
in higher education will also know English. In the majority of

cases, therefore, Gujaratis in India are not merely bilingual, they are multilingual.

Special reference should also be made to Kachchi which is spoken in the province of Kutch within the geolinguistic borders of Gujarat. It is more closely related to the Sindhi spoken in neighbouring Pakistan than to Gujarati (see Ch. 9) and, in recent years has been recognized as a languuage in its own right by the Indian government. However, Gujarati is used throughout the region as the medium of education, government and wider communication. No doubt for this reason, Kachchi has traditionally been regarded as a dialect of Gujarati rather than an independent language, and Kachchi speakers in the UK, too, usually consider their mother tongue to be a variety of Gujarati (Alladina 1989; LMP 1985).

The main focus for the present chapter, however, is Gujarati. Gujarati belongs to the Indo-Aryan group of languages which is a subgroup of the Indo-European family. Modern Gujarati, Rajasthani and Braj (Western Hindi) are all derived from Shaurseni Apabhramsha, a variety spoken between the tenth and twelfth centuries AD. Gujarati has four major dialects: Pattani, spoken in north Gujarat, Surati in south Gujarat, Charotari in central Gujarat and Kathiawadi in the Saurashtra region. There are also slight variations between East African and Indian varieties of Gujarati and some differences between male and female speech, particularly in the area of intonation.

Although there is a great deal of social and geographical variation, everyone also understands the standard language used on radio and television, in education and in literature. The Gujarati dictionary published by Gujarat Vidyapith, a rural university founded by Mahatma Gandhi, was an important landmark in the standardization process, gaining widespread acceptance with publishers and educators when endorsed by Gandhi. Gujarat has a rich literature beginning in the tenth century AD and drawing both on the standard language and on regional dialects. The most coveted literary prize in India – the Gnanpith Award – was recently won by Pannalal Patel for *Malela Jiv*, a novel in which one of the dialects of Gujarati is used prominently.

The Gujarati script is a modification of the Devanagari script used in Hindi, without the continuous line running along the top. Some simplification of the script was attempted by the eminent writer, Kaka Kalelkar, in order to facilitate the reading process for people from other provinces, and also by Mahendra Meghani in his unique Gujarati digest magazine *Milap* (Encounter). These moves never gained widespread acceptance. However, recently it has been necessary to make certain changes to the conjuncts to reduce the number of characters on the keyboard of typewriters, though these difficulties have been eliminated with the introduction of the more flexible word processor.

The Gujarati speech communities in Britain

It is estimated that there are over 300,000 Gujarati-speaking people in the UK, making it the second largest of the South Asian speech communities (Mobbs 1985a). The community is scattered throughout the country but is more concentrated in Greater London and the Midlands. In and around London, the largest settlements are to be found in Brent, particularly in the area of Wembley; in Harrow; in Newham in east London; and Croydon and Wandsworth in south London. The ILEA biennial *Language Census* (see Table 6.1) gives some indication of the size of the community in Inner London where Gujarati speakers currently form the largest single South Asian group after speakers of Bengali.

TABLE 6.1 Data of Gujarati-speaking pupils from the ILEA *Language Census* (1981–87)

Year	Number	% PHLOE*
1981	3,377	7.5
1983	3632	7.2
1985	3,831	6.8
1987	3,930	6.1

*PHLOE = Pupils with a home language other than or in addition to English.

Outside London there are large communities in Leicester, Coventry and the northern textile towns. In Coventry, for instance, Gujarati children form 16 per cent and in Bradford 9 per cent of all the bilingual children attending LEA schools (LMP 1985).

Although many Gujaratis have come directly from the central and southern parts of Gujarat, particularly the districts of Surat and Charotar, perhaps the largest section of the community arrived via East Africa in the late 1960s and 1970s. Although the contact between the west coast of India and East Africa predates Western colonialism, large groups of people from

South Asia went to East Africa at the beginning of the century when the British and German colonial governments were recruiting overseas labour for the construction of a railway in East Africa. Traders and farmers, particularly from the Gujarat area, were invited to open up the colonial territories. People of Gujarati origin comprised approximately 70 per cent of the South Asian communities there.

British colonialism produced an economic stratification of the races whereby, as Tandon and Raphael (1978) point out, the British were the wealthiest and most powerful group, owning most of the financial institutions and many of the production and distribution enterprises, the Asians were a powerless middle class, owning some larger enterprises, most of the retail distribution and providing middle-level professional and artisanal classes; the Africans at the bottom of the hierarchy were labourers and domestic servants.

When the East African countries won their independence, the wealth and privilege of Asians were threatened by the process of Africanization and many looked for suitable opportunities to resettle in other countries. During independence negotiations, Asian minorities had been given the right to a UK passport and entry to Britain and increasing numbers took advantage of this option until 1968 when a special voucher system was introduced, restricting the number of families from East Africa who could enter each year to 1,500. This quota system caused considerable hardship and ultimately was slightly relaxed. The real crisis, however, came in August 1972 when President Idi Amin announced them no more than 1,000 Ugandan shillings (about £55 sterling). Some 50,000 Asians, many of whom were in fact Ugandan citizens, left the country; of these, 27,140 arrived in Britain.

Although Gujaratis share many aspects of kinship and social organization with other north Indian peoples, they remain a very distinctive group. Desai (1963), for instance, comments on the fact that Gujaratis from India are better educated than their Panjabi and Bangladeshi fellow immigrants. The fact that a particularly large proportion of Gujarati speakers in Britain came from East Africa only serves to emphasize this distinctiveness. Before independence in Kenya, for instance, 20 per cent of South Asians were in élite professional and administrative posts, over 30 per cent were in commerce and most of the rest were transport and constructive operatives (Tinker 1977). The Gujarati population in Britain is thus, by and large, well educated with extremely middle-class aspirations.

There are many important divisions within the East African

Gujarati community. Approximately three-quarters of them are Hindus who are further subdivided into various castes. Caste is an extremely important concept which underpins all levels of social organization in traditional India. In classical Hindu scripture, it is conceived in terms of a fourfold *varna* scheme, whereby the priests or Brahmins occupy the highest social slot, followed by the Kshatriyas or warriors, the Vaishyas or merchants and finally the Sudras or labourers. The Harijans or untouchables, form a fifth category which falls outside this classificatory scheme. Within each *varna* there are further subdivisions into *jaats*, birth-ascribed endogamous groups which are also arranged in a hierarchy. The major divisions within Gujarati Hindu society are the Patels, the Lohanas, the Jains and the *choti jaat* (small *jaats*). Caste and *jaat* are thus inextricably linked with a person's social and economic status. It is also linked with ritual purity, one of the consequences of which is that a person cannot accept cooked foods from members of castes below their own (see also Vol. 1, Ch. 5 for discussion of ritual purity in a Romani context). Finally, it determines the choice of marriage partner and has an important effect on the social contacts which people make.

The importance of caste was considerably weakened in East Africa. The legal system did not sanction the division of labour according to caste rules. Moreover, most immigrants had come as traders and since traders are traditionally felt to be relatively ritualistically pure as a group, rules of commensality soon broke down (Barot 1975). However, Gujaratis remained strictly endogamous, thus retaining an important sense of the identity and exclusiveness of the *jaat* which enabled them to reassume their proper place in the local system on their visits home to India.

In Britain, too, there has been a weakening of the caste system even among those who came direct from India. As a Hindu minority, they have come from widely separated parts of Gujarat and live in a society which does not sanction the division of labour according to the rules of caste. Desai (1963) reports that the rules of commensality have completely broken down and that even Muslims (who fall outside the Hindu caste system so that even an Untouchable may not accept food from them) are allowed to share food. Desai also stresses the heightened importance assumed by village kin, not necessarily of the same *jaat*, in a British setting in the early years of migration. However, caste still largely determines social contacts; it is very much alive in relations with society in India and marriage remains strictly endogamous (Michaelson 1979; Tambs-Lyche 1975).

The remaining quarter of the Gujarati community is made up

of Muslims. Within Islam the major division is between the Shia and Sunni groups. The Shia Muslims believe that the Prophet Muhammad passed on his spiritual and secular authority; the Sunni majority deny any succession of authority. Virtually all East African Gujarati Muslims belong to Shia sects. The Ismailis, the most numerous Muslim Gujarati community, are descendants of converted Lohana Hindus from the Kutch region who accept the Aga Khan as their spiritual leader. The Ithna Asaris are another Shia Muslim group. Unlike the Ismailis, who were encouraged to adopt Western dress and to adapt to their new homeland, the Ithna Asaris are intensely traditional: education for women is discouraged and marriage across caste lines is unheard of. The final group, the Bohra Muslims, believe like the other two Shia groups, that God's messenger lives on earth at all times. For historical reasons, however, the 'Imam' must remain hidden and so the Bohras appoint a caretaker through whom the continuing message is conveyed. The home language of these groups, however, is Gujarati or Kachchi with varying degrees of loyalty to Urdu and Qur'ānic Arabic.

Changing patterns of language use

The first generation of Gujarati speakers in the UK use the same range of Gujarati as is found in the home country. Their vocabulary, however, is worthy of comment. Because of the long British rule in India, many English words such as 'station', 'ticket', 'pen', 'court' and 'coat' were, in any case, a part of their everyday speech. These loan words have continued in a British setting with the addition of items like 'video', 'tube', 'computer' and 'rocket'. East African speakers also use certain Swahili words in their vocabulary such as *jugu* (peanuts), *kisu* (penknife), *bakudi* (bowl) and *maramoja* (quick).

All members of the community engage, to some extent, in code-mixing, though this behaviour is more marked in the case of second and subsequent generations. Examples such as the follow- . ing are common:

Kem *olrait* chhe ne?
Are you alright?

Shun, badhun *oke* chhe?
Is everything OK?

Chalo tyare *tek ker, bai*
OK then, take care, bye!

A wide range of code-switching behaviour is also to be found within the Gujarati community. Speakers switch from English to Gujarati from sentence to sentence and even within the course of the same sentence. When talking with South Asian friends they use Hindi as a lingua franca (see also Chs 7–9) and will often switch between Hindi and English. The situation is equally complex for Kachchi children who speak Kachchi at home and Gujarati with their Gujarati friends. They also attend Gujarati classes where they learn standard Gujarati. The speech of Kachchi children is thus often marked by code-switching between all three languages.

English has inevitably had a greater impact on the speech of the second and subsequent generations of Gujaratis than on their parents and there has, inevitably, been a shift to English. Wilding (1982) provides some interesting information on attitudes towards language among adult Gujaratis in Leicester. Parents in the sample were shown to be multilingual. All of them still speak their first language and most of them can read and write it. There is a strong allegiance to the first langauge which is the main language in the home and with the children and it is also used extensively outside the home. A high proportion of the sample could speak and understand others in English and also read and write it. However, a quarter experienced communication difficulties outside the home, and there was a general recognition of the importance of English.

Nearly all the respondents' children learned Gujarati as a first language and most could still speak it. But whereas nearly all of the children could read and write English, very few were literate in Gujarati. This problem was due in part to the fact that at the time of the survey demand exceeded availability of classes. The majority of parents, however, expressed a wish for their children to attend if such facilities were available.

The picture presented by Wilding (1982) is largely confirmed by the findings of LMP (1985) for Coventry and London. Their Adult Language Use Survey, for instance, shows that adult respondents have a higher level of skill in Gujarati and a slightly lower level of skill in English than the household as a whole which includes, of course, younger British-born speakers (Table 6.2).

Further evidence for the shift to English is provided by parental estimates of children's language use. Some 38 per cent of parents in Coventry and 33 per cent in London reported that their children used mostly or only English when talking among themselves (LMP 1985).

TABLE 6.2 Data on language skills of Gujarati speakers, extrapolated from LMP (1985)

		Gujarati	English
% of respondents who know the language very well or fairly well	Coventry	98	74
	London	98	76
% of people (including respondents) who know the language fairly well or very well	Coventry	87	79
	London	85	80

Coventry: N = 203
London: N = 99

Rather less information is available on the language attitudes of the second and third generations than on those of their parents. It would seem, however, that a wide range of responses is to be found among this group of children and young people. Mercer, Mercer and Mears (1979), for instance, studied a group of twenty-nine male and nine female Gujarati students at a sixth-form college and a college of further education in Leicester. The majority expressed an interest in supporting and maintaining Indian culture; most also considered Gujarati to be important in their social lives, particularly in communication with monoglot elders. Yet the group was very much divided as regards the question of identity and attitudes towards the maintenance of Gujarati. Predictably, those who considered themselves as unambiguously Indian were very positively orientated towards the mother tongue while those who opted for a British identity tended to be relatively uninterested.

The shift to English has no doubt been accelerated by the attitudes of the host society. Gujarati, like other community languages, was, for many years, strongly discouraged in school (cf Edwards 1983): children have been told to 'stop jabbering in Gujarati' (Mercer 1981) and parents have been advised to speak English to their children. While the (1975) Bullock Report advocated that bilingualism should be treated as an asset which schools should help to nurture, no guidance was offered as to how this should be achieved. Further, the Swann Report (1985) removed this responsibility from the mainstream and placed it firmly on the various community organizations.

Language, culture and community

Although the Gujarati community is extremely diverse, the various groupings show a very high degree of internal cohesion. We have already discussed, for instance, the importance of religion for social organization. Cultural and religious festivals are celebrated throughout the year. Hindu festivals include *Holi*, a festival of spring; *Shivaratri*, a festival devoted to Shiv; *Janmashtami*, the celebration of Lord Krishna's birthday; and *Diwali*, the festival of lights held at the onset of winter (see also Chs 6, 7 and 10 (Tamil)). The most important Muslim festivals are *'Id-al-Adha,* traditionally associated with Abraham's intended sacrifice of his son, and *'Id-al-Fitr* which falls at the end of Ramadan, the month of fasting (see also Ch. 8).

Hindus and Muslims also observe a wide range of life-cycle rituals, such as birth rituals, the naming of the child, confirmation into the religious group and marriage and funeral rites. Marriage is a particularly important occasion and is marked by a wide range of ceremonies. In Hindu families, for instance, the invitation ceremony where the Brahmin will personally write the invitations to the closest members of the family; the betrothal ceremony; the *haldi* ceremony in which the bodies of the bride and groom are rubbed with a turmeric and mustard seed oil mixture; the *sanjina geet* or independent gatherings of the bride and groom's parties on the evening before the wedding in addition to the wedding ceremony itself.

There is a wide range of cultural activities which support the use of Gujarati. Cultural evenings by the various castes are generally part of their annual general meetings. Community language classes have an annual open day where Gujarati songs, one-act plays and *garba* dances are performed. There are about 500 community organizations in Britain, now united in the National Federation of Gujarati Organizations, many of which promote cultural events. Prominent in this area is the Gujarati Literary Academy, a body established in 1977 to promote Gujarati language, literature and culture. As well as its efforts in the area of mother tongue teaching (see section on Education and language reproduction, below), the Academy has been responsible for organizing several international literary and linguistic conferences, inviting scholars from Gujarat. Each of the conferences has attracted between 300 and 400 delegates.

The Bharatiya Vidya Bhavan, an institute of Indian culture, was founded in India more than 50 years ago by the late Dr K. M. Munshi, a freedom fighter, politician, barrister and

Gujarati littérateur. Every year since 1977 Bhavan's London branch has staged full-length Gujarati dramas, each running an average of twenty nights. Since 1980, the drama department has also run competitions for one-act Gujarati plays performed by amateur groups from London, Birmingham, Leicester and Coventry. Adjudicators are invited from Gujarat and as well as judging the plays they give constructive suggestions on how to foster good Gujarati drama in the UK. Other organizations, like the South Asian Literature Society, also support mother tongue promotions, including Gujarati.

There is a very lively ethnic economy in areas of Gujarati settlement with a wide range of food, clothing and video hire shops. It is also the case that many people work in situations where there are other Gujarati speakers. According to the LMP (1985) Adult Language Usage Survey, just over half the working respondents in Coventry and less than a third of those in London used only or mainly English in the workplace. This would suggest that substantial numbers of Gujaratis continue to use the mother tongue in their daily employment and that, for many people, the workplace is an important factor in language maintenance (see Table 6.3).

TABLE 6.3 Language use in the workplace, extrapolated from LMP (1985)

% of working respondents where at least one fellow worker can speak Gujarati	Coventry London	39 69
% of working respondents where all fellow workers can speak Gujarati	Coventry London	9 21
% of workers who said they use only or mainly English with workmates	Coventry London	57 32

Coventry: N = 122
London: N = 62

A picture thus emerges of a wide range of settings which support the use of Gujarati: religious and life-cycle celebrations; visits to friends and families; membership of community associations; the workplace; shopping expeditions. Again, LMP (1985) provides corroborative evidence (see Table 6.4) of some of the situations in which Gujarati is likely to be used.

TABLE 6.4 Language use in a range of settings, extrapolated from
LMP   (1985)

% of repondents who said they spoke only Gujarati with the first person mentioned as someone they spent time with	Coventry	70
	London	74
% of respondents who said that all or most of their neighbours could speak Gujarati	Coventry	13
	London	6
% of respondents who said that they had seen a video or film in Gujarati in the last 4 weeks	Coventry	64
	London	66
% of respondents who said that they sometimes visited a shop where Gujarati was spoken by the shopkeeper or assistants	Coventry	98
	London	97
% of respondents who had a doctor who spoke Gujarati	Coventry	32
	London	51

Coventry: N = 203
London: N = 99

There are also many other signs of a strong ethnolinguistic
vitality. There is, for instance, a wide range of publications available in Gujarati. Weekly editions of most of the important daily
newspapers from Gujarat, *eg Gujarat Samachar* (Gujarat News),
Janma Bhoomi (Motherland), *Sandesh* (Message), *Samkalin*
(Contemporary) and popular weeklies, *eg Chitralekha* (Illustration), *Yuvadarshan* (Youth Encounter), are available from
many newsagents, providing up-to-date information about life in
India in general and Gujarat in particular. Some Gujarati publications are produced in Britain. The weeklies *Garvi Gujarat*
(Gujarat Pride) and *Gujarat Samachar* (Gujarat News) are London-based while *Ame Gujarati* (We Gujaratis) is a monthly
magazine produced in Leicester. There is also a quarterly
magazine for Gujarati women called *Sangana* ('Togetherness').
   Local government information is available in Gujarati and
many boroughs such as Brent, Harrow, Ealing and Camden
publish their material in the language. Some also run translation
units though the quality of their work sometimes leaves a great
deal to be desired. Audio cassettes of Gujarati songs, *garbas* (folk
music) and *bhajans* (devotional music) and video cassettes of
Gujarati films are very popular: they are readily available from
libraries or can be bought or hired from shops.

Links with India tend to be strong, even in the case of East African Gujaratis. Sons and married daughters keep in touch by letter or telephone, sending gifts with friends visiting India and often airline tickets which allow parents to visit their children in the UK. In cases of famine or other disasters in Gujarat, donations are sent by the UK community. Religious and other leaders often come from Gujarat and are invariably well received here. Many people fly to India on business or for social or religious functions.

Education and language reproduction

Mother tongue teaching, with very few exceptions, is organized by the voluntary sector in the form of community organizations, social institutes, welfare and religious organizations. In many cases, they have a long history, some of the classes in Bradford, for example, dating back to 1957 (LMP 1985). Classes are usually held once or twice a week, mostly on Saturdays and Sundays, and run for one to two hours. Although the main focus of these classes is on the teaching of the Gujarati language, other elements are often introduced. Some Gujarati social organizations have a religious focus; others teach Indian music and dance, yoga and games. A particularly wide range of activities features in the Vidya Vihar, an independent full-day Saturday school in Harrow which teaches Vedic prayers, Yoga, Sanskrit, Hindi, Indian culture, dance, drama and music as well as Gujarati.

The materials for teaching Gujarati are often very limited. Until recently the main source was primary textbooks, alphabet charts and story-books from India. Work towards developing resources suitable for Gujarati children in a British context started in a small way with self-made materials which have been produced by institutions such as the Moat Community College in Leicester. The Gujarati Literary Academy has produced a set of five graded textbooks and a teacher's guide (Dave 1986). These books are now widely used throughout Britain, Africa and the USA. Some commercial publishers have also produced bilingual story-books, but, although the binding, printing and presentation are of good quality, the Gujarati language content sometimes deserves more careful attention.

Some teacher preparation is provided within the community. Gujarati Shikshan Sangh (The Association for the Teaching of Gujarati), for instance, which has its headquarters in Leicester, is involved in teacher training and curriculum development. The

Gujarati Literary Academy is another body which has been involved in teacher training.

In some cases, classes are funded entirely by the community; in others, the local authority provides a variety of support. In Coventry in 1981, for instance, the LEA provided accommodation and teachers' salaries for 4 classes; either salaries or accommodation for 14 classes; and neither salaries nor accommodation for 2 classes (LMP 1985).

Gujarati has also become part of the mainstream curriculum in a growing number of schools. In some LEAs, Gujarati language support teachers or instructors work alongside classroom teachers in a team-teaching situation to provide extra help for bilingual pupils. At primary level, it is often offered as a lunch-time or after school activity; and at secondary level, it sometimes appears as part of a carousel programme of language learning under the umbrella of language awareness teaching (cf Mobbs 1985b). It is also offered as a subject for GCSE by the London and East Anglian Group and in the summer of 1988, for instance, there were some 240 candidates. However, there has been some criticism of the way in which Gujarati is treated as a modern language rather than a community language. British-born children of Gujarati parents are in a special situation: their fluency in Gujarati often falls short of native speakers and yet it is far superior to that of children learning it as a foreign language. The content and design of the examinations fail to take this into account; it also pays insufficient attention to Gujarati literature and culture.

In response to this situation, the Gujarati Literary Academy has developed a syllabus and textbooks for five graded examinations for those settled in Britain and North America where English is the dominant language. The main emphasis in the lower-stage examinations will be on the assessment of language proficiency, but in the later stages greater emphasis will be placed on cultural heritage and literature. The first examinations – first level only – were taken in December 1988 by some 600 students in 20 different centres all over Britain. Assessment was based on all four aspects of language: speaking, listening, reading and writing. Each year a further level will be added until, by 1992, all five levels will be available. The fifth level will correspond to A level standard, although the literary and cultural content will be more developed than is the case for modern language syllabuses. The Academy therefore provides a valuable alternative to mainstream schooling where, in spite of pressure from the community, no examination board offers Gujarati as an A level subject. At university level, the School of Oriental and African

Studies at the University of London has provision for teaching Gujarati. With the acknowledgment of the importance of the mother tongue has come an increased demand for the learning of Gujarati. Although there are many experienced Gujarati-speaking teachers with a first degree or postgraduate degree from India, their qualifications are not always recognized by the Department of Education and Science, and when they are employed, it is usually in the lower status role of instructor. Opportunities for further training which would allow people from ethnic minorities to obtain qualified teacher status are currently extremely limited. Still, hope springs eternal. As the famous poet Narmad reflects: '*Shubha shakun dise madhyana shobhashe, viti gai chhe rat*' (I see good omens, dark night is over and the beatiful mid-day sun will shine).

References

ALLADINA, S. (1989) 'The status of Kachchi in India and in Britain: implications for language teaching'. In T. Acton and M. Dalphinis (eds) *Superliterates and the Struggle for Multilingualism*, London: Karia Press.

BAROT, R. (1975) 'The Hindus of Bakuli'. In M. Twaddle (ed.) *Expulsion of a Minority. Essays on Ugandan Asians*, London: Athlone Press for the Institute of Commonwealth Studies, *pp* 70–80.

BULLOCK, SIR A. (1975) *A Language for Life*. London: HMSO.

DAVE, J. (1986) *Gujarati Bhasha Pravesh* Parts 1, 2, 3, 4 (An Introduction to the Gujarati Language). Wembley: Gujarati Literary Academy.

DAVE, J (1986) *Setu* (Teacher's Guide). Wembley: Gujarati Literary Academy.

DESAI, R. (1963) *Indian Immigrants in Britain*. London: Oxford University Press for the Institute of Race Relations.

EDWARDS, V. (1983) *Language in Multicultural Classrooms*. London: Batsford.

Inner London Education Authority (ILEA) (1981, 1983, 1985, 1987) *Language Census*. London: ILEA Research and Statistics.

Linguistic Minorities Projects (LMP) (1985) *The Other Languages of England*. London: Routledge & Kegan Paul.

MERCER, L. (1981) 'Ethnicity and the supplementary school'. In N. Mercer (ed.) *Language in School and Community*, London: Edward Arnold, *pp* 147–60.

MERCER, N., MERCER, L. and MEARS, R. (1979) 'Linguistic and cultural affiliation among young Asian people in Leicester'. In H. Giles and B. St Jacques (eds) *Language and Ethnic Relations*, Oxford: Pergamon Press, *pp* 15–26.

MICHAELSON, M. (1979) 'The relevance of caste among East African Gujaratis in Britain', *New Community* 12 (3): 350–60.

MOBBS, M. (1985a) *Britain's South Asian Languages*. London: Centre for Information of Language Teaching and Research.

MOBBS, M. (1985b) 'Towards the evolution of the linguistic primate (Angliensis): an argument for a broadened modern languages curriculum', *Times Educational Supplement* 4 October: 56.

SWANN, LORD (1985) *Education for All*. London: HMSO.

TAMBS-LYCHE, J. (1975) 'A comparison of Gujarati communities in London and the Midlands', *New Community* 4: 349–56.

TANDON, Y. and RAPHAEL, A. (1978) *The New Position of East Africa's Asians: problems of a displaced minority*. Revised edn. London: Minority Rights Group.

TINKER, H. (1977) *The Banyan Tree – Overseas Emigrants from India, Pakistan and Bangladesh*. Oxford: Oxford University Press.

WILDING, J. (1982) *Ethnic Minority Languages in the Classroom? A Survey of Asian Parents in Leicester*. Leicester Community Relations Council and Leicester City Council.

Chapter 7

The Hindi speech community

Mahendra K. Verma

निज भाषा उन्नति अहै,
सब उन्नति कर मूल ।
बिनु निज भाषा ज्ञान के,
मिटत न हिय के सूल ॥

nij bhaashaa unnati ahai,
sab unnati kar muul
binu nij bhaashaa gyaan ke,
miṭat na hiya ke suul

One's language is the provenance
of all developed thought;
Until we know our mother tongue
Our hearts remain distraught.[1]

BHARTENDU HARISHCHANDRA (NINETEENTH CENTURY WRITER)

The Hindi speech community constitutes the largest linguistic group in India. Hindi, sometimes known as Khari Boli Hindi, is spoken by more than 200 million people, mainly in the states of Bihar, Uttar Pradesh, Madhya Pradesh, Rajasthan, Haryana, Himachal Pradesh and Delhi, and is the official language of India. It is a new Indo-Aryan language which can be traced back to the Old and Middle Indo-Aryan languages, Sanskrit and Prakrit. During the Moghul rule in north India and the Deccan from the thirteenth to eighteenth centuries, when Persian was the official language, Khari Boli drew heavily on Persian and Arabic vocabulary. During this period we also see the beginning of the development of two different styles of Khari Boli – Hindi written in Devanagari and Urdu written in Perso-Arabic script. Modern educated Hindi usage in India reflects the influence of English on the one hand and the revival of Sanskrit on the other. Together both Sanskrit and English have replaced Persian as a lexical resource.

The early history of Hindi consists of devotional and epic poetry. The nineteenth century saw the beginning of formal attempts at developing prose writing in Hindi. Modern Hindi history has seen extraordinary achievements in poetry, novels, short stories, travelogues and literary criticism. Although in literary and formal registers Hindi and Urdu have been drifting away from one another, the colloquial language of interpersonal discourse is in essence almost identical.

The Hindi-speaking belt in India has had long historical links with Britain in the colonial and post-colonial periods. The abolition of slavery in the British Empire in 1834 led to the recruitment of indentured labourers from India to other colonies. During the mid-nineteenth century thousands of Indians from the Hindi-speaking states of Bihar and Uttar Pradesh were shipped to Mauritius, the West Indies, Fiji and South Africa to work on the sugar plantations. These were largely peasants from rural areas, poor and uneducated. They were predominantly Bhojpuri speakers, with smaller numbers from the Awadhi-speaking area of eastern Uttar Pradesh. The language label they invariably assigned to their mother tongue, however, was Hindi because Hindi as the language of the medium of education in India has prestige value and positive cultural associations. Hindi was also closely linked with the freedom movement in India, with Gandhi as its champion. Hindi is maintained as the second or third language in the repertoire of many Indians in these countries.

In the post-colonial period, following Indian independence in 1947, a large number of South Asians have migrated to Britain on the strength of labour vouchers. But there is a significant difference between the nineteenth-century Indian migration and the more recent one. Unlike the nineteenth century, the twentieth century did not see the emigration of masses of Hindi-speaking people. The majority of immigrants from India to Britain have come from non-Hindi-speaking areas, especially the rural Panjab or Gujarat. Other Panjabis (Hindus and Sikhs) and Gujaratis (Hindus and Muslims) have come from East Africa. Only a small minority of Hindi speakers, almost entirely urban-based, have migrated to Britain.

Hindi in Britain

The sociolinguistic situation of Hindi speakers in Britain differs in many important respects from that of the other South Asian communities. Hindi speakers draw on four main groups. The first group consists of native speakers of Hindi and their descendants. These speakers include a small minority from the Hindi states who speak Khari Boli Hindi as their mother tongue, and others, mostly first generation, who also speak Maithili, Magahi, Bhojpuri or Awadhi in addition to Khari Boli Hindi. The second group consists of Panjabi Hindus who speak and aspire for their children to speak Hindi as a second language for cultural and religious reasons. For both these groups, Hindi is the main language of literacy. As one elderly first-generation Panjabi speaker consulted in the course of fieldwork for this section commented, 'Panjabi is only my home dialect. My religion is Hinduism. Hindi is our language. I am an Indian. Hindi is our national language. Hindi is the common man's religious language. Hindi is our *dharm* (duty).' (Translated from Hindi.)

An interesting sociolinguistic picture thus emerges in the interlocking relationships of the Hindi–Urdu–Panjabi communities. The speakers of Hindi, Urdu and Panjabi perceive their mother tongues as distinct languages through which they project their socio-cultural identity. But whereas mother tongue speakers of Hindi and Urdu owe no allegiance to Panjabi, Hindu and Muslim Panjabis readily identify with Hindi and Urdu in formal domains for their religious, occupational and literary pursuits. For Hindu Panjabis in India and Britain, Panjabi is not perceived as a language of literacy. In both these communities, Panjabi therefore exists in a diglossic relationship with Hindi and Urdu.

The third group is made up of speakers of Hindi as a second language, other South Asians, especially Gujaratis, both Hindus and Muslims, and Sikhs who perceive and use Hindi–Urdu as a lingua franca and as an in-group language of superordinate South Asian ethnic identity. Finally there are the White learners of Hindi as a foreign language who are, by and large, adults who study Hindi in further and higher education. In some places it is a continuation of the colonial legacy of learning and teaching Hindi to civil servants (*cf* Alladina 1986). More recently, however, there has been a surge of interest among teachers of English as a second language and others in professions like social work to study Hindi on short, intensive courses.

Hindi mother tongue (HMT) speakers are an essentially middle-class community in Britain. The vast majority are professionals – doctors, teachers, engineers and civil servants – whose roots lie in any of the seven Hindi states in India. This is in marked contrast with both the early Hindi migrants in the colonial period and the more recent non-Hindi migrants from linguistically and geographically marked areas. Unlike Panjabis, Gujaratis and Bengalis, HMT speakers hardly ever have a network of close relatives in Britain.

In the case of most other South Asian communities in Britain, it is possible to see the replication of the social structure of a village in the main areas of settlement (see, for instance, Chs 5, 6, 8 and 9). Here there is a traditional network of social interaction within and across castes and kinship groups. In contrast, HMT speakers do not constitute a community which has any kind of neighbourhood network. Caste, kinship and community ties do not generally play any significant role in the formation of a strong, close-knit localized group. Even where Hindi professionals live in the inner-city areas, their patterns of settlement are conspicuously isolationist, with the result that their households are scattered. Consequently the children from HMT families are distributed among various schools and are generally growing up alongside monolingual English children. Many of these children are in private schools where there is hardly any chance of ethnic, linguistic or cultural support.

In the entire spectrum of interaction that an adult Hindi speaker has with others, occupational interaction is the most significant. Most Hindi speakers work in jobs outside their own community which entail regular contact with the English-speaking community. A typical Hindi-speaking doctor, for instance, has a wide spectrum of interlocutors in his or her social network, eg White English speakers belonging to various socio-economic classes; speakers of various South Asian languages as patients in the surgery; South Asian friends in their social milieu; and neighbours who are invariably White English speakers. In many linguistic minority communities, the women have generally been the custodian of the mother tongue because of their limited contact with the dominant English society. But Hindi women, like the men, are in jobs where they interact with members of other linguistic groups, particularly English speakers. In contrast, other South Asian groups are either self-employed in small businesses where they interact largely with other members of the South-Asian community, or in restaurants and shops where the interaction with English speakers is restricted to the language of buying and selling.

TABLE 7.1 Data on Hindi speakers from LEA language surveys

LEA	Year	Numbers	% of bilingual school population
ILEA	1981	733	
ILEA	1983	671	
ILEA	1985	738	
ILEA	1987	648	
Bradford	1981	176	
Bradford	1985	137	
Bradford	1987	162	
Barnet	1983	329	4
Brent	1982	371	3
Coventry	1981	197	3
Haringey	1981	7	
Leeds	1988	228	
Peterborough	1981	38	3
Waltham Forest	1981	55	

There is a real dearth of facts and figures on Hindi speakers in Britain, making it very difficult to build a reasonably accurate picture of the number, distribution and patterns of language usage of this group. An analysis of various LEAs' language census data, for instance, as set out in Table 7.1, very clearly demonstrates that Hindi tends to be submerged in statistics.

There can thus be no doubt about the small numbers of children whose first language is Hindi, though there are some indications of growth in certain LEAs. The 1985 and 1987 Bradford surveys, for instance, note a 'bottom heavy' age profile for Hindi speakers, which might indicate both an increase in the number of speakers and in commitment to the language (City of Bradford Metropolitan Council 1988). However, in other areas, especially Leeds, pupils from a Hindi-speaking background are evenly spread throughout primary, middle and secondary schools.

The monolithic approach to data gathering on Hindi speakers has the effect of disguising the true nature of the Hindi speech community. In this respect, the attempts of the 1985 Ealing School Language Survey (see Table 7.2) to break down Hindi speakers into first, second and third language users are considerably more revealing. In this survey, 13,552 pupils reported that they spoke a language other than English at home. Out of these, 85.4 per cent (11,574) reported that they used one

TABLE 7.2 Number of children reporting Hindi as first, second or third additional language in the 1985 Ealing School Languages Survey

Pupils speaking one language in addition to English		Pupils speaking two languages in addition to English		Pupils speaking three languages in addition to English	
13,552		11,574		259	
Hindi as first additional language		Hindi as second additional language		Hindi as third additional language	
620	4.6%	804	40.6%	51	19.7%

additional language, 14.6 per cent (1,978) reported that they used more than one additional language and 1.9 per cent (259) reported using three additional languages. In the case of speakers naming only one additional language, Panjabi was mentioned most frequently followed by Gujarati, Urdu and then Hindi. But when respondents reported that they spoke two additional languages, Hindi was the language most frequently mentioned as the second additional language.

Changing patterns of language use

The extent to which the Hindi community is retaining its language and culture at the same time as developing stable bilingualism is a matter requiring extensive research. On the basis of a pilot study of some five mother tongue Hindi-speaking families undertaken as part of the research for the present Chapter, however, there can be little doubt that there is a significant shift to English among the young generation. There are many reasons for this shift, some of which have been touched upon in the discussion of Hindi in Britain above. These include the size of the group and its patterns of settlement. The smallness of a minority group in itself does not necessarily militate against language and cultural maintenance, providing the patterns of settlement are not diffuse. But, as we have already indicated, the diffuseness of the Hindi community is its hallmark, as is the lack of a Hindi neighbourhood which replicates village structure in India. Similarly the occupational patterns previously outlined make for a range of diffuse social networks (cf Milroy 1980) which involve a large

Table 7.3 Patterns of language choice across the generations

	Parents and community	Spouse	Children	Friends
3A First-generation speakers				
Mostly	Hindi	Hindi	Hindi	Hindi; English
Sometimes		English	English	
Never	English			
	Parents and community	Siblings	Friends	
3B Second generation – pre-school children				
Mostly	Hindi	Hindi	Hindi	
Sometimes		English	English	
Never	English			
	Parents and community	Siblings	Friends	
3C Second generation (older children) – pattern 1:				
Mostly	Hindi	English	English	
Sometimes	English	Hindi–English		
Never				
	Parents and community	Siblings	Friends	
3D Second generation (older children) – pattern 2:				
Mostly	English	English	English	
Sometimes	Hindi–English			
Never				

number of people from English and other South Asian language communities. In such a situation, both parents and children tend to think that English not Hindi will be of help both in education and in the job market. Another factor which shifts the balance from Hindi to English is family structure. Most HMT speakers live in nuclear families and can call neither on the extended family nor on the village network, with obvious implications for mother tongue maintenance.

A survey of patterns of language use for interpersonal transactions conducted by the present writer in five HMT families indicates some very consistent trends. In all the families surveyed, the first generation revealed a uniform pattern of language use. Hindi is used mostly in situations where there are Hindi-speaking interlocutors; English is used sometimes in conversation with both children and spouse, but never with parents or the wider Hindi speech community. The second generation, however, showed very different patterns. Although the adult patterns of language choice are largely mirrored in the case of pre-school children, older children showed very different patterns of language behaviour. In some cases, Hindi is used mostly with parents and the wider Hindi speech community, and English is also used sometimes in these situations. With siblings, however, English is mainly used, with some code-switching between English and Hindi. In other cases, English also replaces Hindi as the main language of interaction with parents and the community, with children only code-switching to Hindi on some occasions. These different patterns are set out in Table 7.3.

The drop-off in the use of Hindi is thus not simply by generation, but also within the same generation across pre-school and school age ranges. In the speech of these children, starting school leads not only to a decline in the use of Hindi but to Hindi – English code-switching/mixing. Living in an English-speaking neighbourhood provides an extra incentive for the shift to English. Children begin to realize that they and their friends have to adopt a language that they can all understand. Over time, English, the language of the classroom, playground, neighbourhood and television, gradually begins to replace Hindi as the language of interaction with parents and siblings.

Language, culture and community

It is worth noting, however, that there are also counter-assimilative forces that continually encourage language loyalty and language maintenance (though not development) among Hindi speakers. These include religion, Indian nationalism with Hindi as the symbol of being a Hindu (as against being Sikh); parental pressure; and the Hindi video industry which provides an extremely popular form of home entertainment.

Disillusioned by the lack of institutional support, the Hindi lobby has set up many educational, cultural and quasi-academic organizations to promote Hindi. Each year a Hindi day is organized by these groups with talks on Hindi themes, poetry and music. The High Commission of India has a Hindi officer who is based in London. The High Commission is generally responsible for a Hindi library, translation work, loan of films in Hindi and the teaching of Hindi language and literature. The Education and Culture Department of the High Commission is concerned with mother tongue projects and the promotion of Hindi. Efforts to promote Hindi include the donation of books and Hindi typewriters to institutions teaching Hindi.

First-generation Hindi speakers received some attention for many years in the BBC's Sunday morning programme '*Nai Zindagi, Naya Jeevan*' (meaning 'New Life' – *Zindagi* from the Urdu; *Jeevan* from the Hindi) though there is nothing currently broadcast which caters to the needs of the literate adult Hindi speaker. Network East, an occasional Channel Four programme, includes songs in Hindi and interviews with well-known Hindi personalities, but remains essentially an English-language programme. There is, however, a network of local radio stations broadcasting songs, announcements and discussions in Hindi-Urdu, alongside other languages. Although Hindi speakers are thinly dispersed, they have not been deprived of their share of entertainment in the mother tongue via songs and films that form part of ethnic broadcasting. The needs of second-generation speakers, however, have received rather less attention from the media. Currently, the only broadcast aimed at this group is the weekly BBC 'Mother Tongue Story'. Publications in Hindi, such as *Amar Deep* and *Naveen*, also cater for the needs of the first generation only.

'The counter-assimilative forces referred to earlier are also evident in the activities of Hindu community centres in areas where there is an active Panjabi Hindu community. Hindu temples and community centres are hubs of religious and cultural activities. Diwali and Holi, for instance, two important festivals that the Hindu community celebrates with enthusiasm, are usually marked by the performance of Hindi plays and music by children. Community centres are also likely to organize weddings and religious discourses. The revival among Hindu Panjabi and HMT communities of the tradition of *Akhand Ramayan* (recitation of the religious book, the *Ramcarit Manas*, in Hindi) brings whole families together at weekends and gives the participants, including the children, some sense of affinity with Hindi and Hinduism. The community's commitment to maintain language and culture is in evidence in these places, and yet it is not Hindi but Panjabi and English that dominate the activities of the temples. This kind of exposure thus does little to create the Hindi atmosphere that is so important for young learners of the language.

Education and language reproduction

According to statistics released by the Department of Education and Science in 1983 in response to the Memorandum on com-

pliance with Directive 77/486/EC (EC 1977), approximately
2,571 school-age children were studying Hindi in LEA schools
in 1982. Relative to the total Hindi-speaking population in
Britain, however, such provision is insignificant. Hindi is almost
non-existent in primary schools, even in areas where parents
would like their children to acquire literacy in the language.
There are only a few secondary schools where Hindi is available
as part of the modern languages curriculum.

Hindi is, however, available as an examination subject. In June
1987, for instance, there were 29 candidates for the A level in
Hindi and 125 candidates for the O level offered by the University of London Examinations Board. These examinations have
often met with considerable criticism from the Hindi community.
Young learners often find them uninteresting and archaic. It is
also felt that they fail to recognize the importance attached within
the community to literacy and the study of literature (cf also
Ch. 5). The Institute of Linguists examination in Hindi is also
viewed by many as an assessment of competence in functional
Hindi only. It is to be hoped that the development of the new
GCSE syllabus will go some way towards alleviating these difficulties and anxieties (cf Broadbent 1983).

The majority of Hindi learners take lessons outside their normal school hours during weekdays or on Saturday and Sunday,
usually on temple premises or in Hindu community centres. The
Hindi community, with some help from the LEAs, has been organizing these classes since 1970, though the extent of this
support is highly variable. In most cases, community schools draw
on relatively small numbers of pupils. It would seem that the
largest number of children is in two Nottingham schools where
the combined classes have 150 pupils on roll.[2]

My experience of pupils learning Hindi in both mainstream and
voluntary classes suggests that the majority come from Panjabi-
speaking homes, with Hindi speakers as the second largest group.
What is interesting is the wide variety of language backgrounds
of learners of Hindi as a second or foreign language, including
Bengali, English, Gujarati, Assamese, Urdu, Nepali, Sindhi,
Tamil and Marathi.

Neither the children nor the teachers find the environment in
community schools conducive to learning. Upadhyay (1988), for
instance, sums up her impressions of one such class in the following terms:

> The most obvious problem the class seems to face is the shortage
> of space, the inadequate supply of teaching materials and the

inappropriateness of the latter. There is a regrettable shortage of teaching aids and equipment – the level of noise and the restriction of movement within the one room available for the class is also a major problem for class organisers. The teachers work with the bare minimum of resources, coping among other things, with irregular attendance and with changing composition of the groups they meet.

There is no provision for the initial training of Hindi teachers other than occasional INSET programmes organized by individual LEAs or the University of York. Although Hindi is offered, for example, as a degree subject at the University of London School of Oriental and African Studies, in the Faculty of Oriental Studies at the University of Cambridge and, in conjunction with linguistics, at the University of York, courses of this kind are designed primarily for native English speakers. There are no degree-level courses that cater for the cultural and literary needs of mother tongue/second language learners.

In conclusion, the Hindi speech community differs in many important ways from other South Asian communities in Britain. It draws on a wide range of groups including both mother tongue speakers and speakers of Hindi as a second and indeed third language. However, HMT speakers are a small, diffuse group whose patterns of occupation, settlement, family structure and social networks all weigh heavily towards a significant shift towards English in second-generation children. On the other hand, various factors might contribute to language stability rather than language death in a British context. These include the status of Hindi as the national language of India and as the language of religion for Panjabi Hindus and other Hindi speakers. Equally important is its role as a lingua franca among the various South Asian groups. Hindi and Urdu come from the same historical and linguistic roots. The survival of Urdu in Britain, in an oblique manner, might contribute to the survival of Hindi.

Note

1. I am grateful to Rupert Snell for providing me with a translation of this extract
2. Personal communication from B. N. Sharma, community languages co-ordinator for the voluntary sector in Nottingham.

References

ALLADINA, S. (1986) 'Black people's language in Britain – a historical and contemporary perspective', *Journal of Multilingual and Multicultural Development* 7 (5): 349–60

BROADBENT, J. (1983) *Assessment in a Multicultural Society. Community Languages at 16+*. Longman for the Schools Council.

City of Bradford Metropolitan Council (1988) 1987 *Schools Language Survey*. Bradford: City of Bradford Metropolitan Council.

European Communities (EC) (1977) *Council Directive on the Education of Children of Migrant Workers*: 77/486. Brussels: EC.

MILROY, L. (1980) *Language and Social Networks*. Oxford: Basil Blackwell.

UPADHYAY, S. (1988) 'Investigation of the social values and meanings associated with language use with focus on strategic uses of bilingual communicative resources in a community class'. Unpublished MA dissertation, University of Lancaster.

Chapter 8

The Panjabi speech community

V. K. Mahandru

----------------ਬੋਲੀ ਹੈ ਪੰਜਾਬੀ ਸਾਡੀ।
ਰੂਹ ਜਿੰਦ ਜਾਨ ਸਾਡੀ, ਗਿੱਦਿਆਂ ਦੀ ਖਾਨ ਸਾਡੀ।

boli hai Panjabi sadi rhoo jind jan sadi gidyan di khan sadi
Our language is Panjabi. It is our life and soul, it is a treasure of
folksongs

DHANI RAM CHATRIK

The Panjab – 'the land of five rivers' – owes its turbulent history
to its strategic position on the invasion route to India in the north-
western sector of the South Asian continent. Within this
geographical area are Muslims, Hindus and Sikhs, all of whom
might be described using the generic term 'Panjabi'. The focus
for the present chapter, however, will be the Sikhs, a
predominantly rural and farming religious community, which
claims the geographical Panjab as its homeland.

Since partition in 1947, the state of Punjab has been divided
between India and Pakistan (see Fig. 8.1). Before this time, however, the majority of the population of this state and others, in
a small number of adjoining areas outside the state itself, spoke
a dialect of Panjabi as their mother tongue. Panjabi belongs to
the Indo-European family of languages and has descended from
Sanskrit through Pali. The variety spoken in the south and east
is very close to Hindi, whereas on the western and northern ex-
tremes Panjabi gives way to Lahnda. It has been estimated that

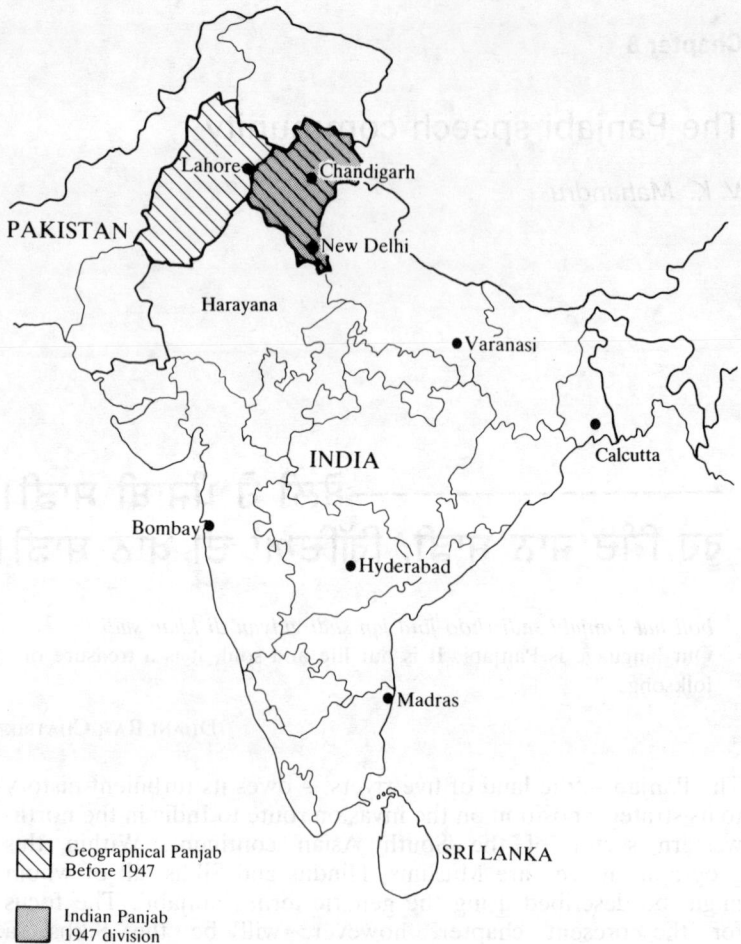

Geographical Panjab
Before 1947

Indian Panjab
1947 division

FIGURE 8.1   Location of Panjab

there are some 50 million speakers of Panjabi in Pakistan and
a further 15 million in India (Katzner 1977).

  The Muslim speakers of Panjabi on the Pakistani side of the
border look to Urdu as their second language and the language
of literacy (see Ch. 9). The southern portion of the Panjab has
a predominantly Hindu population which looks to Hindi as the
language of high culture and in 1966 became the new state of
Harayana, in which Hindi is the official language (see Ch. 7).

Only one group within the Panjab, the Sikhs, owe their primary language loyalty to Panjabi.

The Sikh religion grew from the attempt to unify Hinduism and Islam which began with the fifteenth-century preceptor, Guru Nanak, and his nine successors. It grew from strength to strength, especially in the sixteenth century, under Guru Arjan Dev, with the massive conversion of the dominant high-caste Jats. The religion has always met, however, with considerable hostility from outside. The oppression and persecution to which Sikhs (or 'disciples') have been subjected have given rise to a militaristic, soldier-saint brotherhood known as the *khalsa*. The symbols of this brotherhood are known as the five *ks*: the *kes* (uncut hair); the *karha* (iron bracelet on the right wrist); the *kirpan* (sword); the *kanga* (comb in the hair) and the *kachha* (specially designed underclothing). Although the importance of uncut hair for membership of the *khalsa* remains hotly disputed in both India and Britain (Helweg 1979), it is the *kes* which marks out Sikhs as a physically distinctive South Asian group.

The Holy Book of the Sikhs, the *Guru Granth Sahib*, was compiled by Arjan, the fifth guru, at the beginning of the seventeenth century. According to Sikh doctrine, the first guru Nanak's spirit passed through the next nine gurus. After the tenth guru, the gurudom was vested in the *Guru Granth Sahib*. The Holy Book is therefore treated with considerable reverence, since it is considered to be the spiritual embodiment of the ten gurus. The language of the Holy Book is Panjabi, written in the Gurmukhi script, especially devised by the second guru who reduced the *Pavan Akri*, or the 52 letters of the Hindi alphabet, to 35 and later added a further 5 letters from Persian. The Panjabi language and the Gurmukhi script are understandably treated with deep affection by Sikhs and have been used not only for scripture but also as the vehicle of a strong literary tradition dating back to the fifteenth century, and of a rich folk literature.

The Panjabi speech community in the UK

Sikhs have a history of migration (see Tinker 1974). Traditionally they were migrant traders, settling elsewhere in India and in lands to the west. The British army, which drew heavily on Sikh recruits, scattered members of this community even further afield in Singapore, Hong Kong, Australia, New Zealand and Fiji. Sikh hawkers and pedlars first came to Britain in the early 1920s, travelling around the country but working mainly in rural areas. By the end of the 1930s there were small communities of Panjabi pedlars in almost every British city (*cf* Ballard and Ballard 1977; Helweg 1979; Walvin 1984). There were many other destinations, too, including East Africa, where south Asians played an important role in the construction of the railway, and the west coast of North America.

Following the Second World War and partition, however, the most popular destination was Britain. Sikhs are one of the largest of the South Asian communities in Britain and number somewhere in the region of 400,000. Most of this Panjabi-speaking community who came to the UK between the late 1950s and early 1970s from India settled in the industrial Midlands and south. A number of Panjabis, however, came from East Africa in the late 1960s and early 1970s. They, too, clustered in the urban centres of the Midlands and the south. The main areas of settlement are Southall and Newham in London; Birmingham, Wolverhampton, Coventry; Leeds, Bradford, and a number of other smaller towns, such as Gravesend.

Accurate statistics are problematic for any ethnic minority population, but are particularly difficult to arrive at in the case of the Panjabi community (*cf* Nicholas 1988). When questionnaires are framed with underlying monolingual assumptions, and speakers are required to state which language, rather than which languages, they consider to be their mother tongue, Muslim Panjabis would be likely to declare their mother tongue as Urdu; Hindu Panjabis might say that they were Hindi speakers. The ILEA biennial *Language Census* (see Table 8.1), one of the few sources of information on linguistic minority populations in the UK, thus provides a valuable guide to numbers but is likely to underestimate considerably the number of Panjabi speakers. Even allowing for what may be quite a serious degree of underestimation, Panjabi speakers consistently emerge as one of the larger language minorities within the authority.

The first Panjabi immigrants were mainly agriculturalists and small landowners. They left home for a wide range of reasons

TABLE 8.1 Numbers of Panjabi speakers reported in the ILEA *Language Census*, 1981–87

Year	Number	%PHLOE*
1981	2,879	6.4
1983	3,022	6.0
1985	3,015	5.3
1987	3,200	5.0

*PHLOE = Pupils with a home language other than or in addition to English.

(Helweg 1979), the most important of which were financial. Panjabis, like other immigrant groups, wanted to take advantage of the economic opportunities (often greatly exaggerated by travel agents) available in the new country, and were often escaping from the great poverty and hardship which followed in the wake of partition. Emigration involved considerable expense: some individuals were sponsored by their families; others sold their belongings or rented their land to pay for their passage. As a result, the earlier settlers were males and lived in a state of enforced bachelorhood. They worked hard and saved enough so that they could send money to their families in India (cf Ballard and Ballard 1977).

The work which they took up on arrival in England was, in relative terms, extremely lucrative though often of a far lower status than they had enjoyed in the Panjab. It is interesting, for instance, that, in India, Sikhs who are unable to farm often choose to join the army but very rarely to work in factories. Helweg's (1979) description of the ways in which Sikh settlers in Gravesend accommodated to the new circumstances is particularly illuminating in this respect. He talks, for instance, of the way in which one of the people in his study justified his job as a factory janitor: 'Harbachan Singh had no choice. He had to show the home village that he was successful, even if this meant compromising caste dictates. [Not] maintaining his purity and being a failure in the eyes of his village-mates was far more degrading than being a janitor'.

Panjabis from East Africa, in contrast, came from a very different background and were mostly professionals and businessmen (cf Ch. 5). They arrived with their families and quickly established themselves in well-paid jobs and businesses. In recent years, however, there has been a narrowing down of these differences in the social patterns between Indian Panjabis and East African Panjabis. A number of Panjabis still work as skilled and semi-skilled labourers, but a growing percentage of them are now in banking, education, health care and the civil service. Many of them are also setting up businesses of different kinds.

Changing patterns of Language use

The character and status of Panjabi among its speakers have been greatly affected by life in Britain. The early Panjabi immigrants had to contend with the twin problems of learning a new language and a new urban style of life. They had to acquire English for

their everyday use, which in most cases did not go beyond a form
of 'survival' English. In the same way that words like 'gymkhana',
'jodhpur' and 'pyjamas' became part of the voçabulary of the
British colonizers in India, Panjabi had to change to make room
for new words that defined things that its speakers had not seen
or used before. Some English loan words, eg 'video', 'computer',
'autobank', have retained their English forms, whereas others, eg
boorash for 'brush' and sparnay for 'spanner', have been influenced by Panjabi phonology.

A further development in this borrowing process was that a
number of phrases, colloquialisms and idiomatic expressions were
directly lifted from English and transplanted into Panjabi. They
have become completely assimilated into Panjabi and form an integral part of the speaker's Panjabi repertoire. For instance,

> *uh mere lai **hedek** ban gaya*
> He became a headache for me

> ***reni de** lai kutf sev kar le*
> Save something for a rainy day

The last instance also shows an alternative strategy used by
Panjabi speakers: code-mixing in which elements of English and
Panjabi are fused in a single system. Agnihotri (1979) argues that
this mixed code forms an integral part of the collective verbal
repertoire of the community, the speakers' selection of Panjabi
and English depending on place, person, topic and certain internal linguistic factors, There are, however, intergenerational
differences in both code-mixing, and the related strategy of code-
switching, in which the speaker switches from one language to
another in the course of the same discourse or even the same
sentence (cf Poplack 1979). An older speaker, for example, may
borrow a word or two from English as in:

> *menu **kar** lai pese ud*^{h}*are lene payee*
> I had to borrow money for the car

But the young speaker might say the same thing as follows:

> *menu **kar** lai **mani: boro** karni payee*

As Agnihotri (1979) remarks: 'Sikh children are being simultaneously exposed to Panjabi and English. The social pressures,

TABLE 8.2 Language skills in the Panjabi community, extrapolated from LMP (1985)

		Panjabi	English
% of respondents who know the language quite well or very well	Coventry	99	61
	Bradford	99	54
% of people in respondents' households who know the language quite well or very well	Coventry	89	75
	Bradford	87	75

the intensity of motivation and the opportunities available to learn are different in each case. . . . The use of unadulterated Panjabi has nearly ceased to exist among the Sikh children in Leeds.'

There are many indications of a shift in the linguistic behaviour of second and subsequent generations from Panjabi to English. Confirmation of this trend is found, for instance, in the LMP's (1985) Adult Language Usage Survey (ALUS) (Table 8.2). The inclusion in the second set of figures of British-born children in-inevitably has the effect of depressing the reported level of proficiency in Panjabi and raising the level of proficiency in English. Parental reports of language use among children support this shift to English: some 42 per cent of the children in Coventry and 51 per cent of the children in Bradford use English mainly or exclusively in a peer group situation. However, there is also evidence of language stability: in family settings where bilingual language use is a realistic possibility, the majority of interactions take place in the home language, and it would seem that English is very rarely used to the total exclusion of Panjabi. ILEA *Language Census* data on levels of fluency in English would also lend support to the notion of language stability. In the 1987 census, for instance, only 29.2 per cent of the Panjabi-speaking children were considered to be fluent in English.

A number of patterns are emerging in various families: firstly, those where parents and children all speak Panjabi; secondly, those where parents speak Panjabi to their children, but the children respond in English; and thirdly, those families where both parents and children speak English. Figure 8.2 illustrates this situation.

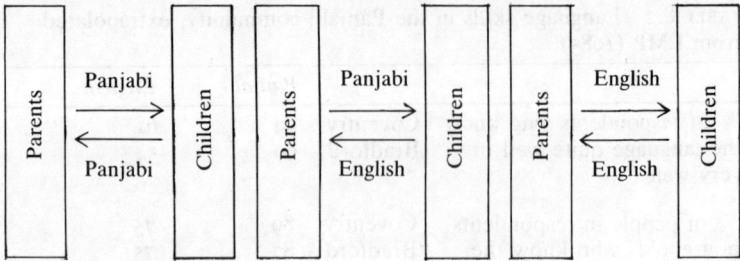

FIGURE 8.2 Three communication patterns in Panjabi families

Language, community and culture

Most Panjabis have maintained very strong contacts with their homeland through frequent visits to Panjab as well as receiving their relatives in the UK. International telephone links have made it even easier to keep in touch with families and relations back home. Moreover, a number of parents still prefer their sons and daughters to bring their marriage partners from India. The family ties between the various generations seem to be quite durable though there are signs that the youngest generation may break away from some of these connections (Ballard and Ballard 1977).

Helweg (1979) comments on the remarkably efficient communication networks between the home village and the UK and indeed with other Sikh communities elsewhere in the world:

> [Settlers in Gravesend] knew details of each other's salaries, family, caste, degree of faithfulness to spouse, personal habits, bank accounts and social ranking in the home village. Having contacts in various cities and villages, it was possible to learn as much as desired about a fellow immigrant. The migrant's awareness of the tightness of the network is exemplified by the dilemma of one Panjabi girl who desperately wanted to marry a boy out of caste, but deeply feared her family's wrath. Her English girl-friend suggested that she emigrated to Canada or the United States. She replied, 'There are Panjabi Jats in Canada and the United States. There is no escaping from our people!'

Links such as these make it easy to exert a strong social control on members of the community and to maintain traditional values to a far greater extent than would be the case in a more loose-knit society and inevitably have implications for language maintenance.

The *gurdwara* or Sikh temple (from 'Guru's door') is primarily a place of worship. However, it also plays a vitally important role as a community centre and a focus for political activity. It houses a hospice and a refectory which serves free meals. It also acts as a focus for a variety of socio-cultural as well as religious events, held all the year round. These reinforce the links that bind the Panjabi community, and these events are instrumental in supporting and promoting the use of Panjabi. Baisakhi, the New Year celebration in April, Diwali, a festival of lights held at the onset of winter, and a number of Sikh gurus' days commemorating various landmarks in the history of Sikhism attract large audiences, where the only language used is Panjabi. Birthdays, weddings and funerals are also conducted in accordance with the traditional Sikh rituals and accompanied by Panjabi music. At weddings in particular, the tradition of women singing folk-songs where they taunt and tease each other still survives. For example:

baribar si k^{h}atan gaya si k^{h}at ke leaya kan
b^{h}angra tan sajeda jee natfe munde di man

Roughly translated, it means:

The bridegroom went out to earn and earned himself a crow,
The dance'll swing when the groom's mother to the floor will go.

Political developments in India are, to a large extent, mirrored in the UK. The growing dissatisfaction which led to the storming of the Golden Temple of Amritsar by Indian government troops has gathered considerable momentum in recent years for the formation of an independent Sikh state. The political sectarianism within the Panjab has also created parallel divisions within Sikh communities in Britain, *ie* those who support Akali Dal (the Panjabi Independence Movement) and those who do not. The level of activity within the UK Sikh community was sufficient for the Indian prime minister, Rajiv Gandhi, to appeal to the British government for support. Political groups, however, are also heavily concerned with local issues and bodies like the Indian Workers' Association are active in many different spheres, including welfare and culture.

There is an active Indian Writers' Association which includes many Panjabi writers among its members and which sponsors regular seminars and conferences. British-based periodical publications include *Des Perdes* (Home and Abroad,) and the *Panjabi Times*.

TABLE 8.3 Language use in the workplace extrapolated from LMP (1985)

% of working respondents where at least one fellow worker can speak Panjabi	Coventry	72
	Bradford	80
% of working respondents where all fellow workers can speak Panjabi	Coventry	16
	Bradford	33
% of working respondents (who work for someone else) where the boss can speak Panjabi	Coventry	10
	Bradford	8

The tight-knit nature of the community creates many opportunities for the use of Panjabi. The existence of a strong ethnic economy has implications, for instance, not only for employment within the community, but for patterns of language use. Many Panjabis work in places where their own language is spoken with little or no need to communicate in English. The Linguistic Minorities Project's (LMP) (1985) Adult Language Usage Survey (ALUS) shows the pattern described in Table 8.3.

The findings of LMP (1985) also point to a wide range of settings, other than the workplace, which offer opportunities for using and maintaining the mother tongue (see Table 8.4). Most social life is conducted within the community around the *gurdwara*, visiting friends and relatives and viewing videos of Indian films. In the wider community, many neighbours are also Panjabi speakers; Panjabi is often used in shopping for food and clothing and in many legal and medical interactions.

In areas of important Panjabi settlement, most local authority and government publicity material is translated into Panjabi and is readily available in local council offices and libraries. Leaflets and pamphlets about school education, health education and police information are often distributed with Panjabi texts alongside the English.

Education and language reproduction

The Sikh community sees that the teaching of Panjabi is an important means of maintaining cultural and ethnic identity. Unlike many other linguistic minority communities, there is no dilemma over which variety of Panjabi should be taught: there is universal agreement on the standard form of Panjabi. For many years, mother tongue teaching was organized by Panjabi religious bodies and based at the *gurdwaras*. The teaching of Panjabi was combined with religious instruction and classes were held in the

TABLE 8.4 Language in a range of settings, extrapolated from LMP (1985)

% of respondents who used only Panjabi with the first person mentioned as somebody they spent free time with	Coventry	75
	Bradford	78
% of respondents who said that most or all of their neighbours could speak Panjabi	Coventry	25
	Bradford	32
% of respondents who said they had seen a film or video in Panjabi in the last 4 weeks	Coventry	70
	Bradford	67
% of respondents who said they sometimes visited a shop where Panjabi was spoken by the shopkeeper or assistants	Coventry	98
	Bradford	96
% of respondents who said they had a doctor who could speak Panjabi	Coventry	70
	Bradford	69

Coventry: $N = 200$
Bradford: $N = 98$

evenings or on Saturdays and Sundays. More recently, however, parents themselves have stepped in and arranged for classes to be run after hours in schools. Although the organization of these classes is secular, the teaching of the language is closely connected with religion and culture.

Recent figures on numbers of community classes are difficult to locate. As a very rough guide, however, LMP (1985) report that there were some 30 classes in Coventry in 1981, some of which had started as early as 1970, while in Bradford during the same period there were 29 classes, the longest established of which also dated back to 1970. Classes in both cities ranged between one and four hours in duration. Support from LEAs for these community classes was highly variable (Table 8.5).

TABLE 8.5 Patterns of support for community classes in two LEAs

	Coventry	Bradford
LEA provides both teachers' salaries and accommodation	13	6
LEA provides either teachers' salaries or accommodation	11	0
LEA provides neither teachers' salaries nor accommodation	6	23

Increasingly, however, there has been pressure for Panjabi to be acknowledged within the mainstream curriculum. Some LEAs, including ILEA, Birmingham and Coventry, have taken the initiative of introducing Panjabi into the state schools and are preparing students for their GCSE and A level examinations. In the summer of 1988, for instance, there were almost 1,000 candidates for the GCSE in Panjabi offered by the Midland Examining Group, the Joint Matriculation Board and the London East Anglian Group. There are, however, important differences between modern languages and community languages and these differences need to be addressed by both teachers and examinations boards (*cf* EC Community Language Project).

There has also been a small number of research and curriculum development initiatives involving Panjabi. The EC Bedfordshire Project (Simons 1979) which took place between 1976 and 1980 produced teaching materials in Panjabi for children aged between 5 and 8 and attempted to develop strategies for co-operation between mother tongue and mainstream teachers. A second project, the Mother Tongue and English Teaching Project (MOTET, see Fitzpatrick 1987), worked with two groups of Panjabi speakers in the first year of primary education. The first group was taught through the medium of English, the second through the medium of Panjabi. It was established that at the end of this experimental period, the level of achievement in English was comparable for both groups, whereas the children taught through the medium of Panjabi performed better in the mother tongue than the English-medium control group. This evidence, supported by other longitudinal studies of bilingual programmes from around the world (Skutnabb-Kangas and Cummins 1988), makes it imperative that the multilingual skills of schoolchildren in British schools are recognized and validated in our educational system.

References

AGNIHOTRI, R. K. (1979) 'Processes of assimilation: a sociolinguistic study of Sikh children in Leeds'. Unpublished D. Phil. thesis, University of York.

BALLARD, R. and BALLARD, C. (1977) 'The Sikhs: the development of south Asian settlements in Britain'. In J. Watson (ed.) *Between Two Cultures*, Oxford: Basil Blackwell, *pp* 21–56.

FITZPATRICK, B. (1987) *The Open Door*. Clevedon, Avon: Multilingual Matters.

HELWEG, A. W. (1979) *Sikhs in England: The Development of a Migrant Community*. Delhi: Oxford University Press.

Inner London Education Authority (ILEA) (1981; 1983; 1985; 1987) *Language Census*. London: ILEA Research and Statistics.

KATZNER, K. (1977) *Language of the World*. London: Routledge & Kegan Paul.

Linguistic Minorities Project (LMP) (1985) *The Other Languages of England*. London: Routledge & Kegan Paul.

NICHOLAS, J. (1988) 'British Language Diversity Surveys (1977–1987): a critical examination', *Language and Education* **2**(1): 15–34.

POPLACK, S. (1979) '*Sometimes I'll start a sentence in English y termino en Espanol': towards a typology of code-switching*'. Language Policy Task Force Working Papers No.4, New York, Centre for Puerto Rican Studies, City University.

SIMONS, H. (1979) *Mother Tongue and Culture in Bedfordshire*. EC Pilot Project, First External Evaluation Report, Cambridge, Institute of Education.

SKUTNABB-KANGAS, T. and CUMMINS, J. (eds) (1988) *Minority Education: From Shame to Struggle*. Clevedon, Avon: Multilingual Matters.

TINKER, H. (1974) *The Banyan Tree: Overseas Emigrants from India, Pakistan and Bangladesh*. Oxford: Oxford University Press.

WALVIN, J. (1984) *Passage to Britain*. Harmondsworth: Penguin.

Chapter 9

The Urdu speech community

Farhat Khan

یہ اُردو زباں کامِل و پُر اثر

زبانوں کی سُورج، ادب کی قمر

فصاحت میں پایہ ہے اِس کا بلند

سراپا بلاغت، دَہن پُر گہر

ye Urdu zabaan kaamil wa pur asar zabaano ki suraj adab ki
xamar fasaahat men paayaa he is kaa buland saraapaa bilaarat
dahan pur gohar

Urdu is an accomplished and forceful language. It is like the sun
among the languages and the moon (of the world) of literature. It
has a great potential for eloquence. It is full of rhetoric and has
pearl-like beauty.

Hasan Jahangir Hamdani

The present chapter presents a brief profile of the Urdu speech
community living in Britain. This community comprises a small
number of native Urdu speakers from India and others who
migrated to Pakistan after partition from India in 1947. There are
also relatively small numbers of Gujarati Muslims who use Urdu
for religious purposes (see Ch. 6). The vast majority of Urdu
speakers in the UK, however, are Muslims from the Pakistani
Panjab for whom Panjabi is the main language of the home. This
community of speakers can be distinguished, for instance, from

Sikh and Hindu speakers of Panjabi, by their commitment to Urdu as the symbolic expression of their religious identity. The main focus will therefore be on this numerically dominant group of Urdu speakers in the British context.

The historical development of Urdu

Urdu was originally one of the varieties spoken in the 'Hindi Region' alongside Braj, Bihari and Kari Boli Hindi. During the sixteenth century, large parts of India fell under Muslim rule. Although the ruling Muslim dynasties were mainly Turkish or Afghan in origin, their language and culture were predominantly Persian. While Urdu remained an essentially Indian language in structure, the linguistic influence of the invaders created an extensive Persian superstructure. Persian remained the official language, but Urdu spread all over India via army encampments, bazaars and administrative channels. A clue to this diffusion process is, in fact, contained in the etymology of the language name: 'Urdu' comes from the Farsi Zaban-e-Urdu-e-*mu'alla* ('language of camp and court'). It was also cultivated as a literary language by Indian Muslims in the independent Muslim kingdoms of central India, drawing much of its vocabulary from Persian and using the Perso-Arabic script, and by the eighteenth century this literary use of Urdu had spread from central India to the north. Today the Urdu spoken in the central Indian area is known as 'Dhakani'.

The question of description and definition of Urdu has been hotly debated since the beginning of the twentieth century. Many writers (eg *Census of India* 1961; Mobbs 1981) have suggested that Urdu and Hindi should be treated as a single linguistic entity in the spoken mode, differing mainly in the choice of lexical items for certain word classes. Others (eg Grierson 1927) point also to differences in word order between the two varieties. Still others point to the importance for language definition of culture (Alladina 1985), choice of scripts (Pattanayak 1981), language loyalties and identity (Mehdi 1974), all of which would point towards the treatment of Urdu and Hindi as separate varieties. This question continues to generate a great deal of emotion. Alladina's (1985) argument for the autonomy of Urdu and Hindi, for instance, provoked an extremely hostile response from Russell (1986b).

In India today Urdu is one of the 15 official languages and is spoken either as a first or second language by some 30 million Muslims. On partition from India in 1947, it became the official language of Pakistan where it is the mother tongue of approximately 5 million people who fled from India after partition. It is also used as a second language by perhaps 40 million more speakers (Katzner 1977).

In Pakistan, the main role of Urdu is therefore seen to be as a unifying national language. The four regions of Pakistan have their own regional languages – Panjabi in the Panjab, Sindhi in Sindhi, Baluchi in Baluchistan and Pashto in Sarhad; in addition to these regional languages, there are also many local varieties. Urdu, however, is the language of education and government and as such it is associated with power and prestige. While Urdu has not been universally welcomed in Pakistan – it has met with resistance, for instance, from the Pashto-speaking communities of Sarhad – it has none the less gained widespread acceptance.

Urdu speakers in Britain

Although there is a small number of Urdu mother tongue speakers from both India and Pakistan in the UK, by far the largest section of the Urdu speech community comes from the west Panjab and the Mirpur district of Azad Kashmir. Originally the Panjab formed a single state in which the majority of the population spoke various dialects of Panjabi (see Ch. 8). After partition, however, there were major population movements, with Hindus crossing to the Indian side of the border and Muslims moving to the new state of Pakistan. Although these speakers use Panjabi in most family and informal contexts, they consider Urdu to be the language of religion, literacy and culture. A smaller group of Gujarati Muslims from both India and East Africa (see Ch. 5) also use Urdu for religious purposes.

The presence of Urdu speakers in Britain is by no means a recent phenomenon. Shipping companies recruited vast numbers of Indians, including many from the Panjab, into the Merchant Navy during the First World War, and many more joined the British army and navy during the Second World War. The much larger numbers of Panjabi–Urdu speakers arriving in Britain in the 1950s and 1960s in response to the labour shortages created by the post-war boom economy were therefore a continuing part of a migration chain which had been in existence for many years.

As was the case for other immigrants, the main destinations were the major industrial cities of the UK. A high proportion of the new arrivals made their homes in the north of England, particularly in the textile towns of Lancashire and Yorkshire which sent recruitment officers to the Panjab to ensure a steady flow of workers. It is estimated, for instance, that there are 30,000 Pakis-

TABLE 9.1 Numbers of Urdu speakers reported in the ILEA *Language Census*, 1981–87

Year	Number	% PHLOE*
1981	2,778	6.2
1983	3,326	6.6
1985	3,642	6.4
1987	3,808	5.9

*PHLOE = Pupils with a home language other than or in addition to English.

tanis in Bradford, mainly from Mirpur, out of a total city population of 300,000 (Saifullah Khan 1977). Panjabi–Urdu speakers also settled in relatively large numbers in Birmingham, parts of east London, Southall and other towns and cities in the south of England.

It is difficult to estimate the numbers of Urdu speakers in the UK. One problem is that they are a very heterogeneous community which draws on speakers from both India and Pakistan, and from both the Panjab and other areas of India. This situation is further complicated by the fact that there is very little statistically reliable information available on British-born Urdu speakers. One source of information, however, is the ILEA *Language Census* (Table 9.1). These figures may also be compared with the findings of LMP (1985) for four other LEAs (Table 9.2). However, these figures do not include the large numbers of speakers who might, in surveys of this kind, report Panjabi or Gujarati as the language of the home, but who none the less are also able to speak Urdu.

TABLE 9.2 Numbers of Urdu speakers in four LEAs (extrapolated from LMP 1985)

Bradford	Coventry	Peterborough	Waltham Forest
2,698	503	433	1159

Changing patterns of language use

The linguistic situation within the Urdu speech community is rapidly changing. Some factors seem to favour the maintenance of Urdu in the community, others favour language shift towards English. There can be little doubt, for instance, of the fundamental importance of Urdu in defining the religious, cultural and national identity of its speakers. This feeling emerged rapidly in the course of fieldwork on the Urdu speech community. One speaker, a 35-year-old man, commented, 'Urdu is our national language, symbol of our cultural heritage and religion. Our community is nothing without Urdu. It keeps the community united.' This is a sentiment frequently expressed by much younger speakers, too. One 16-year-old respondent, for instance, remarked that: 'We'd feel isolated without our language – we'd feel funny if we didn't know our language.'

The importance of English in a British setting, however, especially for second-generation speakers, should not be underestimated. The second generation of Urdu–Panjabi speakers have access to two cultures and two identities: they have loyalties to both their community and to mainstream British society. Young people who have grown up in the UK share many of the social and economic ambitions of their English peers which require a thorough command of English. Comments on this subject included:

> English is the most important language because we live in England. . . . .We learn Urdu because our parents want us to. It is really not very important.

> I don't know why we have to learn Urdu – we use it only when we go to Pakistan. Here English has more value than Urdu.

However, the second generation is also subject to strong pressure from their parents to retain their religious and cultural identities which are closely associated with language. The linguistic behaviour of the second generation is thus often seen as a function of the tension between these two forces.

The process of language shift which is currently in progress can be clearly illustrated by considering the different patterns of language use common among first- and second-generation speakers which emerged from a survey undertaken by the present writer of some ninety-six Urdu–Panjabi speakers in the London borough of Newham in 1988. Speakers came from widely differing social backgrounds, from factory workers and shop assistants to students, teachers and doctors. The sample included equal numbers of male and female speakers and equal numbers of first generation (ages 31–50) and second generation (ages 16–30) speakers. Respondents were asked to provide information on their linguistic preferences when speaking with members of their own family other than their siblings; with their brothers and sisters; with blood relatives and people belonging to the same

TABLE 9.3 Patterns of language use in different domains (%)

Mostly E		Mostly U	Mixture of P/U/E	Sometimes P, Sometimes U	Always P
Members of the immediate family other than siblings					
1st gen.	15	17	8	14	46
2nd gen	22	8	10	20	40
Brothers and sisters					
1st gen.	0	15	10	9	66
2nd gen.	75	0	5	0	20
Biradari or kinship network					
1st gen.	0	32	15	0	53
2nd gen.	52	7	10	0	31
Other Panjabi–Urdu speakers					
1st gen.	15	40	20	0	25
2nd gen.	74	12	14	0	0
South Asian friends and neighbours					
1st gen.	0	22	6	20	52
2nd gen.	60	8	7	0	25
At work					
1st gen.	49	28	8	0	15
2nd gen.	78	9	0	0	13

E = English; P = Panjabi; U = Urdu.

biradari, or kinship network; with Panjabi–Urdu speakers from outside this immediate community; with other South Asians, such as Gujarati speakers from India or Sylheti speakers from Bangladesh; and at work (see Table 9.3).

Urdu thus emerges as having greater currency for first-generation than second-generation speakers. There are indications of a shift towards the use of English, which is least marked in domains outside the home and in the case of interactions with parents and grandparents but particularly noticeable in conversations with siblings. Figures from the present survey may be compared with the findings of LMP (1985), where 40 per cent of the parent sample in Coventry and 25 per cent of the Bradford sample reported that their children spoke to each other mainly or only in English. Interestingly those respondents who reported using English most with their children were professionals who

believed that English was more important for their children's future than either Urdu or Panjabi. Anwar (1978) has made a
similar observation about the linguistic preferences of middle-
class Asian parents.

It is also interesting to note the extent of code-switching which
was reported for both first- and second-generation speakers. The
nature of this switching, however, is different for the two generations. Older speakers use English with friends and neighbours;
with their Panjabi–Urdu-speaking friends and neighbours, however, they will tend to use Panjabi, sometimes switching between
Panjabi and English. With other Asian neighbours, such as
Gujarati, Bengali and Hindi/Urdu speakers, they generally speak
Urdu and sometimes code-switch between Urdu and English.
Code-switching between Panjabi and English is also very common
in the domain of family (see also Ch. 7). Second-generation
speakers, however, for whom English is the dominant language,
report a lower incidence of code-switching behaviour, either between Panjabi and Urdu or between English and Panjabi.

Language, culture and community

Religion is a central part of life in the Urdu-speaking community.
Social customs are justified in terms of religious belief and it is
one of the most important bonds in the maintenance of the
community's social solidarity and cultural maintenance. The goal
of mosques and religious organizations is to preserve religious and
traditional values and also to offer support to the Muslim community, mostly in non-economic spheres.

Mosques are used for religious instruction, daily prayers and
for teaching Urdu and the Qur'ān to children, mainly in the evenings or at weekends. They also serve as a meeting place where
the imam, or priest, gives a sermon on Islam after Friday prayers
and reminds the community of their obligations in terms of family
and *biradari* (or kinfolk). There are over 300 mosques, religious
centres or Muslim organizations in Britain, including the Islamic
Foundation, the UK Islamic Mission, the Muslim Welfare Association, the Muslim Youth Organization, the Pakistan Welfare
Organization, the Pakistan Social and Cultural Circle and Urdu
Markaz (Urdu Centre), which are responsible for a wide range
of community and religious activities ranging from daily prayers
to social and cultural functions.

The major religious festivals are 'Id-ul-fitr (the celebration of
the end of Ramadan, the month of fasting), 'Id-ul-Azha (associated
with Abraham's intended sacrifice of his son) and Bara-wafaat

(the prophet's birthday). The first two festivals begin with prayers at the mosque followed by visits to friends and relatives. On the prophet's birthday, most Muslims visit the mosque, usually decorated with lights, in the evening and wait until the next day to celebrate by socializing with family and friends.

The Urdu–Panjabi speakers in the UK tend to have extremely dense and multiplex social networks (*cf* Milroy 1980) in which *biradari* – or kin – play a vitally important part. Beyond the extended family it is the *biradari* which structures kinship networks. *Biradari* includes all those who claim and can trace their relationship to a common ancestor. All members of the *biradari* maintain close relationships with each other. Many *biradari* members pool resources to buy a house or start a business and generally lend each other support. They visit each other regularly and meet for family celebrations, such as weddings, birth and childhood ceremonies and religious festivals. Social networks of this kind are an important element in the maintenance of purdah (seclusion) in the Urdu-speaking community. Purdah also refers to restrictions on the physical movements of women who do not normally go out of the home unless it is absolutely essential. Although there is enormous variation, most women do not work outside the home and conduct their social lives entirely within the community. A thriving ethnic economy of clothes manufacturers, grocers, *halal* butchers, sari and clothes shops also makes it easy to live more or less exclusively within the confines of the community.

Most families maintain regular links with the homeland and often send their children to Pakistan for several months in order that they may have experience of life in a Muslim community and understand the significance of their religion in daily life in a way which is impossible in England. Visits from relatives in Pakistan are also common.

Urdu, Hindi and Panjabi film songs are the most popular entertainment among Urdu–Panjabi speakers. A considerable number of video shops conduct a thriving business in areas of Urdu–Panjabi and Hindi settlement. Videos are particularly popular with women who do not very often go outside the home for their entertainment or recreation.

Cultural events particularly popular with the first generation of settlers include *Mushairas* and *Qawwalis*. *Mushairas* are public gatherings where poets recite lyrics known as *gazal*, the most popular of all the classical forms of Urdu poetry. *Qawwali* music is the devotional music of the Sufis, the mystics of Islam, dating back to the tenth century. The lyrics are usually in Urdu, Panjabi or Farsi and the songs are in praise of God. Both *Mushairas* and *Qawwalis* are organized by the community about three or four times a year. These cultural events are organized by groups such as the Pakistan Welfare Association, the Pakistani Social and Cultural Centre and Urdu Markaz.

Commitment to religious and cultural values is reflected in the publication of Urdu books, the emergence of a number of monthly and biweekly magazines and daily newspapers in Urdu and the setting up of South Asian bookshops. There is a limited amount of radio and television broadcasting in Urdu and some local radio stations also produce programmes in Urdu.

Many local libraries in various regions where the Urdu speakers have settled have recognized the community's interest in and need for maintaining its linguistic heritage by providing books, magazines, newspapers, video films and records in Urdu. During the last ten years or so an increasing number of government and local authority departments have published various booklets, leaflets, posters and hand-outs in Urdu. Some local authorities also employ translators and interpreters. Provision of this kind clearly helps to meet the needs of a community, on the one hand, and to foster the ethnolinguistic vitality of the community, on the other.

Education and language reproduction

Community attempts to teach Urdu in Britain date back to the early 1970s. The first classes in Coventry, for instance, were started in 1974 and were followed a year later in Bradford (LMP 1985). Mother tongue teaching at this time was organized entirely by the community, and many classes continue to be community run. They take the form of weekend classes which are held either in local schools or in mosques. Panjabi is usually the medium of instruction. The aim of these community classes is primarily to enable children to read religious books and to have a better understanding of Islam. Children are also taught to read the Qur'ān in Arabic.

Large numbers of children between the ages of 5 and 16 are involved in community language learning. LMP (1985), for instance, reports that over 300 regularly attended classes in Coventry in 1981 while the comparable figure for Bradford was almost 1,800. The amount of time spent in classes is highly variable. In Coventry, class time ranged between 2 and 10 hours a week and in Bradford between 9 and 14 hours.

Initially, the feeling was that the community alone should take responsibility for organizing Urdu teaching. Over a period of time, however, there was increasing pressure for Urdu to be taught, alongside other community languages, as part of the curriculum in state schools. While considerable progress has been made in this direction, the pattern of provision in mainstream education is not uniform. Only in some cases is Urdu taught as part of the curriculum, sometimes being offered as an option under modern languages and sometimes replacing subjects such as PE, cookery and art and craft. In other cases, Urdu is taught in the lunch break or after school.

The teaching of Urdu is beset with many problems including the traditional approach and methods, the low status of teachers whose qualifications are not recognized and therefore are paid as instructors, the lack of effective in-service training and the shortage of suitable teaching materials and resources. Although some progress is being made on all these fronts, there is no room for complacency.

There are few suitable published books and courses in Urdu for pupils in the UK, although there are various local attempts to produce materials which meet the needs of British learners. The University of London School of Oriental and African Languages has some useful publications for teaching Urdu to adults, such as Russell's (1974) *Essential Urdu, A New Course in Hindustani* and (1986a) *A New Course in Urdu and Spoken Hindi*, and some resource material relating to the teaching of Urdu for GCSE is now beginning to appear. For example, the BBC has produced '*Urdu Boliye*', a series of radio programmes on spoken Urdu, along with teacher's notes for Urdu teachers and learners (Khan 1988; Khan and Siddiqui 1988). This is the first time the media have offered Urdu as a subject. Hashmi (1986) has also produced a series of Urdu textbooks for the teaching of Urdu in schools.

With respect to examinations and assessment, three examining groups – the Midland Examining Group (MEG), the London and East Anglian Examination Group (LEAG) and the Northern Examining Association (NEA) – offer Urdu as a GCSE subject. All three have Urdu syllabuses in line with other modern languages. The LEAG offers A level Urdu; it also provides Urdu examination papers with rubric and instructions in both English and Urdu. Nearly 2,900 candidates took the GCSE (MEG, LEAG and NEA) examinations in Urdu in 1988.

Some pioneering work is being done in graded assessment for GCSE in modern languages including Urdu under the auspices of the LEAG in co-operation with a number of LEAs and schools.

The aim of this scheme is to facilitate the progressive and continuous assessment of learning and achievement. The materials used are intended to integrate assessment with normal classroom procedures and learning processes in a less obtrusive way than is the case for other external examinations and tests. The scheme is divided into eight levels which are linked with GCSE grades. As such it is a valuable pointer and a milestone for curriculum development. The graded assessment scheme in Urdu, available from September 1989, is the first of its kind in a community language.

It should be remembered, however, that the problems and challenges of teaching community languages are sometimes very different from those which face teachers of other modern languages in the curriculum. This is a question which has been addressed, for instance, by the European Commission 1984–1987 Project on Community Languages in the Secondary School in relation to the Italian, Panjabi and Urdu-speaking communities (see Ch. 8 and Vol. 1, Ch. 13).

The University of London School of Oriental and African Languages offers short courses in Urdu as well as a number of diploma and certificate courses and postgraduate courses. Bradford and Ilkey Community College, the Polytechnic of Central London and a number of other polytechnics and maintained colleges in London, Birmingham, Manchester, Sheffield and Luton run courses for adults and prepare them for examinations. In addition to these colleges, various organizations such as Urdu Markaz and the Academy of Urdu Studies, also provide tuition in Urdu.

Despite the presence of significant numbers of Urdu speakers in Britain for the last thirty years, there is still widespread ignorance about their background. Teachers, social workers and others who come into contact with the South Asian speech communities often tend to deal in terms of blanket labels like 'Pakistani', which are often generalized to the languages of this group. Many children responding to language surveys such as the LMP (1985) and Rosen and Burgess (1980) have been acutely aware of this ignorance and have attempted to insulate themselves from it by telling teachers and researchers that they speak 'Pakistani'. Many people do not understand the religious significance of Urdu, nor the fact that, in most cases, Urdu is used in addition to another mother tongue.

Urdu speakers in Britain are multilingual. In addition to their knowledge of Urdu, they will have varying degrees of fluency in English and Panjabi or Gujarati. Some will also know other languages such as Kachchi or Hindi. In addition, they are likely to have a range of literacy skills in both Urdu and Arabic and, in the case of Gujarati Muslims, Gujarati, too. The British expectation of monolingualism as the norm is seriously challenged by speakers with linguistic repertoires of this kind. With the growing understanding of the cognitive and intellectual advantages of bi- and multilingualism, it is important that speakers of Urdu and other community languages receive due recognition for their skills and adequate support for their language learning.

References

ALLADINA, S. (1985) 'South Asian languages in Britain: criteria for definition and description'. *Journal of Multilingual and Multicultural Development* **6**(6): 449–66.
ANWAR, M. (1978) *Between Two Cultures*. London: Commission for Racial Equality.
Census of India (1961) Vol. I, Part XI. Report on the Census of the Panjab: 1881 by D. C. Ibbertson, Chapter. V, 'The Languages of the People', Part 1, Introductory and Comparative.
GRIERSON, G. A. (1927) *Linguistic Survey of India*, Vol. 8, Part I. Calcutta: Motilal Banarasidas.
HASHMI, M. (1986) *Phalla Xadam* (First Stage); *Dusraa Xadam* (Second Stage); *Tisraa Xadam* (Third Stage). Bradford: Directorate of Education.
Inner London Education Authority (ILEA) (1981, 1983, 1985, 1987) *Language Census*. London: ILEA Research and Statistics.
KATZNER, K. (1977) *The Languages of the World*. London: Routledge & Kegan Paul.
KHAN, T. A. (1988) *Urdu Boliye*. Brighton: Language Centre, Brighton Polytechnic.
KHAN, T. A. and SIDDIQUI, W. (1988) *Urdu Boliye*. BBC School Radio Productions.
Linguistic Minorities Project (LMP) (1985) *The Other Languages of England*. London: Routledge & Kegan Paul.
MEHDI, B. (1974) 'The Final Cry'. In A. Jussawalla (ed.) *New Writing In India*, London: Penguin. pp. 207–8.
MILROY, L. (1980) *Language and Social Networks*. Oxford: Basil Blackwell.
MOBBS, M. (1981) 'Two languages or one? The significance of the language names "Hindi" and "Urdu"', *Journal of Multilingual and Multicultural Development* **2**(3): 203–11.
PATTANAYAK, D. P. (1981) *Multilingualism and Mother-tongue Education*. New Delhi: Oxford University Press.
ROSEN, H. and BURGESS, T. (1980) *Languages and Dialects of London School Children*. London: Ward Lock Educational.

RUSSELL, R. (1974) *Essential Urdu*. London: University of London School of Oriental and African Studies.

RUSSELL, R. (1986a) *A New Course in Urdu and Spoken Hindi*, 2nd edn. London: University of London School of Oriental and African Studies.

RUSSELL, R. (1986b) 'South Asian languages in Britain; a critique of Safder Alladina's analysis', *Journal of Multilingual and Multicultural Development* 7(6): 443–50.

SAIFULLAH KHAN, V. (1977) 'The Pakistanis: Mirpuri villagers at home and in Bradford'. In J. Watson (ed.) *Between Two Cultures*, Oxford: Basil Blackwell, *pp* 57–89.

Chapter 10

The Sri Lankan speech communities

Sri Lanka, formerly called Ceylon, is a small island state situated at the southernmost tip of India in the Indian Ocean. Sri Lankan society is multi-ethnic, multilingual and multicultural. The most obvious divisions are related to the major ethnic groups – the Sinhala, the Tamils, the Moors or Muslims, the Malays and the Burghurs, who are descendants of the Portuguese and Dutch colonizers of the seventeenth and eighteenth centuries. The present chapter will look in detail at the two most numerically important of these groups – the Sinhala and the Tamils. This focus should not, detract, however, from the extent of linguistic diversity on the island as a whole. The Moors, for instance, arrived as traders in Sri Lanka from the west coast of India and the Middle East. Their home language is a dialect of Tamil strongly influenced by Qur'ānic Arabic. The Veddhas, an aboriginal Sri Lankan community, speak a creolized version of the original Veddha language and Sinhala. In addition, Tamil-based Portuguese creoles in Batticaloa and Jaffna and a Sinhala-based Portuguese creole in Kandy, which developed during the period of Portuguese colonization in the sixteenth century, are still spoken by Indo-Portuguese Christians.

The British colonial presence in Sri Lanka from 1802 also had important linguistic consequences. As is the case in other parts of the world where English is spoken, a distinctive local variety has developed. Sri Lankan English is very close to Indian English, although there are important differences, especially in phonology, intonation and vocabulary. There is also internal variation to the extent that it is possible to distinguish, for instance, between the English of speakers in the north and east, and in the south of the island. There are differences, too, between the English of Sinhala and Tamil speakers though, in the case of educated speakers from the same parts of Sri Lanka, it is virtually impossible to discern the ethnicity on the basis of speech alone.

The Sinhala speech community

Lakshmi de Zoysa

භාෂාව ජාතියේ රුධිරයයි

Bhashava jaathiye rudhirayaii
Language is the lifeblood of a people

Sinhala was brought to Sri Lanka by settlers from north India and, for this reason, is a member of the Indo-Aryan family of languages rather than the Dravidian family which includes Tamil and the other languages spoken in south India. It is closely related to Maldivian, a language spoken in the Maldives, a chain of islands in the Indian Ocean to the south-west of Sri Lanka. The origins of the Sinhala language can be traced to the Brahmi inscriptions of the third century. Geiger (1938) called the language of these inscriptions Sinhala Prakrit because of its similarities with Middle Indian Prakrit in both phonology and morphology. Early Sinhala shows a close relationship to the Indo-Aryan languages of north India, with much of its vocabulary identical with that of Sanskrit and it has continued to draw on Sanskrit vocabulary throughout its history. However, over the centuries, Sinhala has developed features very different from those of the north Indian languages under the influence of the Dravidian languages of south India, particularly Tamil. This Dravidian influence is to be found not only in lexical borrowings but also on the level of syntax (Gunawardena 1959; De Silva 1979). Dravidian influence can be detected, too, in the Sinhala writing system. The earliest writing was based on the northern Brahmi script, but as time went on the letters became more rounded, resembling those of the Dravidian languages. This was perhaps due to the fact that the palm leaf used as writing material did not permit angular writing.

Sinhala has also been subjected to the influences of Western colonization which began in the sixteenth century with the arrival of the Portuguese and was followed by the Dutch and the British in the late nineteenth century. The language of the rulers became the language of government and social prestige and its influence on all sections of Sinhala society was soon reflected in lexical borrowings such as *kamise* (shirt) and *keju* (cheese) from Portuguese, *kokis* (cake) and *almariya* (wardrobe) from Dutch and *buseka* (a bus) from English. De Silva (1979) comments on the ways in which these lexical borrowings operate within a Sinhala grammatical framework. All new verbs in Sinhala take compound forms, *eg* noun + to do – *telifon karanava* (to phone); noun + to look – *telivisan balanava* (to watch television). Singular verbs bear the affix *-eka* meaning 'one', *eg baseka* (bus).

The main dialect divisions are Kandyan and low-country Sinhala, both of which can be further divided into smaller dialect areas. The various dialects are mutually intelligible and differ mainly in vocabulary and intonation. The dialects in the Kandyan area display Tamil influence while those in the low country Portuguese, Dutch and British influence.

The existence of a number of subgroups within the Sinhala community is reflected in a variety of social dialects, such as those of the Rodiyas (or 'untouchables'), and the Ahikuntakayas (or travellers). Most studies of these dialects to date have taken the form of lists of secret vocabularies (*cf* also Vol. 1, Ch. 5). Geiger (1938) refers to 'some secret or conventional languages which are used in conversation by certain castes or groups of persons on certain occasions, though not always with the same intention'. In addition, there is the secret vocabulary of farmers who use certain words to counteract the effects of evil spirits by using a 'lucky' or auspicious word and a forest language to ward off the dangers of the forest.

There are marked differences between the 'low varieties' of Sinhala used in informal interaction by speakers from all classes of society (*cf* Ferguson 1959) and the 'high' variety, acquired through formal instruction at home, at the temple or in school, and used for most written and formal spoken purposes. Closely associated with this variety is the temple and the Buddhist monk, the transmitters of the 'high' culture and religion, including stories from the lives of the Buddha. It is also used in newspapers, books, official documents and public speaking.

The most important differences between high and low varieties are in lexis. Whereas colloquial Sinhala tends to draw mainly on Tamil, Arabic, Portuguese, Dutch and English vocabulary to meet the demands of modern technology and science, literary Sinhala makes greater use of Sanskrit and, to a lesser extent, Pali,

TABLE 10.1 Some differences between literary and colloquial Sinhala

Literary Sinhala	Colloquial Sinhala	English
visin	athin	by
sijallam	akkoma	all
sita	indala	from
saha	ekka	with

the canonical language of Buddhist literature. It also draws on vocabulary from an older stage of Sinhala called Elu which gives it an even more learned ring.

There are differences not only between content words in the different varieties, but also between structural words, as set out in Table 10.1. There are also differences on the level of grammar. Whereas nouns and verbs are uninflected in colloquial Sinhala, in literary Sinhala nouns are marked for plurality and verbs for person and number. Grammatical differences between the varieties, however, would seem to be on a superficial level and even semi-literate speakers have at least a passive competence in literary Sinhala (cf De Silva 1979).

It would be naïve, however, to conclude that there is a neat and rigid division between colloquial and literary Sinhala. Intermediate varieties which incorporate colloquial main verbs while, at the same time drawing extensively on literary vocabulary are to be found, for instance, in children's books, religious sermons, lectures and public speaking.

Sinhala speakers in Britain

Sri Lanka is a small country and the impact of British colonization was very deep. Education was conducted through the medium of English and the people emulated the lifestyles of the British. The rich sent their children to the UK for the 'great British education' and the majority returned to take up leadership positions in all spheres of life. A few remained, others trickled in. Sri Lankans continue to come to Britain for purposes of higher education and research, even today.

With independence in 1948, Sri Lankans did not retain British citizenship but as members of the British Commonwealth they were able to settle in Britain. It was only after 1956 when Sinhala was made the official language that many people decided to emigrate. Some felt unable to cope with changing conditions, others wished their children to have an 'English' education. These emigrants belonged to the educated élite and some of them were eager to assimilate into the mainstream of the English life they valued so much. The preservation of their own language and culture did not have a high priority.

In the 1960s and 1970s Sinhala people began to leave Sri Lanka for political and economic reasons. They were educated professionals, mainly doctors and nurses, lawyers and engineers, accountants and teachers, who were opting for Britain because of their familiarity with the system and their command of the English language. However, with the stricter immigration controls which were enacted in Britain, a voucher system was introduced and professionally qualified people were encouraged to come to the UK. As a result, the Sinhala people – an estimated community of 50,000 – are scattered all over the country with relatively large concentrations in parts of London. They did not intend permanent settlement and it was only rarely that whole families sought immigration. Parents were reluctant to leave home and, as a result, there are very few old people in the community.

As was the case with the earlier settlers, those who made up this second wave of settlement were also proficient in English, having had at least their higher education through the medium of English either in Sri Lanka or the West. However, they had also been subject to the influences of the post-colonial period. They were, by and large, literate in Sinhala and valued Sinhala culture more than the earlier immigrants. Biliterate and bicultural, this group is more conscious of their identity as Sinhala people.

There is no accurate information on the numbers or distribution of Sinhala people in Britain, although a high proportion live in and around London. The ILEA *Language Census* returns for children reporting themselves as Sinhala speakers are the only source of statistical information on the school-age population either in the capital or elsewhere (Table 10.2).

TABLE 10.2 ILEA *Language Census* data on Sinhala speakers (1981–87)

Year	Number
1981	192
1983	165
1985	170
1987	170

Changing patterns of language use

Because the Sinhala population in Britain is essentially a highly educated élite, virtually all were bilingual in Sinhala and Sri Lankan English on arrival. Some found it more comfortable to operate in English than in Sinhala and many genuinely believed that the use of Sinhala might interfere with their children's acquisition of English. As a result, children of Sinhala origin are in the process of losing the language of their parents. Many of them have a passive understanding of the language, with the ability to follow instructions and use a few phrases to express their basic needs. Nor are there any pressing practical reasons for using Sinhala in the home. Whereas children from many linguistic minorities in Britain need to use the mother tongue to communicate, for instance, with their grandparents, many of the older generation in the Sinhala community speak, read and write English.

ILEA *Language Census* statistics on the English skills of Sinhala children are therefore surprising. According to ILEA (1987), for instance, only 50.6 per cent of Sinhala children were considered to be fluent English speakers. This finding is in marked contrast with my own experience in Brent where not more than half a dozen have been identified as needing special help in English during the last fifteen years. The ILEA figure is, of course, based on a sample of only 170 children. It is also possible that, because teachers are unaware of the extent of bilingualism within the Sinhala community or the presence of a distinctive variety of Sri Lankan English, they expect a low level of language skill and categorize the children accordingly (see, for instance, Alladina 1985 and Nicholas 1988, for a critique of language survey data in the UK). These low estimates also bring into question the categories of English proficiency and methods of assessing these and the competence of the assessors themselves.

Contrary to what the ILEA statistics might suggest, the main concern of the Sinhala community is that children are becoming monolingual English speakers. The political situation in Sri Lanka has heightened this concern. The widespread fear among Sinhala people for the extinction of their race – a minority in the context of South Asia – has given rise to a greater consciousness of the need to preserve the Sinhala language and culture. There is a growing desire to encourage awareness of Sinhala among the young and the maintenance of language and culture is now becoming a priority for the Sinhala community in the UK. This is reflected, for instance, in the changing patterns of language choice in a growing number of families. Whereas it was previously the case that English was the dominant, or even the exclusive language of the home, in recent years many Sinhala are making a very conscious effort to use the mother tongue and to transmit the language to their children.

Language, culture and community

The desire to return to Sri Lanka is still strong among the Sinhala community and, as such, the later immigrants, in particular, try to maintain cultural and linguistic ties with the home country and to share their cultural heritage with their children. In the region of 90 per cent of Sinhala people are Buddhist and the focal point of Sinhala cultural life has always been the Buddhist temple and this continues to be the case in the UK. Buddhism is part and parcel of Sinhala life and, for historical reasons, takes a distinctive form. The Sinhala royal families traditionally took Hindu princesses for their wives. Sinhala Buddhist temples contain Hindu shrines and worshippers are also familiar with Hindu ritual.

The London Buddhist *vihara* at Chiswick has been in existence since 1926. A second temple has since been built in Selsdon, south London. Sinhala people gather at the *vihara* for religious observances and meditation on full moon days (Poya days), particularly at Vesak, the period which includes the full moon day in May when followers celebrate the birth of the Buddha, his attainment of enlightenment and his final release from the round of rebirth. The new year, celebrated around 13 or 14 April, is also an important time for the community. Both Sinhala and English are used in the *vihara* since there are many non-Sinhala Buddhists.

There are strong links with family and friends in Sri Lanka as often only one or two members of a family are in the UK. Visits home to Sri Lanka and visits to Britain from relatives and friends are regular. Perhaps as compensation for the lack of an extended family, several associations have sprung up, including past pupils associations of schools in Sri Lanka. Two of them are essentially Sinhala and Buddhist. Another meeting place for many Sinhala Buddhists is the Community of Many Names of God in Llanpumsaint, Dyfed, where worship includes both Hindu and Buddhist elements. There are also the Sinhala Association and the Sinhala Bala Mandalaya (Association of Sinhala People) with their own newspapers in Sinhala. The *Silvarrow* is an English monthly bulletin with news from home and of Sri Lankans in the UK.

Over the years cultural activities have increased, with associations specifically for the arts. Of these the South East London Cultural Group, the Sri Lankan Arts Forum and Namel and Malini Arts have promoted traditional and indigenous dance, song and drama. Occasionally Sinhala films are shown, but Sinhala videos are not in common use.

Education and language reproduction

Language and learning have traditionally been associated with the Buddhist temple and Sinhala classes are therefore organized by Buddhist monks at the London Buddhist *viharas* in Chiswick and Selsdon. Classes usually last two hours and take place once a week. The children are grouped according to age and range from $3\frac{1}{2}$ to 15. The content tends to be oriented towards religion and the methodology is traditional, starting with the alphabet and using books and materials from Sri Lanka. The emphasis is on developing literacy skills. There has been a real increase in recent years in the number of children attending.

There is no provision for the teaching of Sinhala in the state system, other than one LEA-sponsored class in Merton, the only one of its kind in the UK. Here modern approaches to language teaching are used, encouraging oral communication skills and using specially developed materials which ensure a positive view of Sinhala language and culture. Otherwise, Sinhala is taught by a few private tutors in their homes and sometimes by voluntary groups. Until recently there was an opportunity for offering Sinhala as a GCE O level subject. Sadly this opportunity is no longer available.

Acknowledgements

I would like to acknowledge the help of the Venerable Dr Hamallava Saddhatissa, K. D. Somadasa, H. H. Bandara and Dr Subadra Siriwardena in the preparation of this chapter.

References

ALLADINA, S. (1985) 'Research methodology for language use surveys in Britain'. In P. H. Nelde (ed.) *Methods in Contact Linguistic Research*, Bonn: Dümmler, *pp* 233–40.

DE SILVA, M. W. S. (1979) *Sinhala and Other Island Languages in South Asia*. Arts Linguistica 3. Tübingen: Gunter Narr Verlag.

FERGUSON, C. (1959) 'Diglossia', *Word* 15: 232–51.

GAIR, J. W. (1968) 'Sinhalese diglossia', *Anthropological Linguistics* 10(8): 1–15.

GEIGER, W. (1938) *A Grammar of the Sinhala Language*. Colombo: The Royal Asiatic Society, Ceylon Branch.

GUNAWARDENA, W. F. (1959) *First Principles of Sinhala Grammar*. Colombo: Lake House Investments Ltd.

Inner London Education Authority (ILEA) (1981, 1983, 1985, 1987) *Language Census*. London: ILEA Research and Statistics.

NICHOLAS, J. (1988) 'British Language Diversity Surveys (1977–1987): a critical examination', *Language and Education* 2(1): 15–34.

The Tamil speech community

Gnani Perinpanayagam

கற்க கசடற க் கற்பவை கற்றபி
னிற்க வதற்குத் தக.

Katkek kasadara katravai katrapin nitke adhatkuth thaha
Learn and learn thoroughly; having learned, live according to that learning

THIRRUKURAL

To talk about the Tamil communities in the UK is a complex task, especially in the late 1980s when 'the relationship between society and language, culture and language . . . political and official status of languages and, most of all, the perceptions and loyalties of the speakers and users of those languages have to be considered' (Alladina 1985). A purely descriptive-linguistic account might suffice at a superficial level, as an academic exercise, but when it concerns people – which is what sociolinguistics is all about – some underlying forces, however briefly, need to be explored.

The sociolinguistic situation of Tamil

About 75 million people across the world speak Tamil in south India, Sri Lanka, Malaysia, Singapore, Fiji, Mauritius, Trinidad, Guyana, Zanzibar, parts of East Africa, South Africa, Canada, Australia, New Zealand, East and West Germany, Switzerland, the UK and the United States. Of this number about 3.9 million speakers are from Sri Lanka.

Tamil belongs to the Dravidian language family. In India it is completely surrounded by other languages belonging to the same family, of which Telegu, Kannada or Canarese, Malayalam, Gondi, Kurukh, Kui, Tulu and Brahui have sufficient numbers of speakers to be given status among the 197 'recognized' Indian languages (*cf* Katzner 1977). On account of diverse contact situations, there have been mutual influences – especially on the phonology – of these languages. However, unlike the more northern Dravidian languages which are in contact with Indo-Iranian languages, the structure of Tamil has remained Dravidian and the main changes over time have been in lexicon.

There are two major dialects of Tamil in Sri Lanka. The first is an indigenous dialect whose 2.7 million speakers have for centuries lived along the north-western, northern and eastern coastal areas and in the north central regions. The other dialect is Indian Tamil with about 55 million speakers in India, 1.17 million speakers in Sri Lanka and about 15 million speakers elsewhere. Indian Tamils were brought to Sri Lanka by the British colonial authorities in the 1840s. They worked on the tea plantations in the central hills and neighbouring territory as segregated, indentured labour. Because of their isolation from the original Sri Lankan Tamils, these two dialects of Tamil have had no influence on each other, although speakers of the indigenous variety are familiar with Indian Tamil through imported films.

High and low varieties of Tamil exist in a diglossic situation (*cf* Ferguson 1959). On a phonological level, there is little divergence (cf. *aynthu* [H] and *anjchu* [L] which mean 'five' or *vaarungko* [H] and *vaangko* [L] which mean 'come'). On the level of idiom, however, the differences are more significant. Take, for example,

[H]   *naan kooviththeen*
[L]   *enakku paththikondu vandhedhu*   I became angry
[H]   *ennaiy vadhekyaadhe*
[L]   *ennaiy aaykinaiy paduththaadhe*   Don't bother me

The high variety is valued for its propriety and conformity, its wealth of imagery and phonological harmony. It is the language of a literature which extends over two millennia (Somasundaram Pillai 1959) and is associated with formal situations. The low variety is reserved for informal spoken situations and is not found in writing other than in dialect drama. These two forms coexist and a speaker may select either form depending on the context. The low variety is valued for its intensity and vivid imagery.

Following independence in 1948, schools and universities turned from English as the medium of instruction towards the vernaculars – Tamil and Sinhala – except in the fields of engineering, science, law and medicine. Elsewhere English was taught as a compulsory foreign language after three years of primary schooling, but its thrust was feeble since the political climate had changed the 'valorization' (cf. Hamers and Blanc 1982) of the language. The Sinhala-Only Bill of 1956 further detracted from the value of English, though the language was tenaciously maintained by the middle and upper classes. In spite of an amendment which allowed for the restricted use of Tamil, the bill also had the effect of seriously eroding the status of Tamil. Access to Sri Lankan universities became increasingly difficult for Tamil speakers and increasing numbers therefore turned to India for their higher education. It was only in 1987 that Tamil and English were also accorded the status of official languages in Sri Lanka alongside Sinhala.

The Tamil speech community in the UK

Individual Tamils have been coming to Britain for over a century. Some of my own relatives, for instance, came for training as doctors, engineers and lawyers, in the 1870s and 1880s. Throughout the twentieth century, Tamils have continued to arrive in small numbers, usually for the purpose of further study. Many returned to Sri Lanka; some made their home in the UK either permanently or for extended periods of time. Because this migration was very much on an individual level, the Sri Lankan Tamils have tended to be a very dispersed community. Of the 100,000 Sri Lankans which the Sri Lankan High Commission estimate to be in the UK, 65 per cent are Tamils. The rest are Sinhala, Moors and Burghers.[1] The British Tamil community can be divided into three main groups: UK citizens, permanent residents in the UK, and students.

This number, however, does not include those Tamils who have sought political asylum in the UK since the serious escalation of violence in Sri Lanka in 1983 (Piyadasa 1988). The scale of this violence in Sri Lanka is often not fully understood outside the country. As the Tamil Refugee Action Group (1988) point out: 'Between 1981 and 1987, 71,000 Tamil refugees fled to Europe; 160,000 to India; 336,545 within Sri Lanka with a reported 16,000 killed, 14,000 injured and over 2,000 missing: 154 schools and places of worship (some used as refugee camps) destroyed and property worth several billions of Rupees beyond redemption.' Some 4,289 of these Tamils sought political asylum in the UK between 1980 and 1986 (BRCR 1987). Of these, only 27 were granted asylum, 2,610 were granted 'exceptional leave to remain' in the UK; 205 were refused both asylum and 'exceptional leave to remain' and 1,447 cases were still pending decision in this same period. Uncertainty about the status of these Tamils has understandably caused a great deal of anguish within the community as a whole.

Those Tamils who arrived before 1983 were either fully qualified and experienced professionals – accountants, business administrators, computer scientists, engineers, lawyers, doctors, nurses and teachers – or came to Britain for higher education. The common denominator was their high level of education, but this was by no means a homogeneous group: although it was predominantly Hindu, there were significant Muslim and Christian minorities. This earlier group of Sri Lankan Tamils was usually trilingual in Tamil, Sinhala and English. Because of changes in the Sri Lankan education system following independence and the Sinhala-Only Bill, those who sought asylum after 1983 have often been monolingual Tamil speakers who have been exposed to English only as a foreign language in school. They have taken on any kind of work available in order to afford fees for further study which they assiduously pursue if they gain admission.

Changing patterns of language use

It is important in any discussion of language maintenance and shift to distinguish between the two main groups of Tamils in Britain – settlers of long standing and those who have arrived since the political troubles of 1983. Because a very high proportion of the longer-established Sri Lankan Tamils attended English-medium schools in Sri Lanka and went on to English-medium higher education both in Sri Lanka and the West, this group was composed of essentially balanced Tamil–English bilinguals on arrival in the UK who have continued to maintain both languages.

The conversation of these pre-1983 Tamils in the UK is marked by code-switching behaviour. Often without so much as a pause, speakers switch back and forth between Tamil and English. On analysis one might find areas which, if translated into the other language for linguistic consistency, might skew meaning or distort accuracy and are, therefore, preserved in the original language. The code-switching of these speakers is completely unconscious.

As Ervin-Tripp (1972) has remarked, 'Sometimes speakers cannot remember the language in which they just spoke, let alone report it to an interviewer.' Explanation and discussion, however, are usually in the mother tongue or 'the language of confidence' (Perinpanayagam 1973). What is most impressive is the sophistication and very high levels of confidence with which both languages are used.

Possibly as a result of the current political situation in Sri Lanka, there appears to be a renewed vigour to learn and to maintain Tamil among this group. Inevitably, the recent influx of Tamil speakers has had an important impact on the community as a whole. The presence of many people who were, on arrival, effectively Tamil monolinguals has made the whole question of Tamil language and culture more immediate and pressing for the British-born generations.

None the less, there is an inevitable shift to English among second- and third-generation Tamils who recognize it both as the language of greater instrumentality and as the language of the peer group which will allow them to foster friendship networks. There is a certain tension for these young people who, on the one hand, no longer see the relevance of maintaining Tamil in terms of their wider life-plans, but, on the other hand, need to speak Tamil to be included in the Tamil community. The fact that a return to Sri Lanka is not a viable proposition for Tamils in the foreseeable future, further shifts the balance towards the use of English.

Those who have arrived since 1983 are, of course, in a rather different situation. With changes in language policy in Sri Lanka, they have been exposed to English only as a foreign language. On arrival in Britain, therefore, improvement of English skills has been a priority. The growth in the Tamil population in the 1980s and the differences in educational experience between the newcomers and the longer-established Tamil community are reflected in the data on Tamil pupils contained in the ILEA *Language Census*, 1981–87 (see Table 10.3). As the number of Tamil

TABLE 10.3 Data on Tamil speakers from ILEA *Language Census*, 1981–87

Year	Number	% of fluent English speakers
1981	133	58.6
1983	139	54.7
1985	221	51.1
1987	370	31.9

speakers attending ILEA schools has risen, so the proportion of children considered to be fluent speakers of English has fallen, reflecting the different educational circumstances to which the newcomers have been exposed.

In my work as an educational assessor, I have come across bereaved Tamils among whom the trend suggests that the switch to English is likely to be rapid and complete, especially in the case of children who have arrived in the UK via other countries, having witnessed violence in Sir Lanka. There is a widespread reaction among the refugees of never wishing to return home and, while the parents continue to use Tamil among themselves, many of the children switch to English within a very short space of time and avoid using Tamil because of its traumatic associations with their past. Consequently some children have become 'receiver bilinguals' (Haas 1959) who comprehend Tamil but will not speak it.

In this respect the work of Lake (1985) on ego strength is particularly pertinent. Among the nine items of 'personal and social competence' which he lists is the 'capacity to cope with change, loss and uncertainty (eg loss of family member, friends, jobs, money, change of routine, illness)'. Difficulties in this area affect both the post-1983 arrivals and, to a lesser degree, the longer-term settlers anxious about family, friends and property left behind. Any understanding of the sociolinguistic behaviour of Tamils needs to take into account factors such as these.

Language, culture and community

I have yet to come across a Sri Lankan Tamil – even in the nine countries where I have worked – who has severed all connections with Sri Lanka even though they may be citizens or permanent residents of those countries. Given the current political situation in Sri Lanka, there is understandably a great preoccupation with what goes on in the home country. Communication is largely by mail that is usually out of date on arrival, but also by telephone from the country's capital Colombo, and Madras, the capital of Tamilnad in south India.

The very great concern with the current problems in the home country is reflected in the political activity within the British Sri Lankan community. The major Sri Lankan Tamil organizations, including the Tamil Eelam Liberation Organization, the Eelam People's Revolutionary Liberation Front, the Eelam Revolutionary Organization of Students, the People's Liberation

Organization of Tamil Eelam and the Liberation of Tamil Eelam, all have followings in the UK.

Social life revolves largely round the family. Although there is a significant Christian minority, the vast majority of Sri Lankan Tamils are Hindu. As such observance of Divali and the Hindu New Year are an important part of the religious calendar and are observed in the same way as in other Hindu communities (see, for instance, Vol. 2, Ch. 7). Supplementary schools (see section on education and language reproduction, below) are an important focus not only for the transmission of the mother tongue but also for cultural events within the community. Their aim is not only to maintain the language but to develop and encourage an appreciation of culture through music, dance and drama. End-of-term performances are an important event for the whole Tamil community and their guests. At such functions one can often see an *arangeetram* – the public debut of a promising musician, singer or dancer. It is a largely symbolic, religious ritual, infused with strict standards of music (melody and lyric), rhythm and movement.

Videos also play a part in maintaining the vitality of the mother tongue in Tamil homes. There is no Tamil film industry in Sri Lanka, but Indian Tamil films were imported in steady quantities to Sri Lanka. In the UK Tamil video films from India are freely available and are a very popular form of home entertainment in the community.

No newspapers or magazines to my knowledge are published in Tamil in the UK, but the *Tamil Times* and *Tamil Voice International*, two English-language publications, are widely available.

Education and language reproduction

There is currently a regeneration of interest in, and enthusiasm for, Tamil language and culture in those members of the community who have been longer established in the UK. There are some thirty Tamil Saturday and Sunday schools, spread from Glasgow to London. Half of these schools are London-based. The schools often receive small subsidies from the LEA, but the teachers are volunteers who receive only an honorarium to cover their expenses. The numbers of students attending range from 15 to 150 and the total school population is about 1,000. Needless to say, more such schools are being planned for those in more remote areas.

Texts for use in these schools are usually contributed by parents and other interested people and are brought from abroad. The principles of teaching are dictated by the texts but are modified by teachers to be in consonance with educational practice in the UK. For the most part, teachers are already teaching in various local authority schools. Unfortunately, Tamil is not yet offered as a subject by any of the examination boards. With the recent renewal of interest in the mother tongue in the community as a whole, it is hoped that there will be some developments on this front in the not too distant future.

Note

1. Personal communication from His Excellency, the High Commissioner for Sri Lanka in the UK.

Acknowledgements

I wish to acknowledge the detailed information which cannot be included here given to me generously by Mr Pat. S. Mylvaganam of the UK Tamil Refugees Organization. I also wish to thank Mr Malcolm Rogers of the British Refugees Council for the discussion and documents he so kindly gave me.

References

ALLADINA, S. (1985) *South Asian Languages in Britain: Criteria for Description and Definition*. Occasional Paper No. 5, Centre for Multicultural Education, University of London Institue of Education.

British Refugee Council Research and Development Unit (BRCR) (1987) *Report on Tamil Refugees in the UK*. London: BRCR.

ERVIN-TRIPP, S. (1972) 'On sociolinguistic rules: alternation and co-occurrence'. In J. Gumperz and D. Hymes (eds) *Directions in Sociolinguistics – the Ethnography of Communication*, N.Y.: Holt, Rinehart & Winston.

FERGUSON, C. A. (1959) 'Diglossia', *Word* 15 (2): 325–40. Reprinted in D. Hymes (ed.) *Language in Culture and Society*, N.Y.: Harper & Row, *pp*. 429–38.

HAAS, M. R. (1959) 'Results of the Conference of Anthropologists and Linguists'. Supplement to *Journal of American Linguistics* 19: 24–38.

HAMERS, J. and BLANC, M. (1982) 'Towards a social psychological model of bilingual development', *Journal of Language and Social Psychology* 1(1): 29–49.

Inner London Education Authority (ILEA) (1981, 1983, 1985, 1987) *Language Census*. London: ILEA Research and Statistics.

KATZNER, K. (1977) *The Languages of the World*. London: Routledge & Kegan Paul.

LAKE, B. (1985) 'Concept of ego strength in psychotherapy', *British Journal of Psychiatry* **147**: 471–8.

PERINPANAYAGAM, G. T. (1973) 'On becoming bilingual: cognitive and semantic considerations in language acquisition'. Unpublished Ph.D. dissertation, the University of New Mexico.

PIYADASA, L. (1988) *Sri Lanka – the Unfinished Quest for Peace*. London: Marram Books.

SOMASUNDARAM PILLAI, J. M. (1959) *Two Thousand Years of Tamil Literature*. Madras.

Tamil Refugee Action Group (1988) *Tamils: The Right to Live*. London: Tamil Refugee Action Group.

Part three

East Asia

This section examines the sociolinguistic situation of the various speech communities in Britain who came originally from Japan, the Philippines, Hong Kong, Vietnam, Singapore and Malaysia. The same startling diversity of languages which marked South Asia, is also a hallmark of East Asia. Few outside observers, however, appreciate the degree of this diversity. A large proportion of East Asian settlers in Britain are ethnically Chinese and the widespread tendency to talk in terms of different Chinese *dialects*, rather than *languages,* sometimes has the effect of oversimplifying the highly complex linguistic situation in this area of the world. It is not difficult to understand why this should be the case. Various scenarios world-wide demonstrate that the decision as to whether a particular variety is a different dialect or a different language depends far more on political than linguistic factors. Spanish and Portuguese, for instance, are considered to be separate languages. Yet the differences between these two varieties are qualitatively and quantitatively far less striking than those found between, say, the different 'dialects' of Arabic or Chinese. In the case of Spanish and Portuguese, independent political development over many centuries leads speakers to emphasize differences rather than similarities. In the case of Arabic and Chinese a common political – or religious – commitment has led to the minimizing of linguistic difference.

None the less, linguistic diversity is a fact of everyday life in East Asia. In Hong Kong, Hakka, Chiuchow, Hokkien and Cantonese coexist with English, though the numerical dominance of Cantonese speakers has resulted in Cantonese becoming the lingua franca of the various Chinese communities. Cantonese is also the lingua franca of the ethnic Chinese minorities in Vietnam. The different colonial histories of Hong Kong and Vietnam have, of course, produced very different overall configurations and, in addition to varieties of Chinese and Vietnamese, this latter group is likely to know French not English.

Malaysia and Singapore are a major crossroads in East Asia. In addition to the indigenous population of Malays, there are large Chinese communities and also a significant South Asian presence of mainly Tamil descent. Again colonial history has made its mark on the linguistic landscape, though in a slightly different way: English is a powerful force in Hong Kong, but tends to be restricted to those who complete secondary and higher education. The majority of Hong Kong Chinese in Britain, however, come from the New Territories where it was rare, during the main years of migration to the UK, for children to stay in school beyond the primary level. In contrast, in the more ethnically diverse populations of Singapore and Malaysia, English has fulfilled the same function as Cantonese as a lingua franca. In many cases, it is also a native language. The situation in Malaysia has, of course, changed a great deal since independence with Bahasa Malaysia taking over many of the domains previously associated with English. Nevertheless, a highly distinctive form of English has emerged in both countries which serves as a marker of national identity.

The influence of English is to be felt, too, in the Philippines, though, in this case, the ongoing contact has been with speakers of American rather than British English. The adoption of Tagalog (renamed Filipino) in 1962 as the national language might suggest that the sociolinguistic situation in this part of the world is a good deal simpler than is the case. However, in addition to English and Filipino, it has been estimated that over eighty other languages, all belonging to the Malayo-Polynesian family, are spoken.

Japan, in comparison, is a great deal more homogeneous. Apart from the small but significant number of Korean immigrants, Japanese is the first language of the entire population. English as the language of wider communication, is widely taught in schools and a substantial proportion of the population have at least a reading knowledge of the language.

Settlers in Britain from East Asia thus come from a wide range of social, educational and linguistic backgrounds. Singaporeans and Malaysians will be fluent speakers of a variety of English which differs in important respects from standard British English. For the most part they will be professionals who have chosen to stay on after completing their higher education in Britain.

Filipinos will also have a good knowledge of English as a second language. They come from a wide range of social and educational backgrounds, but, for the most part, have accepted low-paid jobs in the catering and hotel industry, which are none the less more financially rewarding than the jobs which they left at home. Until very recently, Filipinos have regarded themselves as temporary residents and have strongly nurtured 'the myth of return'. Hong Kong Chinese, for the most part, will have come from peasant backgrounds, will have received little education and speak very little English. Whereas the myth of return featured strongly in this community, too, the planned return of Hong Kong to the Chinese in 1997 has meant that most people now accept Britain as their permanent home. Similarly, the Vietnamese Chinese also have no possibility of return. In contrast, most Japanese see themselves very much as temporary residents, most families spending only a few years in Britain before returning to Japan.

These different social and linguistic scenarios have implications not only for the ways in which the first generation adapts to life in Britain, but also for their aspirations for their children. For most Singaporeans, Malaysians and Filipinos, mother tongue maintenance is not a priority, though the situation is now starting to change at least in the case of the Filipino community. For the Japanese, however, the importance of maintaining the mother tongue is paramount if children are to reintegrate successfully into the Japanese education system on return. Hong Kong and Vietnamese Chinese also attach considerable importance to mother tongue maintenance. The longer families are settled in the UK, the more marked the shift to English in their children. In communities where first-generation competence in English often remains at a 'survival' level, mother tongue maintenance in British-born children is an urgent community priority.

Chapter 11

The Filipino speech community

Amy Thompson

Ang hindi marunong magmahal sa sariling wika, ay masahol pa sa malansang isda.

(JOSÉ RIZAL, NATIONAL HERO, 1861–96)

(Anyone who does not love their own native language is disgustingly worse than a smelly fish.)

Since the 1970s, Britain has been playing host to migrant workers from the Philippines. With the passage of time, it seems that these people, following the pattern of other earlier immigrants, are transforming from migrants to immigrants to settlers. In other words, the Filipinos in Britain are here to stay, thus adding to the multi-ethnic composition of Britain today.

Because English is an official language in the Philippines, the Filipinos who have come to Britain all possess a degree of knowledge of English. Their silence and invisibility here have been interpreted as easy integration into British society; the facility with which they have supposedly been integrated being, in turn, attributed to their prior knowledge of English. Another reason suggested for the easy integration of Filipinos into the British way of life is their orientation towards Western culture as a result of a long history of colonization first by the Spanish (1565–1898) and then by the Americans (1898–1946).

On the face of it the Filipinos in Britain appear to have settled with ease in the host country. We do not hear about problems with cultural or language gaps; there has been no public outcry about underachievement of Filipino students or racism against the workers; they have not made demands for mother tongue teaching in schools. Not only are they a silent minority in Britain, they have also been for all intents and purposes an invisible minority. It seems, on the surface at least, that the Filipinos have successfully carved a niche for themselves in Britain and are happy and contented with their lot. Yet how much do we in fact know about the Filipinos in Britain – in terms of their languages and culture? What is the quantity and quality of interaction between Filipinos and the mainstream host society? How integrated are the Filipinos in actuality? Little attention has been paid to this new group in British society. It is hoped that the following sociolinguistic report on the Filipinos in Britain will go some way towards redressing the situation.

Published information on the Filipinos in Britain is scant. Therefore, unless specific references are given, the information on which this report is based has been derived from a series of interviews I conducted between April and November 1988 with members of the Filipino community, including the Philippine Consulate, the Filipino Chaplaincy, leading members of Filipino organizations, nurses, students, parents and university teachers. I am indebted to them all for their co-operation, so generously proffered.

The sociolinguistic situation in the Philippines

The Philippines is a country comprising 7,107 islands divided into 51 provinces which in turn constitute the 3 main island areas of Luzon in the north, Visaya in the centre and Mindanao in the south. The number of languages that exist in the Philippines is usually cited as being at least eighty-seven (Sibayan 1975). The major languages are commonly cited as Tagalog, Ilocano, Bicolano (or Bikol), Pampangan, Pangasinan (all spoken in the Luzon area), Cebuano, Hiligaynon, Waray (spoken in Visaya and northern Mindanao) and Maranao, the largest language group in southern Mindanao. All these languages belong to the Austronesian, or Malayo-Polynesian, family of languages which encompass a vast area stretching from Madagascar to the Indonesian archipelago, across the Pacific Ocean taking in the aborigines of Taiwan and Hawaii, and through the Pacific islands to Easter Island west of Chile. More specifically, the languages of the Philippines belong to the Indonesian branch of the Malayo-Polynesian family, to which Indonesian, Malay and the aborigine languages of Taiwan also belong (cf Katzner 1986).

Before the Philippines gained independence in 1946, the official languages were Spanish and English. It was under Spanish rule that the Roman alphabet was adopted for the Philippine languages. In the latter days of Spanish colonialism, as part of the reaction against colonial rule and the desire to assert a Philippine national identity, the notion of a need for a national language began to be expressed. In the 1930s the search for a national language was conducted in earnest. Numerous studies were made with the intention of finding a language among the indigenous languages which could serve as the national language of the people. In 1937 Tagalog was declared the language on which the national language would be based. It was by no means a unanimous choice since language loyalties are strong in the Philippines and many non-Tagalog speakers questioned the bases on which Tagalog was selected. Nevertheless, it was the language spoken in Manila, the major city in the Philippines, and in the nearby provinces where the major industries were located. Tagalog as a national language began to be taught in 1940. In 1959, Pilipino was designated as the official name of the national language. Since 1987, the term 'Filipino' has been used instead of Pilipino to refer to the national language. However, these terms do not seem to have had any significant impact on the population who continue by and large to call the language Tagalog. English has been retained as an official language and all the major institutions (government, education, legal system, media) are still heavily reliant on English. Spanish, on the other hand, is spoken only by a small minority today although the Spanish influence is very much in evidence in Filipino culture, not least being its legacy of Catholicism.

Since 1957, the country has pursued a policy of bilingual education which has allowed the use of the local language as a medium of instruction in the early grades with Filipino and English taking over as media of instruction thereafter. For pragmatic reasons, the curriculum has been divided between social studies, health and PE being taught in Filipino and science and maths subjects being taught in English. Nevertheless, up to and including the present time, the balance has tilted in favour of English as the dominant language in education since university exams are conducted in English and all major businesses and transactions in government and legal institutions still require the use of English.

With the promotion of Tagalog as the national language through education and through the media, it is estimated that by now about 85 per cent of the population can speak Tagalog (the Philippine Consulate). The bilingual educational policy aims to ensure that every schooled Filipino possesses a degree of knowledge in both Filipino and English. It is reckoned that 85 per cent of the population are literate in Filipino and English, though proficiency varies. The maintenance of the regional language in the home means that many Filipinos know at least three languages – their own regional language, the national language which is Filipino/Tagalog and English. In addition, it is not uncommon for Filipinos to be able to understand one or more neighbouring dialects (see Barcelona 1977).

Although English and Filipino are the official languages and are the media of instruction in school, it cannot be assumed that all Filipinos are proficient in these languages. The main reason is that, unless they live in a Tagalog-speaking region and/or are professionals, the language used in their everyday lives, in the home and in the community, will be their own regional language. In certain regions, Filipino and English are learnt in schools but are not used. Their use depends on a number of factors such as the proximity to Tagalog-speaking regions or urban areas, the type of work they do and the person to whom they are speaking (whether peers or subordinates or superiors). On the whole, Tagalog/Filipino is used with people who do not speak their regional language and has gained ground as the lingua franca, gradually replacing English in this respect. However, English is still the language for more formal contexts and proficiency in it is more important for professionals than proficiency in Tagalog (see also Sibayan 1975; Barcelona 1977).

English is still regarded as being important because it remains the language of officialdom, of the media, of the legal system and of education. As a concomitant to this the notion of status has developed, associating English with high status and local dialect with low status (Loveday 1982). Proficiency in English is regarded as a sign of an educated person and as the key to upward mobility and personal advancement. English, therefore, is learnt for instrumental reasons while Filipino is learnt for integrative reasons – to identify with the Philippine nation (Sibayan 1975).

The growth of feeling for the national language gained renewed impetus recently with the post-Marcos government which is now trying to promote the use of Filipino instead of English wherever possible. The University of the Philippines, the leading university in the country, is at present undergoing a 'social transformation programme' whereby all teaching is to be conducted in Filipino as far as possible. This has not been without problems since many university teachers have come through an English-medium education themselves and find it difficult to deliver lectures in a language they have not hitherto used in such a domain; the problem is compounded by a lack of teaching materials in Filipino. Even though Filipino is now standardized, there is still a need to develop specialist and technical terms in Filipino (to replace English words) and to develop materials for use in the classroom and for the legal system. When the 'social transformation programme' was first introduced, university teachers were given additional monetary incentives to teach in Filipino; now such incentives are allocated for material production. There are plans to introduce the use of Filipino in addition to English for the entrance exam to the University of the Philippines. It is hoped that other universities in the country will follow the example of the University of the Philippines. However, there is resistance to this initiative not only from teachers but also from students.

The simultaneous promotion of English and Tagalog has led to a great deal of code-mixing between the two languages and the development of 'Taglish' as a popular form of communication, especially among the young people. Not only is Taglish widely used among young people, but it is also used in advertisements and some newspaper journalists even write their columns in Taglish. Taglish is a social language only and is not used in formal situations.

In the Philippines, most publications are in English or Tagalog. At present, there are more newspapers in English than in Tagalog. Many novels, regional newspapers and magazines are published in the major regional languages. Until the major institutions adopt a wider use of Filipino, all official documents will continue to be in English. One area where the use of Filipino has been accelerated is in television where programmes in Filipino, especially current affairs programmes, are becoming more popular since they are more accessible to the masses than English.

Filipinos in Britain

The Filipinos started to arrive in Britain in the 1970s. The majority were women who had come in answer to job advertisements placed by overseas employment agencies back home in Manila. They saw these as a golden opportunity to escape from unemployment and the ailing economic situation in the Philippines. When they came to Britain they took up lowly jobs, mainly as hotel workers, nursing auxiliaries in hospitals and domestics in private homes. Many of these Filipinos were college graduates and teachers. Yet they were willing to take up employment in low-paid jobs because they could earn more here than in the Philippines. For example, in the Philippines a teacher would earn about £50 a month which was hardly enough to cover the average monthly cost of living of nearly £90 a month for a family of six (Paganoni 1986). In contrast, working in Britain as a domestic helper she could earn up to £250 a month.

The Philippine Centre estimates that there are now over 30,000 Filipinos living in Britain. This would appear to be a reasonable estimate given that the Philippine Embassy gives the conservative figure of 20,000 while the Filipino Chaplaincy in London claims that it could be as high as 40,000. Filipinos are located in most of the major cities in Scotland, England and Wales. The largest concentration is found in London (about 12,000) (cited in Paganoni 1986). The largest settlement outside London is Epsom in Surrey where, according to the Filipino Chaplaincy, there are about 2,000 Filipinos, most of whom are working in the various hospitals in the area.

The concentration in particular areas does not mean that the Filipinos in Britain are community-centred. On the contrary, in Britain they have tended to align themselves according to regional/dialect groups. Adherence to one's own language group is a salient feature back home in the Philippines – that is why Tagalog has not been universally recognized by everybody in the Philippines as the national language. Since the areas in Britain with Filipino settlement comprise mixed language groups, there have not been strong organizations that are local community based. If they belong to any groups at all, it is usually to a group based on regional dialect or political affiliation.

Filipinos came as migrant workers on fixed-term contracts and conditions of work and immigration rules did not allow for them to bring their children and dependants to Britain with them. The practice of enforced separation from dependants is widespread among Filipino migrants; so much so that in the Philippines where more than a quarter of the population is dependent on remittances from abroad, a phenomenon of what the Scalabrini Migration Centre has called 'seasonal orphans and solo parents' has developed as a result. As the term suggests, material gains from working overseas have been at the expense of the children and spouses that have been left behind (Cruz 1987).

Up until 1978 Filipinos who had gained resident status after four years working in Britain could apply for their dependants to come and join them, as long as the stipulations as set out by immigration rules were met. These were usually proof of adequate accommodation and a healthy bank balance. However, in 1978 the Home Office ruled that dependants would no longer be allowed to enter Britain because the applicant was himself or herself an illegal immigrant having falsified information on the original entry papers by not declaring that they were married, or that they had dependants under the age of 16. Between 1978 and 1980, many workers were themselves deported as illegal immigrants for the above reasons. In 1980, the quota for semi-skilled workers was terminated altogether, and work permits are now issued to professionals and skilled workers only. Faced with the threat of deportation, the Filipinos mobilized themselves to organize a series of compaigns. In 1982, the Home Office took the decision to grant amnesty to those who had arrived in Britain before 1979. In 1986 the European Court of Human Rights decreed that married Filipino women should have the right to bring their husbands into Britain.

Nowadays, apart from the arrival of dependants, professionals and students from the Philippines, some Filipinos manage to enter Britain via other means. One way is via the Middle East where Filipinos have been recruited as domestics. Often they travel to Britain as members of Middle Eastern households. Once here, some will leave the service of their Middle Eastern employers and seek unofficial employment in Britain, known in the community as *tago nang tang* or *TNT* (hide and hide). Some Filipinos enter Britain with a tourist visa hoping that once here they will be able to find work through their Filipino contacts, or *kababayan*. A small number arrive in Britain as brides of English men. Such marriages usually involve a transaction of £3,000–£4,000.

The number of children coming to join their parents has increased dramatically during the 1980s. This trend is confirmed, for instance, by ILEA *Language Census* data set out in Table 11.1. With the arrival of children in Britain, the Filipinos are becoming more visible. Hitherto they have been hidden from the

TABLE 11.1 Data on Tagalog speakers from ILEA *Language Census* (1981–87)

Year	Number
1981	223
1983	448
1985	765
1987	968

mainstream of society by a number of factors. Firstly, as single workers, they usually lived at their workplace and so made few demands on the Housing Department and other institutions. Secondly, for them the sole purpose of coming to Britain was to earn enough money to send home; therefore, many Filipinos would seize every opportunity to earn extra by doing overtime or taking on secondary jobs. There was little time left to interact with the host society.

Things are changing now with a second generation growing up in Britain. When the Filipinos first came to Britain, their intention was to earn enough money to enable them to return home and buy land or start a business. They did not intend to stay here; indeed, many still harbour the intention of retiring to the Philippines eventually. However, there are certain indications that the Filipinos are to all intents and purposes settling in Britain. The main indications are the arrival of children, the increasing length of stay here, the beginning of success stories of Filipinos who have managed to break out of the traditional low-paid jobs and improve their job prospects or start up businesses here, the fact that many Filipino women have married British husbands and lastly, many more Filipinos are applying for British citizenship thereby forfeiting their Filipino citizenship.

Changing patterns of language use

Filipinos in Britain prefer to use their own language when speaking among themselves. Those who are in low-paid jobs (for example, waiters) are especially vulnerable to the feeling of inferiority *vis-à-vis* the majority group in society. As a result, they tend to keep to themselves and speak their mother tongue. They use English only in their jobs and for some (particularly waiters and domestic helpers) this has created a limited domain for the use of English, so making it difficult for them to improve their proficiency in it.

Yet many Filipino parents in Britain use English at home with their children, especially if the latter were born here or came when very young. Those children who came at the age of 10 or above are more inclined to speak to their parents in their own language. It has been noticed that when the children speak English with their parents they adopt a Filipino accent and intonation but when they speak with English people they sound very English. It is true to say, however, that most Filipino parents do not feel strongly about their children learning Tagalog. Interestingly, in mixed marriages, it is usually the English fathers who encourage their children to learn Tagalog.

As is the case in the Philippines, a popular form of communication is the use of Taglish – the use of English words and phrases when speaking Tagalog. This is especially prominent among young Filipinos in Britain. It is a social language, used on informal occasions. It is also used in writing.

Because of the existence of many different language groups in Britain, Filipinos tend to use English on their first encounter with another Filipino. Thereafter they switch language accordingly. The feeling is especially strong among young Tagalog speakers (those who came to Britain in their late teens) here that one should speak Tagalog rather than English – a feeling born out of a mixture of loyalty to the Filipino identity and the notion of 'snobbishness' associated with those Filipinos who use English by preference.

Language, culture and community

Most Filipinos maintain regular contact with their families back home. After all, their family is their *raison d'être* for being in Britain. The remittances that they send back regularly through the Philippine National Bank are used to support not only the immediate family including grandparents but also the extended family to whom the Filipinos have an obligation to help out. The money sent home is not just for family upkeep either. It has to provide for the education of the children, pay for the building of the family house, be used to buy land, start a business and repay debts. In a way, the money sent home is their investment for the future – many dream of retiring to the Philippines and becoming landowners or having their own business.

Meanwhile, strong links are preserved with their families back home through regular visits every two or three years. Often these visits take the form of extended holidays of four to five weeks. In this way parents endeavour to foster a link with the Philippines in their children as well. The importance of maintaining close contact is shown by the fact that long-distance telephone calls are regularly made to their families.

Their concern is not just limited to their families. The Filipinos take a lively interest in the political situation in the Philippines. Although an increasing number have applied for British citizenship, many still hold a Filipino passport, unwilling as they are to relinquish their claim to their native country. For the privilege of having their Philippine passport endorsed, the Filipinos living in Britain and paying British taxes are subject to what is known as 'double taxation', which means that they have to pay about 1–2 per cent of their earnings to the Philippine government each year. Although there are administrative inconveniences arising from this, many Filipinos do not begrudge this contribution to their native country.

In Britain, many Filipinos have grouped together to form various Filipino organizations.[1] But they have tended to align themselves in factions. The functions of the various organizations range from promoting cultural, social, fund-raising and sport events to running language classes in Tagalog and English. Several basketball teams have been formed and they play in league matches against each other. Out of all these teams a UK–Philippine basketball team is selected which will then represent the Filipinos in Britain against other British teams. The Philippine Centre, formed in 1985, was set up specifically to try and unite all the different groups under one umbrella. It is the main organizer of the annual Barrio Fiesta.[2] The last Barrio Fiesta held in Holland Park in London was attended by an estimated 4,000 Filipinos who had come from all over Britain and even as far away as Edinburgh. At the moment eight or nine associations are affiliated to the Philippine Centre.

In addition, the Catholic Church takes an interest in the Filipinos here. The Filipino Chaplaincy in London celebrates mass every Sunday in Filipino. Westminster Cathedral also organizes social and cultural events and holds a Filipino mass annually when the celebrant is a visiting bishop from the Philippines. The Consulate is supportive of all events and these lends its premises after hours to organizations such as the PANSAPI[1] for holding language classes.

The proliferation of Filipino organizations and events is a sign that Filipinos are no longer an invisible silent minority. More and more, and especially among the younger Filipinos, it is felt that there is a need for cultural and linguistic revitalization. All these events provide just such opportunities for Filipinos to come together and reassert their common cultural identity. At such times, the use of Tagalog or one's own regional language – the language of intimacy, of the home, of friends – is bound to take place. It is certainly the case that though most of the Filipinos in Britain have been here for fifteen to twenty years, the preferred language of communication among themselves is still their own language. Therefore these events play an important role in maintaining the use of the mother tongue and the Filipino identity, as do the two Filipino newspapers in Britain. One is the *Pahayagan*, published under the auspices of COFOO,[1] which has reports and articles in both English and Tagalog on Filipino communities in Europe as well as news about developments in the Philippines; the other is *The Filipino*, published under the auspices of the Philippine Centre, which is mainly in English and is concerned with Filipinos in Britain.

Education and language reproduction

The teaching and maintenance of the mother tongue among the Filipinos is very much a do-it-yourself job. There is no provision for it in mainstream schools. Filipino does not feature in the newly instigated GCSE exams in community languages. Nor is it a language that is taught in any of the tertiary institutions in Britain. There has not been a perceived need for official documents and public information to be translated, such as for other speech communities in Britain. In short, there is no official recognition of Filipino as a community language even though it is used by the Filipino community in Britain. The situation may seem rather unjust *vis-à-vis* other ethnic minority groups. However, it must be pointed out that, though Filipino is widely used among the adult community, there are many Filipinos who see no need for their children to learn it. Although many parents are anxious for their children to maintain cultural ties with the Philippines, mother tongue learning does not appear at this point in time to be a very important issue to them. With no vociferous demand from the community itself, mainstream institutions do not see any need to cater for the linguistic needs of Filipinos.

Basically, the community in Britain is divided into three 'schools' of thought. Firstly, there are those who do not feel any urgency for their children to learn their own language since they see English as the key to their future success. They are here for economic reasons and so they want their children to speak English.

Secondly, because of the language division that exists back home in the Philippines and the fact that many have not accepted Tagalog as the national language, many Filipinos here show no strong conviction with regard to their children learning Tagalog. They are inclined to feel that it would be more useful for their children to learn their own regional language so that they could communicate with their family when they go to the Philippines.

Thirdly, there are those who feel strongly that if any language is taught it should be Filipino/Tagalog because it is the language that all Filipinos understand. They feel that teaching the regional language to the children is the responsibility of the parents, not an endeavour that needs community support and orchestration. The Filipinos are not sufficiently united on this issue to form pressure groups. At present the few mother tongue classes that exist are organized by interested parties within the community itself. Because of the large number of Filipinos in the Kensington area in London, they have arranged for a teacher to run a class in a primary school there. The class takes place every week during school hours and Kensington LEA pays the travelling expenses of the teacher. Other classes are run on Saturdays. One location is at Bonham Carter Hall in London where Filipino classes are run for adults (mostly for the English husbands of Filipino women) and children. Another is known as the 'Saturday club' where children up to the age of 15 are taught conversational Tagalog. These community-run classes are financed by fund-raising events organized by community organizations such as PANSAPI and the Philippine Centre. There is virtually no support from outside the community for these classes.

Given that many of the Filipinos in Britain are qualified teachers in their own country, one may wonder why so few are involved in running community classes. One reason, as mentioned above, is that not all Filipinos regard mother tongue teaching as a main concern. Another reason is that many Filipinos are already holding two or even three jobs and being a community class teacher is not seen as worthwhile in terms of monetary recompense.

Apart from teaching Tagalog, the classes also make a point of teaching cultural aspects such as Filipino music and dance, the history of the Philippines, and Filipino games. Because mother tongue teaching is on a relatively small scale, the teachers here make use of what teaching materials are available from the Philippines.

It has not been in the scope of the present discussion to investigate more fully the main issues concerning the Filipinos in Britain. However, it is hoped that this study has provided some indication as to what the main concerns might be. Certainly, further research is required particularly with regard to the educational needs of the Filipinos. More information is needed on the acquisition of English as a second language (for example, what aspects of English would be likely to present problems to the Filipino second-language learner), on the provision of English as a second language, mother tongue support and mother tongue maintenance. A better understanding of the community could be obtained with more information on the different Filipino language groups in Britain (for example, what language groups are represented, in what number and where). The main motivation in life for Filipinos in Britain has been financial security. Their aim in coming to Britain has always been to earn as much money as they can here to remit home. Their orientation has always been towards the Philippines and not towards putting down roots here. In this respect they regarded themselves as sojourners rather than settlers. However, with the passage of time and the arrival of children growing up in Britain, Filipinos are in effect taking root here. Consequently, questions of better job prospects as well as cultural identity *vis-à-vis* mainstream society and the maintenance of the mother tongue are beginning to take on more import.

When the Filipinos first came to Britain, they took on low-paid jobs even though many of them had college degrees. This was because such jobs were the only form of employment available to them at the time as migrant workers. At first, they were restricted to such jobs because immigration rules and work permit regulations precluded access to skilled occupations that would have been more commensurate with their educational qualifications. Later, lack of confidence, financial security and proficiency in English (compounded by their conditions of work) have made it difficult for them to compete on the job market and transfer to more prestigious and regarding occupations.

Although too early to say for certain, the danger is that this pattern is being repeated with the younger Filipinos here. Many of the children of the early Filipino immigrants have only recently come to join their parents in Britain. For many of them, it is a struggle to cope with the demands of the education system here since many of them are of the older age group (*ie* 15 plus). Lack of proficiency in English means that they fare badly at school exams and this, together with problems encountered in obtaining grants, militates against their admission into tertiary education. Filipino parents place a high value on education and see it as the key to good jobs and financial success. Despite their parents' aspirations, these young Filipinos find themselves unable to compete on equal terms for the better jobs. Failure at school, frustration with the work situation and lack of interest from the host society may serve to promote a strong in-group feeling among the younger Filipinos.

Whereas financial security has been the most important issue for first-generation Filipinos, questions of cultural identity and mother tongue maintenance may be more important for second-generation Filipinos growing up in Britain. This change is gaining recognition among the community. Since 1983, after immigrant status had been granted to Filipinos in Britain, there has been a growth and expansion of Filipino organizations. The organizations have been small in terms of membership and have tended to be factional. Among those who have settled in Britain there are now signs that they are beginning to think more in terms of a single unifying Filipino identity rather than their old regional differences. The Philippine Centre, which as yet has not found a permanent place of abode, was set up specifically to try and bring all the different organizations together to work towards the common goals of promoting Filipino culture and identity among young people growing up in Britain. Judging from the growing number of participants in recent events and the publication of a second newspaper (*The Filipino*), there seems to be a trend away from separateness towards increased aggregation.

Though the feeling for a national identity has not been strong among the Filipinos, who prefer to direct their loyalties to their own ethnolinguistic groups, it appears that a process of revival in national identity is taking place in the Philippines. The Philippine government is trying to promote the use of Filipino in major institutions. Because of the close ties the Filipinos in Britain maintain with the Philippines, such developments there will have an influence on the fostering of national and cultural identity here. Although many Filipinos here remain silent and unconcerned about the fostering of Filipino culture and language, an increasing number, albeit still a minority, are voicing concern about their cultural and linguistic vitality – some even teasingly accuse their children of being 'disgustingly worse than smelly fish' (see quote at the beginning) when they catch them speaking English at home!

Notes

1. Filipino organizations in Britain include:
   COFOO (Confederation of Filipino Overseas Organizations)
   Commission for Filipino Migrant Workers
   Filipino Athletic Association (FAA)
   Filipino Professionals and Students Association (FPSA)
   PANSAPI (Pandamayang Samahan ng mga Pilipino)
   The Philippine Centre
   Philippine–British Residents League (PBRL)
   Philippine–British Society
   Philippine–UK Heathrow Association (PUKHA)

Philippine–UK Heathrow Association II (PUKHA II) – the youth
branch
Tapayan (Filipino Art Collective)
Tayo-Tayo Club
2. Barrio Fiesta means 'village festival'. In the Philippines, it is the
celebration of the village saint's birthday. It originated in Spain and
is now part of the Filipino tradition.

References

BARCELONA, H. M. (1977) 'Language usage and preference patterns of
Filipino bilinguals: an NMPC survey'. In E. M. Pascasio (ed.) *The
Filipino Bilingual: Studies on Philippine Bilingualism and Bilingual
Education*, Ateneo de Manila University Press, pp. 64–71.
CRUZ, V. P. (1987) *Seasonal Orphans and Solo Parents: The Impact of
Overseas Migration*. Scalabrini Migration Center, Quezon City.
Inner London Education Authority (ILEA), (1978, 1981, 1983, 1985,
1987) Language Census. London: ILEA Research and Statistics.
KATZNER, K. (1986) *Languages of the World*. London: Routledge &
Kegan Paul.
LOVEDAY, L. (1982) *The Sociolinguistics of Learning and Using a Non-
Native Language*. Oxford: Pergamon Press.
PAGANONI, A. (1986) *Paano Ba Ang Mabuhay Sa Ibang Bansa? (Beyond
Philippine Shores: What's it like?)*. Scalabrinians, Quezon City.
SIBAYAN, B. P. (1975) 'Survey of language use and attitudes towards
languages in the Philippines'. In S. Ohannessian, C. A. Ferguson and
E. C. Polome (eds) *Language Survey in Developing Nations: Papers
and Reports on Sociolinguistic Surveys*, Center for Applied Linguistics,
Virginia, pp. 115–143.

Chapter 12

The Japanese speech community

Yoshiko Namie

郷に入りては　　郷に従え。

Gou ni iritewa   Gou ni shitagae
When in Rome   do as the Romans do.

The Japanese language is spoken by 121 million Japanese and
0.85 million aliens in the four main Japanese islands and the
small islands scattered around them (Statistics Bureau Management and Coordination Agency 1986:25, 45). Japanese is also
spoken by Japanese immigrants who settled on the west coast of
the USA, in Hawaii and Brazil in the first half of the twentieth
century. For the last twenty years, the number of Japanese living
abroad has been steadily increasing along with the expansion of
the Japanese economy. The overseas Japanese tend periodically
to move from one place to another, eventually returning to
Japan. Problems arise from this pattern of migration in two ways:
firstly for individuals experiencing different cultures and languages, and secondly for the host countries which accept Japanese
children unfamiliar with these new cultures and languages. The
Japanese community in Britain is a part of this world-wide migration.

The sociolinguistic situation of Japanese in Japan

Japanese belongs to the Altaic language family. With 121 million
speakers, it ranks as one of the top ten languages in the world
(Katzner 1977). It is said that speaking Japanese is relatively easy,
but reading and writing are difficult. The Japanese language is

written in a combination of three orthographies: *kanji*, which is derived from the Chinese ideographs; *hiragana* and *katakana* which are phonetic scripts of forty-six letters each. The National Language Council, under the Ministry of Education, from time to time publishes a guide on the basic rules of the Japanese language for public use. Public organizations such as government offices, media or schools follow these guidelines. The latest report, published in 1986, recommended about 2,000 *kanji* characters for public use. Each of the 2,000 *kanji* characters is read in more than two different ways. Words are usually written in a combination of *kanji* and *hiragana*. *Katakana* is used for foreign words or for describing various sounds. A typical sentence in written Japanese would look like:

Kanji hiragana	*Katakana hiragana*	*Kanji hiragana*
私　は	ロンドン　に	住んでいます。
Watakushi wa	*London ni*	*sun de imasu*
I	London in	am living
I am	living in	London.

In the first year, primary-school children start by learning the *hiragana* and *katakana* syllabary. *Kanji* characters are introduced gradually starting with the easier and more familiar ideographs. By the end of six years in primary school, Japanese pupils are expected to have 866 *kanji* characters in their reading and writing repertoire.

The oldest written form of the Japanese language, based on contemporary Chinese characters, can be traced back to the fifth and seventh centuries. From the Chinese characters, *hiragana* and *katakana* were developed between about AD 800 and 1200 (Sawagata 1987:22–58). With the development of *hiragana* and *katakana*, expressions in Japanese widened. In the literature produced at this period, diaries and essays were mainly written by women. *Genji Morogatari* (Tales of Genji), for instance, produced around 1000 by Shikibu Murasaki, a woman writer, is one of the highly praised classics.

From this period, Chinese culture exerted an immense influence on language, philosophy, literature, arts, medicine and on life in general in Japan. The influence of European and American languages and cultures, however, has been replacing that of Chinese for over 120 years, particularly since the Second World

War. Accordingly *katakana* words are increasing. There is a tendency to truncate the loan word, using only the first few syllables. The following words are some examples:

テレビ	terebi	television
ビル	biru	building
デパート	depaato	department store

The present writing form for *hiragana* and *katakana* was laid down by the Primary School Act in 1900 (Nakata, Wada and Kitahara 1983:13).

The Japanese language is standardized. Although regional differences exist, from the viewpoint of communication, problems arising from dialects are minor. However, the presence of minority races such as the 17,000 Ainu, living in Hokkaido, north of Japan (Japan National Tourist Organization 1975:945) and the 683,313 Koreans (1985 figures: Statistics Bureau Management and Coordination Agency 1986:45) also need to be taken into account. About 20,000 Korean children study at 153 schools which follow the North Korean educational system, and about 2,000 Koreans study at a further 12 schools which follow the South Korean educational system (Yun 1986:253).

The Japanese in Britain

The Japanese people in Britain can be roughly divided into two groups from the viewpoint of settlement. The majority of the Japanese stay in Britain for a limited number of years – usually from one to ten years. They are either sent by Japanese companies or the government, or come to Britain for personal reasons such as study. The second group has settled permanently for business purposes, to cater for the Japanese community, running restaurants, estate agencies, travel agencies or shops, or are married to British subjects.

The number of Japanese living in Britain has shown a marked increase over the last twenty years along with the expansion of the Japanese economy. Accordingly, geographical distribution of the Japanese population is concentrated in the areas where Japanese companies (legally, UK companies) are set up. Although accurate statistics are not available, estimates of the number of Japanese,

TABLE 12.1   The number of children at Japanese schools in Britain

Registered number at the Embassy			Company-based record		
Region	Number		Number of families	Total number	Recorded date
England (London) Wales	24,360 (16,072) 402	London NW England Wales	3,600 83 50	12,000 280	End of 1987 March 1988 March 1988
Scotland N. Ireland	459 9				
Total (children)	25,230 (7,949)				

Sources: (1) Enquiry to Information Centre, Embassy of Japan, the Japanese Association in Wales, The Association of Japanese Companies in North West England; (2) *Youroppa no Kurashi* (Living in Europe), Monthly Newspaper in Japanese, January 1988: 4–8.

based on figures supplied by the Embassy of Japan and other sources, are set out in Table 12.1.

Language, culture and community

Since residence in Britain is, in most cases, temporary, contact with Japan, in the form of visits and new arrivals, is frequent. In addition, there is a wide range of services and activities which ensure a strong ethnolinguistic vitality for the Japanese community in Britain. For instance, two major daily Japanese newspapers, edited in Japan, are printed in Europe everyday on the same day as in Japan: *Nihon Keizai Shinbun*, which specializes in economic affairs, and *Asahi Shinbun*, a more general newspaper. In addition to these, weekly and monthly newspapers in Japanese are published. For example, *Youroppa no Kurashi* (Living in Europe), *London Dayori* (Letter from London), *Nyuusu Daijesto (News Digest)* and *Biggu Ben* (Big Ben) provide news and information about life in Britain. There are three Japanese bookshops in London where many Japanese books are available. Video tapes are also available on loan at Japanese stores.

Apart from the services for the Japanese by the Japanese, organizations such as *The Japan Foundation* have been formed to promote better relations between Britain and Japan. These organizations help to organize exhibitions on Japan, and concerts or plays by the Japanese as a part of the popularization of Japanese culture among the British people. A friendly association, Anjinkai, was organized mainly by British people who had been to Japan through the Japanese Government English Teaching Recruitment Programme. In 1987, 123 teachers were sent to Japan under this programme (Yamazaki 1988:4). Anjinkai has organized the traditional Japanese Summer Festival in London since 1985. Television and cinemas also put on Japanese programmes or films from time to time. In conjunction with these activities, well-known public figures are invited to give public lectures.

In this way, although some of the cultural activities are initially planned for British people, Japanese people also use these opportunities to keep in touch with Japanese culture.

Education and language reproduction

Among the Japanese in Britain, attitudes to language maintenance depend on whether the families are temporary residents or permanent settlers. For children who will ultimately return to Japan, it is important not only to maintain the Japanese language but also to keep up with Japanese standards for their age groups. For permanent settlers, mother tongue maintenance is a matter of individual preference. Although the number of those who intend to settle permanently in Britain has been increasing, the total number seems to be small and the majority of settlers are the first generation in Britain. For these reasons, this section will attempt to describe the present situation of the temporary residents in Britain.

The majority of Japanese children in Britain will go back to Japan after a few years. They experience culture shock twice, once at the time of starting schooling in Britain and again on return to Japan. It is said that difficulties in readjusting to the Japanese system are greater than the problems faced in adjusting to British or other systems. Children face difficulties back in Japan with the level of studies, their behaviour as well as the Japanese language. Children are expected to reach a certain level of knowledge in each subject every year according to the curriculum laid down by the Ministry of Education. Children spending some years overseas will often fail to reach this level. Behavioural differences in children brought up in a society with different expectations stand out in a largely monocultural society like Japan.

In order to cope with the situation, two measures are taken: first, special consideration is given to the returnees from abroad from primary to university levels, and, second, Japanese schools (full time, or Saturday) are set up in areas of Britain and elsewhere where the Japanese live. In 1987, the number of compulsory school-age children abroad was 41,155 (Omukai 1988:8). Out of a total of 41,155, 32,307 pupils (or 78.5 percent) were studying either at 82 full-time Japanese schools (in 54 countries) or at 120 Saturday schools (in 50 countries). The Japanese Ministry of Education supplied 1,039 teachers to staff these schools (Omukai 1988:8). In addition to this number, around 1,100 pupils are also enrolled at private Japanese schools abroad (*Kaigai Shijo Kyouiku* July 1987:17).

In Britain, there are six Saturday schools and one full-time Japanese day school. Each school has classes for children from 6 to 15 years of age. The Japanese School, London, Limited manages one full-time and one Saturday school with three branches. In London, one of the three Saturday school branches has classes for children up to the age of 18. In addition to this, there are three boarding schools, each of which provides for children from the ages of 9 to 18. The number of children enrolled in these schools is as shown in Table 12.2.

Schooling from primary to high school in Japan is controlled by the Ministry of Education. Every school uses textbooks for each subject, which are chosen from textbooks recommended by the Ministry of Education.

The Japanese day school in London and the three boarding schools follow the Japanese curriculum. At Saturday schools, the Japanese language is taught as a subject with textbooks used in Tokyo and other areas in Japan. Saturday schools are conducted in the same way as schools in Japan. For example, the academic year starts in April with an opening assembly. A special ceremony (with the headmaster's speech) for the first-year primary-school children is also held. On Saturdays, there are three lessons, each forty minutes long with ten-minute breaks between. In London each class has about thirty pupils. Textbooks for primary-school children (from 6 to 12), secondary (from 12 to 15), and high school (from 15 to 18) follow a standard format. For example, expression, comprehension and grammar will be gradually learned from simple to complex, step by step, through different genres of literature such as fairy-tales, stories, poems, biographies, folk-tales and plays. Any unit at a given grade is also related to other grades. Pieces of foreign literature, translated into Japanese, are also used in textbooks. At Saturday schools,

TABLE 12.2 The number of children at Japanese schools in Britain

	Primary school (6–12 years old)		Secondary school (12–15 years old)		High school (15–18 years old)		Recorded date
	Full time	Saturday	Full time	Saturday	Full time	Saturday	
London	450						31.10.87
London (3 buildings)		1,118	266	184		71	31.10.87
Manchester		37		14			31.10.87
Telford		51		6			30.09.87
Wales		38		13			31.10.87
Scotland		19		6		International 3	31.10.87
NE England		52		20			30.09.87
Boarding schools							
Rikkyo Eikoku (Guilford)	20		119		209		31.10.87
Eikoku Gyousei Kokusai (Milton Keynes)	25		112		161		1.03.88
Eikoku Shitennouji (Suffolk)	9		59		113		30.09.87
Total	504	1,315	556	243	483	74	3,175

Sources: (1) *'Kaigai Shijo Kyouiku'* January 1988:66 67;(2) Enquiry to the Japanese School, London. Eikoku Gyousei Kokusai Gakuen (School), London. Eikoku Shitennouji Gakuen (School), in March 1988.

children spend only half to two-thirds of the amount of time on
the same Japanese language textbooks as would be expected in
Japan. Usually, they sit in rows facing the front. Pupils are all
expected to do the same thing at the same time. It seems that
the younger children have more problems in being taught this way
than the older age groups. For children at Saturday schools, who
go to British or international schools during the week, it is a hard
task to learn yet another subject, but it can also be a relaxed and
enjoyable opportunity to express themselves in their own language. At the end of the term, pupils receive a school report. In
the Saturday schools in London, four classes are open to children
who were born in London or who have one Japanese parent. Fifty
pupils from 6 to 18 years old are learning Japanese in these
classes.

   At the Japanese day school in London, classes are available
from the second year of primary school (7–8 years) to the third
year of secondary school (14–15 years). The Japanese School
in London is a company and a private school under British law.
There is no subsidy from the Japanese government for upkeep,
but the Japanese government pays the full salaries of the teachers
sent from Japan (about two-thirds of the teaching staff for the
full-time school) and a small subsidy towards payments of local
staff. A public organization *Kaigai Shijo Kyouiku Shinkou Zaidan*
(Japan Overseas Educational Services) which receives money
from the Japanese government and from supporting companies
(about 730 companies in 1987) (Omukai 1988:8), allocates equipment or textbooks, which are free for all children of compulsory
school age (6 or 7 to 15 years), through the Embassy of Japan.
Although the Japanese School, London, is an independent institu-
tion, having its own management committee, Japanese companies
in London have been offering financial assistance as a part of
their interest in the welfare of the Japanese community in London. Japanese schools outside London are managed in a similar
way to the one in London. Outside London where there are fewer
opportunities for cultural activities relating to Japan, there is also
an emphasis on traditional events or studies about Japanese culture at Saturday schools (Inoue 1988:7). In addition to Saturday
schooling, special summer schools with help from London Saturday schoolteachers and a seasonal guidance programme by
teachers of the Japan Overseas Educational Services are arranged
outside London. As a supplementary means of study, the Japan
Overseas Educational Services provides correspondence services
in mathematics, social studies, science and Japanese language for
14,000 primary and secondary pupils in over 100 countries (*Kaigai*

Shijo Kyouiku December 1987:99). This is roughly 34 per cent of the total number of compulsory school-age children abroad (14,000:41,155). In London as in other cities, supplementary classes for other subjects run by nationwide crammer companies, are also becoming popular. These classes are open outside school hours. According to ILEA's latest Language Survey, there were 140 speakers of Japanese, 37.9 per cent of whom were recorded as fluent in English (ILEA 1987: Appendix 5). In mainstream British schools, the Japanese language has been taught in only a few schools. The University of London School Examinations Board is the only board which sets examinations for GCE A level in Japanese. The candidates for the examinations in Japanese are mainly Japanese pupils. The University of London School Examinations Board, the London Regional Examining Board and the East Anglian Examinations Board jointly form the London and East Anglian Group for the GCSE examination: a GCSE syllabus is being developed for the first examination in 1989 or 1990

Japan's expectations of Japanese children overseas are high, but at the same time their education is a complicated issue. Some children move to two or three countries where they must adjust to different cultures and languages. Educational standards vary from one country to another. In some countries, the political situation makes it impractical for children to accompany their parents. Not all children can easily adjust to a different environment. For these reasons, three boarding schools exist in Britain as a centre for children with parents in Europe, the Middle East and Africa. The educational environment for Japanese children in Britain is unique in comparison with other parts of the world in terms of the choices available.

Transmission of the Japanese language and culture, which is dealt with as a problem for the returnees from overseas, is a major topic in Japan. In 1988, the Japanese government earmarked 16,148 million yen (£64.6 million) of its education budget for the education of children overseas and those who have come back to the country. This money is intended to provide aid for school buildings overseas, expenses of teachers sent overseas and programmes relating to the returnees in Japan. The burden of accepting Japanese children in host countries is also recognized by the Japanese authorities concerned (Hasebe 1988:95; Kitashiro 1987:19) although positive measures have not yet been taken.

The main anxieties of the children on return to Japan are

choice of school and future employment. Internationalization of Japanese companies is one of the reasons that people who possess language skills and who understand different cultures are in demand. However, while overseas experience has its merits, it is, at the same time, a source of anxiety for the Japanese employer. The question is whether the employees can adjust to the Japanese environment, and whether they have a good command of Japanese as well as foreign languages (*Kaigai Shijo Kyouiku* December 1987:39).

According to Mr Satou, deputy headmaster of the London Saturday school, the proportion of boys to girls at the full-time Japanese school in London is 2 to 1 at almost every grade. Conversely, the proportion of girls at the London Saturday school increases at higher grades. This implies that it is regarded as more important for boys to be educated in the Japanese way than for girls. This trend would appear to be related to future employment prospects.

The number of students who take the GCE A level examinations is gradually increasing as the A level is accepted as an entrance qualification at some Japanese universities. Some parents prefer the British educational environment, especially British public schools, to the competitive Japanese educational environment. In any case, whether children go to a Japanese school or a British school, the Japanese language seems to be a key element when the children eventually return to Japan.

This chapter has concentrated mainly on children who attend Japanese schools of some description. There are, however, the silent minority who have lost touch with the Japanese schools at some stage. Although these children seem to be performing well at British schools, it is difficult to predict problems which may arise from a British – only education. The psychological problems in each child in the long term are yet another area to be studied.

References

HASEBE, M. (1988) 'Tenki o Mukaeru Kaigai Shijo Kyouiku' (Education for the children overseas at a turning point) *Kaigai Shijo Kyouiku* (Education for the Children Overseas), January: 92–5. Tokyo: Kaigai Shijo Kyouiku Shinkou Zaidan (Japan Overseas Educational Services).

Inner London Education Authority (ILEA) (1987) 1987 *Language Census*, RS 1157/87. London: ILEA.

INOUE, T. (1988) 'Chiiki Shakai tono kou yuu o Fukameru toshi ni' (For the year of strengthening communication with local communities),

Youroppa no Kurashi (Living in Europe, monthly newspaper in Japanese), January: 7. London: M. Furuzawa Overseas Courier Service (London) Ltd.

Japan National Tourist Organization (1975) *Japan*. Tokyo: Japan Travel Bureau.

KATZNER, K. (1977) *The Languages of the World*. London: Routledge & Kegan Paul.

KITASHIRO, J. (1987) 'Nichibei Kyouiku Masatsu o Sakeyo' (Avoid educational conflicts between America and Japan), *Kaigai Shijo Kyouiko*, August: 19. Tokyo: Kaigai Shijo Kuouiku Shinkou Zaidan.

NAKATA, N., WADA, J. and KITAHARA, Y. (eds) (1983) *Kogo Daijiten* (Dictionary of Archaic Words). Tokyo: Shougakkan.

OMUKAI, S. (1988) 'Shinnen no Goaisatsu' (New Year greetings), *Kaigai Shijo Kyouiku*, January: 8. Tokyo: Kaigai Shijo Kyouiku Shinkou Zaidan.

SAWAGATA, H. (Editing Committee for the Dictionary of Joudaigo) (1987) *Kokugo Daijiten: Joudai Hen* (Dictionary of the National Language: Joudai). Tokyo: Sanseidou.

Statistics Bureau Management and Coordination Agency (1986) *Japan Statistical Yearbook*. Tokyo: Japan Statistical Association.

YAMAZAKI, T. (1988) 'Sekai no Naka no Nichieikankei Kyouka o Mezashite' (Aiming at strengthening Anglo-Japan relations in the world), *Youroppa no Kurashi*, January: 4. London: M. Furuzawa Overseas Courier Service (London) Ltd.

YUN, K. (1986) '"Zainichi" ni okeru Minzoku to kokka' (Race and nation for Koreans in Japan as aliens), *Sekai* (World), February: 248–64. Tokyo: Iwanami.

Chapter 13

The Hong Kong Chinese speech community

Lornita Yuen-Fan Wong

"yǔ yán zhè gè dōng xi, bú shi sui biàn kě yi xuě hǎo de,

语言这个东西，不是随便可以学好的

fēi xià kǔ gòng bū kě . . .

非下苦功不可。

di yi, yào xiàng rén mén qún zhòng xué xi yǔ yán.

第一，要向人民群众学习语言。

di èr, yào cóng wài guó yǔ yán zhōng xi shōu wǒ mén soǔ

第二，要从外国语言中吸收我们所

xú yao de chéng fèn

需要的成份。

di sān, yào xué xi gǔ rén yǔ yán zhōng yǒu sheng ming de dōng xi."

第三，要学习古人语言中有生命的东西。

> It is not easy to have a good command of a language. It requires hard work:
>
> 1. Learn the language from common people, the masses;
> 2. Learn the foreign language(s) to supplement our own; and
> 3. Learn the vivid elements of the old language.
>
> MAO TSE-TUNG (1960, 3:838)

The Chinese have been the third largest ethnic group in Britain since the 1950s though, for a variety of reasons, they have received a disproportionately small amount of attention from researchers and educationalists alike. Based on the present writer's knowledge of the language situation in Hong Kong and research on the Hong Kong Chinese attitudes towards language learning and maintenance, this chapter will attempt to outline the language needs of Chinese children in the UK.

The sociolinguistic situation in Hong Kong

In order to understand the sociolinguistic situation of the Hong Kong Chinese, it is important to provide some background information on both the situation in Hong Kong and, in turn, the wider situation of Chinese as a world language. Varieties of Chinese, which form a branch of the Sino-Tibetan family, are now estimated to be spoken by about 1 billion people (DeFrancis 1984; Li and Thompson 1979). The Technical Conference of the Standardization of Modern Chinese which was held in Peking in 1955 agreed on some eight *fanyan* or regional varieties as set out in Fig. 13.1: Putonghua (Mandarin), Wu, Yue (Cantonese), Xiang, Hakka, Gan and Northern and Southern Min (DeFrancis 1984). Although these different varieties are mutually unintelligible, they share a common writing system, based on thousands of distinctive characters or ideograms which have no relation to the sound of the word.

In the People's Republic of China during the language reform movement of the 1950s and 1960s an attempt was made to promote Putonghua, the official language, among the masses by introducing a Pinyin system based on the Latin alphabet (DeFrancis 1984; Lehmann 1975). However, the Chinese abroad, including those in Hong Kong, who left before the language reforms, still maintain the traditional non-alphabetic writing system and speak the variety of the province or district where they came from.

Hong Kong became a British colony in 1843 under the Treaty of Nanking after China's defeat in the first Sino-British Opium War (Taylor 1987). English was the only official language from that point until Cantonese was accorded joint official status in 1974, and English continued as the teaching medium in about 80 per cent of secondary schools throughout the 1970s (Gibbons 1982). However, although English has high official status and is important for the development of international trade, Hong Kong remains what Luke and Richards (1982) describe as a diglossic

FIGURE 13.1 Linguistic geography of China

society without bilingualism in which the use of English is confined to certain domains of intergroup contact.

Ninety-eight per cent of the total population of Hong Kong are
Chinese. Among them approximately 60 per cent were born in
Hong Kong. The rest of the ethnic Chinese are mostly from
Guangdong (Kwangtung) Province (see Fig. 13.2) where Yue or
Kwang Dong Wa (Cantonese) is spoken. Other Chinese varieties
such as Hakka, Chiuchow (Teochiu) and Hokkien (Fukien) are
spoken by a small proportion of the Hong Kong Chinese but Can-
tonese remains the lingua franca (Gibbons 1984; Luke and
Richards 1982; Taylor 1987).

Hong Kong Chinese in Britain

Although there are records showing that Chinese were brought
into Britain as seamen as early as the nineteenth century (Krausz
1971; Lynn 1982; May 1978), and scattered Chinese settlements
were found in Limehouse, Liverpool, Cardiff and Bristol (HAC

FIGURE 13.2 Hong Kong: Hong Kong Island, Kowloon Peninsular and the New Territories

1985), the Chinese community only began to grow after the Second World War in response both to large-scale labour shortages in Britain (Gordon and Klug 1985; Ng 1968) and to local conditions. In the 1960s, the Hong Kong government requisition of land from farmers in the New Territories for development purposes, produced a shortage of farming land. The influx of refugees from the People's Republic during the Cultural Revolution added to these pressures. In the city, as a result of political instability and economic recession, unemployment was quite serious. People in Hong Kong, especially the less educated from the New Territories, tried to look for jobs overseas (Aijmer 1967; Jones 1979; Krausz 1971; Ng 1968; Shang 1984).

Following changes in the law in Britain in the 1960s, the immigration of Chinese from Hong Kong became easier and, with the introduction of the employment voucher system by the 1962 Commonwealth Immigrants Act, the number of Hong Kong workers in Britain increased from 20,000 in 1962 (Aserappa 1962) to 25,000 in 1964 (Aserappa 1964). Later the Commonwealth Immigrants Act of 1968 and the demand for additional labour by the prosperous Chinese catering business accelerated the rate of

TABLE 13.1 Data on Chinese-speaking pupils from the ILEA
Language Census (1981–87)

Year	Number	%PHLOE*
1981	2,237	5.0
1983	2,825	5.6
1985	3,546	6.3
1987	4,325	6.7

*=Pupils with a home language other than or in addition to English.

immigration. The 1971 Census showed that there had been a rise of 107 per cent in the Chinese population in Britain in the ten-year period since the previous census (General Register Office 1966; OPCS 1974). By the early 1980s, there were in total about 100,000 Chinese in Britain, making them the third largest ethnic minority group.

At present about half of the total Chinese population in Britain lives in London. The Chinese community in London therefore is the largest, followed by Manchester, Liverpool, Birmingham and Glasgow. Because there is no question in the population census relating to language (*cf* Ch. 1), it is difficult to arrive at precise statistics for the size and distribution of the Chinese population, though the ILEA *Language Census* (Table 13.1) gives some indication as to the situation in London. Chinese speakers are currently the third largest linguistic minority in the schools of the capital.

This concentration of Chinese children is much higher in inner London than elsewhere in the country. For instance, LMP (1983), report that Chinese speakers made up 1 per cent of the bilingual children who took part in their School Language Survey in Bradford and Coventry, 2 per cent in Haringey and Waltham Forest and 4 per cent in Peterborough.

About 70 per cent of the Hong Kong Chinese in Britain speak Cantonese (HAC 1985; Taylor 1987; Watson 1977). However, approximately 25 per cent come from the New Territories (see Fig. 13.2) where Hakka is commonly spoken (Clough and Quarmby 1978; Watson 1977). Hakka, in the UK, is confined to intragroup communication among those who want to demonstrate affection and solidarity.

Changing patterns of language use

Educational provision in Hong Kong is very uneven; in the New Territories, for instance, only a small proportion of the population is educated beyond the primary level. This pattern has implications for the level of English spoken by immigrants from Hong Kong. A sample survey conducted by the Haringey Chinese Group (1986), for instance, indicated that twenty-seven out of fifty-two Chinese parents had received only primary-level education. Thus it is not surprising to find in another survey in Lambeth (Yau 1983) that most people over the age of 25 did not have a working knowledge of English. In a similar vein, an unofficial estimate given by the Home Affairs Committee (HAC 1985) suggests that about 65–75 per cent of first-generation Chinese immigrants in Britain are unable to speak English.

The widespread employment of Chinese in the catering and restaurant industry is another important factor in language maintenance. The most important source of information on this particular area is the LMP (1985) Adult Language Use Survey. More than any other group included in the survey, the Chinese tend to work within their own ethnic economy, usually self-employed or as part of small family businesses. In this environment, it is only natural that the main language of communication will be Chinese and not English (see Table 13.2).

Other factors, particularly education, militate in favour of a language shift from Chinese to English. Etherton et al.'s study (1974) of parental motivation in the choice of secondary schools indicates that most Chinese parents in Hong Kong preferred their children to be educated in English. After arriving in Britain, however, parents' choice of education for their children seems to have

TABLE 13.2 Language use in the workplace extrapolated from LMP (1985)

% of working respondents where at least one fellow worker can speak Chinese	Coventry London	76 81
% of working respondents where all fellow workers can speak Chinese	Coventry London	72 64
% of working respondents (who work for someone else) where the boss can speak Chinese	Coventry London	* 53
% of working respondents who use mostly or only English to workmates	Coventry London	16 18

Coventry: N=25
London: N=67

* Very few Chinese respondents in Coventry had a boss, since most were in small family businesses or self-employed.

changed. According to Fitchett (1976), Garvey and Jackson (1975) and Jones (1980), some British-born Chinese children were, in the early days of immigration, sent back to Hong Kong to be brought up by their grandmothers. This is partly because Chinese parents wanted to free themselves for work and partly because they worried that their children would be assimilated by British culture if they went to school in this country.

Family reunion in the late 1960s and the fear of Communism when Hong Kong is returned to China in 1997 (for details, see Hong Kong Government 1984) have led the Chinese to abandon their sojourner mentality. Consequently their children are no longer sent back to Hong Kong and now attend British schools. Since British education is English-oriented and the lingua franca in the majority society is English, language shift among the school-age Chinese children is inevitable. The majority of Chinese children manage to speak to their parents or grandparents in the mother tongue. The rest of the children, about 20 per cent, tend to use a mixture of English and Chinese. When they talk to their siblings or friends, more than half indicate that they use English and Cantonese. A further 6 per cent of these children only use English to speak to their friends and siblings (Wong 1988).

The LMP's (1983) Survey of Adult Language Use confirms these changing patterns of language use. Comparisons of reports of language skills for the adult respondents to the survey with those for the household as a whole (which will, of course, include a large proportion of British-born Chinese) point to an inevitable process of language shift from Chinese to English (see Table 13.3). The survey (LMP 1985) provides further evidence of this shift to English in parents' reports of their children's language use between themselves. Some 60 per cent of the parents in Coventry and 20 per cent of the parents in London said that their

TABLE 13.3   Data on language skills in the Chinese community, extrapolated from LMP (1983)

		Chinese	English
% of respondents who speak and understand the language fairly well or very well	Coventry (N=43)	79	51
	Bradford (N=50)	88	28
	London (N=137)	96	65
% of people in respondents' households who speak and understand the language fairly well or very well	Coventry (N=213)	49	55
	Bradford (N=233)	66	81
	London (N=504)	82	61

children used English 'only' or 'mostly'. None the less, it is noteworthy that these estimates of English usage for the Chinese community were considerably lower than for most of the other ten speech communities included in the survey.

According to Saifullah Khan (1977), the shift from one's mother tongue to a foreign language which the parents do not know usually causes a certain degree of frustration and psychological insecurity for the non-English-speaking parents. The children's tendency to speak English among themselves signals that they are gradually being assimilated by the majority culture, at least in terms of language. Since many Chinese parents in Britain do not know English and the children's Chinese competence begins to deteriorate once they start schooling in Britain, it is not unusual for there to be a communication failure between Chinese parents and their children. Some children consulted in the course of my research explained that they sometimes find it difficult to express themselves in Chinese to their parents. Reluctance to speak to parents at home may be interpreted by some parents as not giving respect to their authority in the family, behaviour which is highly incompatible with Confucius's concept of filial piety.

Because the Chinese community in Britain is so dispersed, families are quite isolated from one another. In the neighbourhood where Chinese people live, they are usually surrounded by non-Chinese-speaking people. The inability to communicate with neighbours may aggravate parents' frustration as they cannot find any outlet for their anxiety, such as talking to their friends and relatives in their mother tongue. Under these circumstances, Chinese parents are especially anxious to have their dignity affirmed by being able to talk to and receive the respect of their children, and Chinese-language education, with its associated cultural values, is seen as a priority.

Language, culture and community

As the Chinese population in Britain is growing, their sense of cultural maintenance is becoming stronger and more explicit. Almost all Chinese institutions, including Chinese supplementary schools, organize some sort of celebration of the Lunar New Year which usually falls in either January or February. The lion-dance parade in the London Chinatown, held on the Sunday following the Lunar New Year, is the most exciting event of the celebration which always attracts a lot of foreigners as well as Chinese. The

Mid-autumn Festival is another major Chinese festival that most Chinese in Britain also celebrate. The focus of this celebration is on the 'mooncake', a kind of pastry with lotus seed filling, and the Chinese lanterns hung up in Chinatown. Traditionally Chinese families are supposed to have family reunions and eat a big meal together on that day.

In addition to the major community-oriented festive celebrations, the maintenance of Chinese culture by the Chinese in Britain also finds expression in the mass media. In the London Chinatown in Soho, there are book shops, video hire shops and cinemas where Chinese books, newspapers, videos of Chinese television programmes and films from Hong Kong, China or Taiwan are available.

In recent years, Chinese community centres funded by local councils have been set up in London boroughs such as Camden, Westminster, Haringey and Hackney where there is a sizeable Chinese population. Besides providing welfare services to the Chinese within their borough, these centres also help to maintain and promote Chinese culture in Britain by organizing classes to teach Chinese martial arts, painting, calligraphy, cookery and *Tai-chi* to different age groups of Chinese people.

The Chinese community in Manchester is smaller than in London but it is none the less extremely active. BBC Radio Manchester has broadcast a weekly bilingual programme called 'Eastern Horizon' since December 1983 and the Chinese Information Centre Co-operative produces a bilingual magazine, *siyu*, which acts as a channel for cultural exchange. One particularly ambitious project undertaken by the Chinese community in Manchester was Chinese View '86, a two-week festival to promote Chinese culture with live performances of contemporary and traditional music, events and exhibitions.

In spite of the dispersed nature of the Chinese community as a whole, and the tendency of Chinese people to settle in areas where there are very few other Chinese friends and neighbours, community life is now well-developed. The LMP (1983) Adult Language Usage Survey confirms this picture of a strong, varied and well-developed community life in areas of important community settlement. Most Chinese conduct their social life within the confines of their own community. They are able to do their shopping in Chinese shops as well as carrying out a wide range of other interactions. In London, many people can even consult a Chinese-speaking doctor. All of these activities reinforce the importance of the mother tongue and make for a large degree of language stability within the community (see Table 13.4).

TABLE 13.4 Language use in a range of settings, extrapolated from LMP (1983)

% of respondents who said they only spoke a Chinese language with the first person mentioned as someone they spent time with	Coventry	61
	Bradford	96
	London	89
% of respondents who said most or all of their neighbours spoke a Chinese language	Coventry	2
	Bradford	14
	London	5
% of respondents who said they had seen a film or video in a Chinese language	Coventry	37
	Bradford	24
	London	56
% of respondents who said they sometimes visited a shop where a Chinese language was spoken by the shopkeeper or assistants	Coventry	95
	Bradford	96
	London	99
% of respondents who had a doctor who could speak a Chinese language	Coventry	5
	Bradford	0
	London	42

Coventry: $N=43$
Bradford: $N=50$
London: $N=137$

Education and language reproduction

Because of the language barrier, ignorance of the bureaucracy in Britain and the British government's reluctance to change their language policies in schools, the Chinese community had already taken on the responsibility for providing Chinese-language education by organizing Chinese classes outside school hours as early as 1928 (Chann 1982; *China Journal* 1935; Jones 1980; Ng 1968; Shang 1984). As the number of Chinese children began to increase with the change in the immigration laws in 1968 (CRE 1978; Home Office 1974; NCC 1979, 1984), and as a result of natural growth, Chinese classes were revived in the 1960s and reached the peak of expansion between the late 1970s and early 1980s. According to Chann (1982) about 71 per cent of the Chinese classes registered at the Hong Kong Government Office in London were established within a few years of the late 1970s.

Tsow (1984:20) points out that although Chinese parents want their children to study Chinese, they do not want to see their children 'learn the mother tongue at the expense of learning English or to [have] priority over English'. In order not to interfere with mainstream studies, the majority of Chinese classes are held at the weekend in state school premises, private houses, centres or church halls (HAC 1985; Tsow 1984). Since many parents have to go to work in the evening and the time allowed for the use of these premises is limited, most of the classes last for about one to two hours, or a maximum of three hours.

The academic year of the majority of the Chinese schools is similar to that of the state schools – starting in September and finishing in July, with about thirty to forty teaching weeks. During the summer holiday, the closure of the LEAs' school premises and the lack of teachers means that most of the Chinese classes are suspended. If extra funds are available, some Chinese schools organize various activities related to Chinese culture such as calligraphy, and video shows to help Chinese children to develop a positive image and appreciation of their own culture.

Since Cantonese is the lingua franca within the Chinese community and the majority of the teachers of Chinese are Cantonese-speaking, most of the schools have adopted Cantonese as the medium of instruction. Of the thirteen schools visited by the author in London, twelve were Cantonese-medium. However, a small proportion, about 5 per cent of the Chinese in Britain, speak Putonghua (HAC 1985) and parent groups have founded two schools in London where Putonghua is used as a medium of instruction. As has been mentioned, most Chinese school-age children have become dominant in English, and some English is occasionally used by the bilingual teachers in order to facilitate learning. At present there is no syllabus providing guidelines for the structure and content of Chinese-language teaching in Britain. Individual schools or teachers simply use the textbooks available to introduce Chinese children to a basic knowledge of the Chinese language.

Although Chinese teachers realize that many British-born Chinese children are unable to speak Cantonese fluently, no specific time seems to have been allotted to the development of spoken skills. Teachers seem to have assumed that Chinese children will learn the spoken language within the community or from their family. Most of the Chinese classes therefore tend to focus on the development of reading and writing skills.

For the teaching of reading, most of the Chinese schools use *Modern Chinese*, a Chinese textbook published in Hong Kong and provided free by the Hong Kong Government Office in London. In the process of developing reading skills, most teachers also aim to help children maintain their Chinese identity. Therefore texts related to the glamorous history and great inventions of China, the major Chinese festivals and customs and Confucius's concept of filial piety are chosen for teaching reading. To supplement the reading materials, some teachers like to introduce classical poems which are usually regarded as the essence of Chinese literature or culture.

Although teaching materials are available, it is in fact not easy for Chinese children in Britain to acquire reading skills. According to Wang (1973), one needs to have a knowledge of 4,000–7,000 characters in order to be able to read a newspaper. Unlike English, all these characters are formed by ideographs which provide no clues to their pronunciation. Children studying at the weekend Chinese schools, where the teaching medium is Cantonese, are expected to learn the pronunciation by heart. Since many Chinese children in Britain make relatively little use of Chinese, they easily forget what they learn at school. To help them to memorize the pronunciation, most children put English transliterations alongside the Chinese characters while their teacher is reading the text to them. Although teachers have noticed this phenomenon, very few choose to build upon it: they are not trained to teach Chinese to children who are trying to maintain or 'redevelop' their mother tongue, and most simply use the traditional method – rote learning.

The development of writing skills is another core element in Chinese education. Younger children are taught how to write the various types of strokes – lines, sweeps, angles and hooks (Chang and Chang 1978) (Fig. 13.3) and the basic sequence (left to right, top to bottom, etc.) of putting all the strokes together to form a Chinese character. Most Chinese children get the sequence confused (see Fig. 13.4). Dictation is usually regarded as a way of helping children to memorize the writing of the Chinese characters. After students have acquired a certain number of words, they will be taught to make sentences with the words they have learnt. From the ages of 10 or 11 they will be required to write short essays and family letters.

There is a strong literary tradition not only in China but in the various overseas Chinese communities, including Britain. Literacy rates reported by Chinese children in the LMP (1983) School Language Survey, for instance, were second only to those of Polish and Italian-speaking children. (Table 13.5).

In the upper primary and junior secondary levels, in addition to essay and letter writing, pupils will also have to learn translation from English to Chinese and vice versa. In point of fact,

1. Lines

   Horizontal line: ———

2. Sweeps

   Long sweeps: 丿 乀 丿

   Short sweeps: 丿 ⟋

3. Angles

   Right angle: ⌐

   Acute angle: ⌐ ∟

   Obtuse angle: ⟨

4. Hooks

   Horizontal: ⌐

   Vertical: 亅 ∟

   Curve hooks: 乛 乚 ⟋ ⟍

FIGURE 13.3 Basic strokes of Chinese characters (Source: Chang and Chang 1978: 25–6)

Proper sequence

丨 　 冂 　 ⼎ 　 田 　 田

1. Vertical   2. Right   3. Horizontal   4. Vertical   5. Horizontal
   line   angle   line   line   line

Improper sequence

丨 　 冂 　 ⼎ 　 ⾙ 　 田

1. Vertical   2. Right   3. Horizontal   4. Horizontal   5. Vertical
   line   angle   line   line   line

(*Mistake*: Steps 4 and 5 have been reversed.)

FIGURE 13.4 Sequence of strokes. A Chinese character (field) is used for the illustration

TABLE 13.5 Literacy rates for Chinese in five LEAs (extrapolated from LMP 1985)

LEA	(%)
Bradford	56
Coventry	61
Haringey	69
Peterborough	69
Waltham Forest	57

the development of translation skills was not a priority for Chinese schools when they were set up. It became important mainly because translation was one of the skills to be tested in the O level (later the General Certificate of Secondary Education) and the A level examinations in Chinese. (Some 677 children, for instance, entered the London East Anglian Group GCSE in Chinese in the summer of 1988 and there were 333 candidates for the University of London School Examination Board's A level Chinese in June 1987.) Chinese schools also realize that at home some of the non-English-speaking parents have to rely on their children to do translation for them on various occasions. For practical and examination reasons, translation has therefore become a component of the Chinese curriculum. Translation aside, the curriculum content in general is quite similar to that in Hong Kong at the primary level.

In addition to the language teaching which takes place within the community, some LEAs offer support for Chinese-language education. Within the ILEA, for instance, twelve Chinese classes organized on a voluntary basis by the Chinese community have received grants ranging from £1,000 to £2,000 per year, depending on the size of the school population and money which the school obtains from other sources (ILEA 1986). Besides grants, the waiving of rents for the use of the ILEA school premises to run Chinese classes is another form of financial assistance.

The ILEA has also taken some initiatives to promote Chinese-language teaching in some of its schools. With grants from Section 11 of the Local Government Act 1966 (see, for instance, Home Office 1986; NUT 1978), the ILEA was able to appoint one full-time and two part-time teachers of Chinese in the early 1980s to be responsible for the teaching of Chinese to pupils studying at ILEA schools. In total, nineteen school-based Chinese classes have been set up with the highest concentration in Divisions 2 (Westminster and Camden) and 5 (Tower Hamlets).

Because of the lack of Chinese teachers and the limited number of Chinese pupils at each age level in individual schools, it is not always practicable to provide Chinese-language education for the complete age-range. A solution adopted by one school is to attempt to teach Chinese to both Chinese and non-Chinese speakers from the second to the fifth year. In addition to the school-based Chinese classes held within the timetable, the ILEA also provides some financial support for the setting up of after-school classes as an extra-curricular activity to meet the needs of the Chinese pupils within a school. Two secondary schools where the author has previously taught had set up their Chinese classes in this way. Both Chinese and non-Chinese-speaking pupils, as well as the staff, could join the classes.

The ILEA Resources Centre provides a valuable service for teachers of community languages. Books in various languages, including Chinese, are available for loan to language centres, primary and secondary schools and teachers' centres. In the reference section, community language teachers can share the unpublished materials produced by other teachers. The ILEA also provides in-service training in the form of workshops to meet the immediate needs of untrained and inexperienced language teachers and a special scheme of initial employment and subsequent secondment on full pay for the Post Graduate Certificate in Education (PGCE) has been set up for five instructor posts (ILEA 1986).

My investigation of the sociolinguistic background and the problems encountered by Chinese parents with their children suggests that there can be little doubt of the need to provide Chinese-language education for Chinese children in Britain. Despite initiatives such as those taken by the ILEA to give support to Chinese-language teaching within its administrative area, the extent and nature of provision are far from satisfactory. The dispersed nature of the Chinese community means that it is not possible to provide a full language education integrated into the mainstream curriculum; and where Chinese children are taught alongside native English speakers it is very difficult for the teacher to attend to the very different needs of all the learners. In addition, the perceived aims of language education within the mainstream do not always coincide with the aims and aspirations of the parents and the wider Chinese community.

Nor are community-based classes problem free. Although Chinese community schools have a better understanding of the aspirations of Chinese parents, their reluctance to make innovations in teaching Chinese to their younger generation in a foreign country, together with other constraints such as school premises, finance and teacher education in supply, have similarly prevented Chinese community schools from achieving their aims. It is clearly very important for mainstream educators and the Chinese community to work together so that the effectiveness and efficiency of Chinese-language teaching can be improved.

References

AIJMER, G. (1967) 'Expansion and extension in Hakka society', *Journal of the Hong Kong Branch of the Royal Asiatic Society*, 7: 42–79.

ASERAPPA, J. P. (1962) *New Territories Annual Report 1961–62*. Hong Kong: Government Printer.

ASERAPPA, J. P. (1964) *New Territories Annual Report 1963–64*. Hong Kong: Government Printer.

CHANG, R. and CHANG, M. S. (1978) *Speaking Chinese*. New York: W. W. Norton & Company Inc.

CHANN, V. (1982) 'Chinese mother-tongue teaching in the United Kingdom.' Unpublished paper, London, Hong Kong Government Office.

China Journal (1935) 'Educational notes and intelligence', *The China Journal* 22(1) (January): 46.

CLOUGH, E. and QUARMBY, J. (1978) *A Public Library Service for Ethnic Minorities in Great Britain*. London: The Library Association.

Commission for Racial Equality (CRE) (1978) *Ethnic Minorities in Britain: Statistical Background*. London: CRE.

DEFRANCIS, J. (1984) *The Chinese Language: Facts and Fantasy*. Honolulu, Hawaii: University of Hawaii Press.

ETHERTON, A. R. *et al.* (1974) *Parental Motivation in the Choice of Secondary schools*. Hong Kong: Chinese University of Hong Kong.

FITCHETT, N. (1976) *Chinese Children in Derby*. National Association for Multicultural Education.

GARVEY, A. and JACKSON, B. (1975) *Chinese Children. Research and Action Project into the Needs of Chinese Children*. Cambridge, England: National Educational Research and Development Trust.

General Register Office, London (1966) *Census 1961. Great Britain Summary Tables*. London: HMSO.

GIBBONS, J. (1982) 'The issues of the language of instruction in the lower forms of Hong Kong secondary schools', *Journal of Multilingual and Multicultural Development* 3(2): 117–28.

GIBBONS, J. (1984) 'Interpreting the English proficiency profile in Hong Kong', *Regional English Language Centre (RELC) Singapore Journal* 15(1) (June): 64–74.

GORDON, P. and KLUG, F. (1985) *British Immigration Control: A Brief Guide*. London: Runnymede Trust.

Haringey Chinese Group (1986) 'A survey of the needs of the Chinese living in Haringey'. Unpublished report.

Home Affairs Committee (HAC)(1985) *Chinese Community in Britain.* Second Report from the Home Affairs Committee, Session 1984–5. London: HMSO.

Home Office (1974) *Immigration Statistics 1973.* London: HMSO.

Home Office (1986) *Home Office Circular No. 72/1986: Section 11 of the Local Government Act 1966.* London: HMSO.

Hong Kong Government (1984) *A Draft Agreement between the Government of the United Kingdom of Great Britain and Northern Ireland and the Government of the People's Republic of China on the Future of Hong Kong.* Hong Kong: Government Printer.

Inner London Education Authority (ILEA) (1981, 1983, 1985, 1987) *Language Census.* London: ILEA Research and Statistics.

Inner London Education Authority (1986) *Review of Languages Education.* London: ILEA.

JONES, D. (1979) 'The Chinese in Britain: origins and development of a community', *New Community* **3**(3): 379–40214

JONES, D. (1980) 'Chinese schools in Britain: a minority's response to its own needs', *Trends in Education* (Spring): 15–18.

KRAUSZ, E. (1971) *Ethnic Minorities in Britain.* London: MacGibbon & Kee.

LEHMANN, W. P. (ed.) (1975) *Language and Linguistics in the People's Republic of China.* Austin and London: University of Texas Press.

LI, C. N. and THOMPSON, S. A. (1979) 'Chinese: dialect variations and language reform'. In T. Shopen (ed.) *Languages and their Status,* Cambridge, Mass: Winthrop Publishers Inc., *pp.* 285–335.

Linguistic Minorities Project (1985) *The Other Languages of England.* London: Routledge and Kegan Paul.

LUKE, K. K. and RICHARDS, J. C. (1982) 'English in Hong Kong: functions and status', *English World-Wide* **3**(1): 47–64.

LUKE, K. K. and RICHARDS, J. C. (1982) 'English in Hong Kong: functions and status', *English World-Wide* **3**(1): 47–64

LYNN, L. L. (1982) *The Chinese in Liverpool: Their Unmet Needs with Respect to Education, Social Welfare and Housing.* Liverpool: Merseyside Area Profile Group.

MAO TSE-TUNG (1960) *Selected Works of Mao Tse-tung.* Peking: Jen-min Ch'u-pan-she.

MAY, J. P. (1978) 'The Chinese in Britain'. In C. Holmes (ed.) *Immigrants and Minorities in British Society,* London: George Allen & Unwin pp 114–24.

National Children's Centre (NCC) (1979) *Report on the Third National Conference on Chinese Children in Britain.* Huddersfield: NCC.

National Children's Centre (NCC) (1984) *'The Silent Minority'. Report on the Fourth National Conference on Chinese Children in Britain.* Huddersfield: NCC.

National Union of Teachers (NUT) (1978) *Section 11 – an NUT Report.* London: NUT.

NG, K. C. (1968) *The Chinese in London.* London: Oxford University Press.

Office of Population, Census and Surveys (OPCS) (1974) *Census 1971, Great Britain, Country of Birth Tables*. London: HMSO.

SAIFULLAH KHAN, V. (1977) *Bilingualism and Linguistic Minorities in Britain: Developments, Perspectives*. Briefing paper: London: Runnymede Trust.

SHANG, A. (1984) *The Chinese in Britain*. London: Batsford Academic and Educational.

TAYLOR, M. (1987) *Chinese Pupils in Britain*. Windsor: National Foundation for Educational Research.

TSOW, M. (1984) *Mother Tongue Maintenance: A Survey of Part-time Chinese Language Classes*. London: CRE.

WANG, W. (1973) 'The Chinese language'. In *Human Communication: Language and its Psychological Bases. Readings from Scientific American* (no editor), San Francisco: W. H. Freeman & Co., *pp.* 52–62.

WATSON, J. L. (1977) 'The Chinese: Hong Kong villagers in the British Catering Trade'. In J. Watson (ed.) *Between Two Cultures*, Oxford: Basil Blackwell, *pp.* 181–213.

WONG, L. Y. F. (1988) *Education of Chinese Children, a Comparative Study with the United States of America*. London: Institute of Education, University of London (unpublished PhD thesis).

YAU L. (1983) Report on the Chinese Community in Lambeth. Mimeo, London: Lambeth Community Relations Council.

Chapter 14

The Singaporean and Malaysian speech communities

Ronald Chan

Words need people to fill their blanks

(FROM THE POEM 'WORDS' BY ARTHUR YAP)

One way of introducing this subject is to alert the reader to the potentially bewildering sociolinguistic context in which Singaporean–Malaysian English (SME) has to be understood. It is potentially bewildering in the first place for those without much experience of the linguistic diversity found (typically) in many urban areas of South East Asia. Even those familiar enough with the multi-ethnicity of present-day London (for instance) will find the SME situation remarkable. For one thing, the multi-ethnicity of London (and other British cities) is not reflected in the mass media (except in marginal form) while that of Singapore and Malaysia is. If one were to imagine a situation where both BBC and ITV channels broadcast in such a way as *to take account* of (not necessarily 'use the language of') the four numerically most dominant language communities in London, one would have arrived at an approximation of some of the social consequences of the linguistic situation in (especially) Singapore. Such diversity is also characteristic of Malaysia, but to a lesser extent, for here the multilingual situation has been increasingly modified since 1965 – the year when Singapore and Malaysia became two independent countries – by the gradual rise in importance and prestige of the Malay language (officially labelled now as 'Bahasa Malaysia', 'bahasa' meaning 'language').

In the second place, the sociolinguistic context for SME is potentially bewildering because to understand it at all, a larger than usual number of descriptive terms (*eg* the meaning of terms ending in '-lect') have to be defined or redefined for this specific purpose. The next section therefore has an unavoidably large proportion devoted to terminology.

Finally, a special difficulty in this study is that the question, 'What has been happening to SME *in Britain?*' has probably never been posed before in this context of discussion. Given the paucity of our encyclopaedic knowledge on this question, there is little choice but to hope that relevance will compensate for being (as Grice might say) 'brief'. On the other hand, recent research on SME in the countries of origin has been vigorous and informative. (See introduction to references section below.)

The sociolinguistic situation in Singapore and Malaysia

Until about 1965, it would still have been feasible (up to a point) to speak of a *single* sociolinguistic situation in both countries, since Malaysia and Singapore have evolved into modern states from what was in many ways a single geo- and socio-political unit. Since 1965, however, linguistic diversity in Malaysia has been tempered by the rise in prestige and socio-political status of Malay – one of the consequences of independence from Britain. The sociolinguistic consequences of this development will be discussed below.

In Singapore, however, there has been no parallel rise in dominance of one of the locally spoken languages. Singapore (since independence) has had *four official* languages: English, Malay, Mandarin (Chinese) and Tamil.[1] Of the four, the dominant official language is English. Leaving aside the case of Malaysia for the moment, English in Singapore is best described as a 'post-creole continuum' (Platt and Weber 1980; Platt, Weber and Ho 1984). At the lower ('basilectal') end of this continuum, SME may be regarded as a 'creoloid'. It is used by some speakers as one of their varieties/languages, contains borrowings and mixtures from the local languages, and has developed a sufficiently distinctive grammar and vocabulary to cause some intelligibility difficulties for (say) a British English speaker new to the region. Some examples are discussed in the section on language contact and shift. At the upper end of the continuum (the 'acrolect') SME is a very close approximation to standard British English (hereinafter, simply Br.E) though even here, there are significant differences, some of which will be discussed below.[2] Some of the terminological issues in describing this continuum are handled by other writers in greater detail than can be provided here (*eg* Platt and Weber 1980; Todd 1984; Bickerton 1973). It is important to emphasize that SME, for both Malaysians and Singaporeans, can often be *both* a lingua franca and a native language.

Equally, it is important to note that SME may be used by a speaker who is just as comfortable in a dialect of Chinese or in Tamil or Malay, or in two of the three, or in two dialects of Chinese. In other words, the situation is not so much diglossic as '*poly*glossic'. Code-switching, not only within a discourse, but within one speaker's 'turn', is common. It is not at all uncommon, for instance, for a housewife to buy her fish in the fish market using Teochew, order her lunch in a café or food stall using either Malay or English (or both) and then return home after giving instructions to a taxi-driver in Hokkien. (Riding in a taxi is not necessarily a sign of affluence here.) Moreover, such a person would not be considered an unusually versatile language user.

At the acrolectal (high status) end of the continuum, SME is not only sufficiently like Br.E to function as an international language, it is also a very high-status prestige language – indeed, in most situations it is *the* highest-status language in the country. In Malaysia, Malay ('Bahasa Malaysia') has higher status than English, though even here, English retains a prestige position very near the top. The high prestige given to English (*ie* both Br.E and SME) is the single most relevant factor to be borne in mind when we come later to a discussion of the sociolinguistic situation in the UK.

The reader may wish to consult some standard works for further details (*eg* Platt and Weber 1980). However, some features of the sociolinguistic situation must be mentioned here because these help us to understand the SME speaker's *attitudes* towards language use.

We come therefore to the terminological discussion anticipated earlier. First, in addition to the four 'official' languages mentioned earlier, there are communities (by no means small minorities) in both Singapore and Malaysia who speak either Malayalam (another south Indian language) or some other Indian language (*eg* Panjabi). The description 'four official languages' therefore by no means exhaustively describes the diversity of the situation.

Next, the term 'dialect' has to be understood in at least *three* different senses when applied to this region. First, when used for Chinese, dialects in this language are not mutually intelligible and the SME speaker who also speaks two Chinese dialects (*eg* Hokkien and Cantonese) – and such speakers are not uncommon – is in a sense a user of *three* languages. Second, when used for

Malay, 'dialect' has also the *regional* denotation carried by (for instance) the term 'Yorkshire English', for there are systematic differences between, say, the Malay of the east coast and the Malay of the southern and western towns. And third, the term 'dialect' has the connotation 'sociolect' (*ie* social class dialect) when we speak, for instance, of 'Cockney' or 'Scouse' in the UK. There is only a very weak correspondence in Singapore and Malaysia between 'dialect' in the other two senses and dialect as sociolect. Partial associations are sometimes made between 'dialect' (in both the first two senses) and social status, but these have very weak significance as sociolinguistic factors.

Of course, there are numerous ethnic–occupational stereotypes (of the kind used for the Irish, Jews, etc. in Britain). But the social consequences of such stereotypes (which rarely exist beyond the context of tasteless or offensive jokes) are far more muted than might be expected since it is not that common to find, for instance, a Cantonese speaker who speaks *only* Cantonese. Thus, it is possible in many cases for the fact of your ethnicity to be irrelevant, at least in Singapore. This is so, even in what might seem to an outsider to be clear-cut cases, for a person who looks for all the world as if he/she *ought* to be a Tamil speaker (*ie* has a dark skin) may have a family name such as De Souza and may speak *only* SME, not Tamil.

While ethnicity is similarly irrelevant in many respects in Malaysia, it is highlighted here in one particular respect: there are crucial *constitutional* implications depending on whether one is considered a 'Malay', and one constitutional definition of a 'Malay' is *that the person speaks Bahasa Malaysia*. (Professing Islam is another.) Among other things, constitutionally defined Malays are given a preferential 4:1 ratio in all government posts. (Constitutionally defined Malays make up roughly 50 per cent of the population in Peninsular Malaysia, while the Chinese make up roughly 35 per cent; Ministry of Culture, Singapore 1980: 66.) Such political factors help to account for the high prestige of Malay over SME in Malaysia.

The only language which has widespread and wide-ranging functions as a socioliect is SME. This observation has crucial significance for the discussion in the next section.

One of the more obvious everyday indicators of linguistic diversity in this region is the multiplicity of *written* scripts in daily use. Chinese, Malay and Tamil each have their own traditional orthographies, none of which is based on the Roman alphabet (Malay also has a Romanized alphabetical script as well as the Arabic-based 'Jawi'). All three scripts, along with English, are in use in public notices and government announcements. The most authoritative daily newspaper in Singapore is an English-language paper, followed closely by newspapers in Chinese, but newspapers written in both Romanized Malay and Jawi are also read. *Written* English in the region is largely Br.E, with very few SME traits. It is a regular occurrence for television programmes in both Singapore and Malaysia to be broadcast in one language (*eg* English) accompanied by subtitles in *two* other languages; and while there are some TV and radio channels dominated by English, or Malay, or Chinese, it is unusual (especially on TV) to find a channel broadcasting *entirely* in one language.

Finally, a curious feature of SME is that while it has many sociolinguistic and developmental features reminiscent of (say) West Indian Creoles (WIC), it cannot be understood as a creole in quite the same sense. For instance, like WIC, SME is best described as a continuum, with a sub-variety at the lower end that may seem little like English to a British person with no previous exposure to the variety, and a sub-variety at the higher end that approximates to Br.E. Like WIC, it is influenced by languages other than English, but retains an English base as a consequence of political history. It even shares with WIC the specific characteristics which also seem to characterize a very large range of 'new' or 'modern' Englishes (Todd 1984) in the former countries of the British Empire, *viz* absence of {-s} affixation for subject–verb concord for third person singular ('He go' vs. 'He goes'), dropping of final /-d/ for past tense ('He call out' vs. 'He call*ed* out') and absence of the copula ('He very wicked' vs. 'He is very wicked'). The one distinctive (possibly unique) difference is that SME did not develop from a pidgin and did not evolve through spontaneous use and modification of English for practical daily purposes. It developed because Br.E was taught in schools, *as a matter of educational policy.*[3] If SME is a creole, it is one which originated in the *classroom.*

As to an indigenous literature, local writers using SME have been active since the 1960s in attempts to create drama, poetry and fictional prose distinctive of the region. A writer using SME, Catherine Lim, has had her short stories adopted in several Commonwealth countries as an 'O' level text (Lim 1978). A local poet who has had his work favourably reviewed in London is the Singapore linguist and artist, Arthur Yap. But a feature that again distinguishes SME from some typical creoles is that there is no folklore – no folk-tales or folk-songs – in SME, nor is there an SME version of the Bible, unlike the case in (for instance) Sierra Leone, Nigeria and the Solomons (Todd 1984: 258–78).

Singaporeans and Malaysians in Britain

The largest single group of SME speakers in the UK are students (eg Singapore alone has about 1,600 students registered with the Singapore High Commission in London). Since the decline in numbers of Iranian students after about 1980 Malaysian–Singaporean students now form the largest group of overseas students in the UK.[4] However, SME speakers have lived in the UK either as permanent residents or as British citizens since at least as far back as the 1930s. The number of these were, however, very small. Even today, the number of SME speakers resident in the UK is probably not very large in comparison with most other minority groups. For instance, at the time of writing, there are approximately 3,000 Singaporeans *registered* with the Singapore High Commission as being resident in the UK. However, since registration with their respective High Commissions (both Singapore and Malaysia) is on a voluntary basis, one can only guess at the actual total number of Singaporeans and Malaysians resident in the UK. A reasonable guess, based on figures supplied by the two High Commissions, would be a figure of somewhere between 10,000 and 20,000 SME speakers. Despite the uncertainty over actual numbers, the two High Commissions are fairly certain that there has been no appreciable increase over the last two decades either in the number of students or the number of those permanently resident in the UK. Among reasons given for this pattern by the two High Commissions are (a) the increase in university fees and (b) the lower cost and comparable standard of living in urban Malaysia and Singapore. The SME speakers resident in the UK are engaged in the following typical range of occupations – as dentists, computer analysts, accountants: in other words, professional occupations, though there are also some in non-professional occupations, such as the catering trade. A striking difference between SME speakers and, say, the Hong Kong Chinese is their different *attitudes* towards their own ethnicity. The fact that a Singaporean is of Chinese origin does not guarantee that he/she speaks Chinese or adopts a way of life that is distinctively Chinese or necessarily eats Chinese food as often as possible. He or she may indeed do all these things, but equally he/she may not. A Chinese from Hong Kong almost certainly will (*cf* Ch. 13). Most Singaporeans or Malaysians (whether Chinese, Malay, Tamil, etc.) have little difficulty making the small cultural adjustments needed to understand most British TV or radio programmes and read English newspapers. A Chinese from Hong Kong on the other hand may not understand enough English to do so.

Changing patterns of language use

In striking contrast with the situation of WIC, there has been no consciously motivated movement towards maintenance of SME as a *public* solidarity marker in Britain. A speaker of SME who has been living in the UK for (say) ten years (particularly one who used the acrolectal end of the scale) will have developed, without necessarily trying to do so consciously, a variety of SME that is close to but not quite Br.E but which is nevertheless not used in Singapore and Malaysia either. In particular, the following features, which are typological for SME except in the most formal contexts (*eg* news broadcasts), will tend to drop out of public use in the UK:

1. Copula deletion ('He is very wicked' now preferred to 'He very wicked').
2. Third person subject–verb concord {-s} affixation ('He goes' now preferred to 'He go').
3. Deletion of word-final consonants, including consonantal past tense affixation (*eg* /-d/). This deletion characteristic is more resistant to standardization towards a Br.E model than the first two since – as with the /-d/ deletion observed by Labov (1968) for Black English Vernacular (BEV) – it is *both* a phonological and morphological feature, so that adjustment has to occur on two levels.[5]

Speakers of SME, including those using the acrolectal end of the scale, will use forms typical of the mesolectal (middle) or basilectal (low) end to signify solidarity, informality, intimacy and so on (Platt and Weber 1980; Tay 1978). Among the most vivid markers of this informal variety of SME are:

1. Use of 'already':
   eg 'He came already' = 'He has finally, emphatically come';
   ie 'already' = 'completive aspect'.
2. Use of {la} and {man}:
   eg 'Come on, la' or 'Come on, man' or even 'He came already la'. These are semantically empty morphs attached to lexical stems. They appear to have at least two functions: (a) they act as 'pure' solidarity markers, *ie* they mark SME as being distinctively SME; and (b) they take part in the *tonicity* of the tone unit.[6]

The point here is that SME speakers will hardly ever use such features from the meso/basilect when in the company of a Br.E speaker. This is not just a matter of courtesy. The meso/basilectal end of the SME scale has very low prestige connotations which are felt to be even lower when put alongside Br.E. (The fact that the Br.E speaker overhearing all this has not the slightest awareness of this prestige association is, of course, irrelevant.) Speakers of SME may even be *embarrassed* about using non-acrolectal SME in a Br.E context. This last observation is, however, applicable only to SME speakers who possess something like the full sociolectal range of the continuum. Even for non-acrolectal SME speakers newly arrived in the UK, however, basilectal features like {la} and {man} disappear almost at once – either through a strong awareness that a Br. E speaker will not understand these forms, or through intuitively knowing such solidarity features are inappropriate in the new context, or through a sense of its low prestige. And there are some permanent residents in the UK (*eg* some in the catering trade) who have *never* spoken the acrolectal variety of SME in their lives and therefore have never developed a variety of SME that approximates to Br.E in spite of having settled here since almost 1960.

For those who *do* modify their speech, possibly the most interesting indicators are on the phonological level, because certain features here – compared with features such as copula deletion and use of {1a} – are highly *resistant* to change.

Moreover most of the phonological features exemplified below – unlike the syntactic and morphological features already mentioned – are characteristic of *all* SME, irrespective of sociolect. In other words, while an SME speaker will quite likely have dropped the other ¹meso/basilectal features from usage in the presence of a Br.E speaker (sometimes within a year's residence in the UK) the phonological features take several years to modify. Some remain – even among those speaking acrolectal SME – throughout the lifetime of the speaker in the UK.

1. First, SME is a syllable-timed rather than stress-timed language (Wells 1982: 646).
2. Speakers of SME avoid 'liaison' between 'open' syllables and therefore also linking and intrusive /r/.
3. Consonant clusters tend to be reduced, both word finally and ʳ medially, *eg* recent → rɪsən (Platt and Weber 1980: 50), hundred → hʌnrəd (Wells 1982).
4. Closely tied to (3) above, word-final consonants are often replaced by glottal stops. As a result (Wells 1982) the following are sometimes homophonous: rip = rib = writ = rid = rick = rig, etc. = /lɪʔ/. Such relentless homophony is, however, unusual outside the meso/basilectal end.

These four features are vulnerable to modification towards Br.E pronunciation, especially the last. But any detectable shift may take several years. As these four features have the combined effect of producing a staccato rhythm, one of the more apparent signs of modification towards the prestige Br.E model is loss of this rhythm. But the change from syllable-timed rhythm to stress-timed (Br.E) rhythm must be understood to be dependent on all four factors acting together.

5. Back vowels in SME generally take less rounding than in Br.E. Hence, 'lot' /lɒt/ and 'thought' /θɒt/ have the same vowel /ɒ/ in SME (Wells 1982). Also, 'start' is pronounced stʌt/ (Wheré/ʌ/approximates to Cardinal /a/).
6. 'Shwa' (neutralization) is used far less in SME than in Br.E. (This ties in with the syllable-timed rhythm.)
7. However, word stress is present but systematically different from Br.E, eg 'character' is pronounced cha'racter, 'faculty' → fa'culty (Wells). Two not mentioned by Wells or Platt and Weber: category → kə'tɛgərɪ/, logarithm →/lo'gɛrɪðəm/, with the resultant sub-phonemic changes indicated.

As with the first four, the features (5)–(7) may take years to modify. Of these three features, vowel rounding is the 'Anglicizing' feature most consciously registered by SME hearers, since it is not used in non-British SME even in the acrolectal range. Loss of features (1) and (2) are, of course, regarded as certain signs of 'Anglicization' as well since, like vowel rounding, they are found only in Br.E or SME in the UK. On the other hand, (7) above, is not on its own an Anglicizing feature, since it tends in any case to be less common in the acrolectal range.

Finally, *tonicity* differs most sharply in that SME rarely employs a contrastive nucleus. For instance, a contrast between 'Hŏw aře yóu?' (Where R̂ + R̂ = compound fall–rise) and 'How ARE you?' is virtually never found ın SME, not even at the acrolectal end of the range. In other words, contrasts of this kind in Br.E are, strictly speaking, untranslatable into SME, though a close approximation to the second one might be achieved with SME 'How are you, man?', with tonicity falling on 'man'. Systematic use of contrastive nucleus is therefore a sign of Anglicization. Acquisition of an intonational contour typical of RP is virtually the last and least likely of the modifications that SME will undergo in response to the sociolinguistic situation in the UK.[7]

Language, culture, and community

Remarks made in the preceding section help to explain some special features in the matter of ethnolinguistic vitality in a British context. Ethnic identity can be a peculiarly difficult thing to define for an SME speaker – *eg* one may regard oneself as *both* Singaporean and Tamil or both Singaporean and Chinese, and within this kind of grouping, there may be those of Chinese origin who speak Malay and English in preference to Chinese (these are the 'Straits-born' Chinese – 'Straits' here referring to the Straits of Malacca – or *peranakan*, the Malay word, which means 'locally born', used to refer to those Chinese communities settled in Malaysia and Singapore for so many generations that they have lost all familial ties with China and speak and dress more like Malays). Indeed, while the notion of ethnicity may be of some limited use in defining Malaysians (since 50 per cent of them are ethnically Malays) it is practically useless in defining a Singaporean – and not even a Malay Malaysian would wish to claim that there were not other kinds of Malaysians.

In the light of all this, one of the best defining features of the people of this region is that they speak some form of SME. (Another by no means negligible one is certain common denominators in their taste for food.[8])

When SME is transported to Britain, however, one other sociolinguistic variable that is largely latent in the countries of origin is activated, *viz* a tendency to use a variety of English that most approximates to Br.E. It has been said that SME – at the acrolectal end – is in a high prestige position in Singapore (and to a lesser extent, Malaysia) and this prestige factor presumably falls in with a tendency partially to identify with the speech habits of the parent population in the UK. There are, of course, politico-historical reasons for this as well, Br.E. being, until around 1960, the language of the ruling class in Malaysia and Singapore.

Partly because the number of SME speakers resident in the UK is relatively small, partly because the size of the community is either static or marginally in decline and partly because there are such strong linguistic and cultural points of contact between SME speakers and the dominant indigenous culture of the UK, there is little evidence of a separate, distinct cultural life associated with this linguistic group in the UK, although such a community and culture undoubtedly exist. For instance, the main English-language newspapers in Malaysia and Singapore produce a weekly or monthly version available by air mail to residents in the UK. Malaysians and Singaporeans may gather in sizeable groups, either informally or, more officially, at the invitation of their respective High Commissions, to commemorate special public occasions (*eg* 'National Day', the feast of Ramadan or, as it is known in Malay, Hari Raya, and so on). There are plans at the moment to start a 'Singapore Association' in London for so-cial and recreational purposes and, in a sense, a 'Malaysian Association' has been in existence in the UK for decades, centred on what used to be 'Malaya House' in London's West End. Quite emphatically, the one essential ingredient in all these gatherings is the sharing of *food* peculiar to Malaysian and Singaporean cuisines – even more so than drink.

Education and language reproduction

Obviously, this is no more applicable to SME speakers than it is to speakers of WIC (Ch. 3). Where the SME speaker is also a member of (say) the Tamil-speaking or Cantonese-speaking com-munity in the UK, the desirability of mother tongue teaching for children may be acknowledged but not necessarily acted upon. In practice, many SME speakers are likely to be more anxious that their children speak and write standard Br.E to a high level of proficiency. Indeed, in a small but by no means eccentric propor-tion of SME speakers, part of the point of coming to live in an English-speaking country such as the UK, Canada or Australia is precisely to *get away* from the compulsory mother tongue teach-ing in languages such as Mandarin (Chinese), Malay or Tamil in Malaysia and Singapore, for it is not unusual to find, in families which speak SME by choice, a feeling that the compulsory Asian-language element (*ie* Mandarin/Tamil/Malay) in Singapore and Malaysian schools depresses the child's examination results, in ways which do not reflect the child's academic ability, had he/she only English to contend with. Most SME speakers in the UK would probably say, if asked, that mother tongue teaching was desirable, but very few would be convinced that such teaching had to be provided as a matter of course.

In the final analysis, the most potentially interesting question for speakers of SME is that of ethnic identity. No person from Singapore/Malaysia is able to say 'I am a Singaporean' or 'I am a Malaysian' without admitting the relevance of the next question that is sometimes asked 'Yes, but are you also Chinese, or Malay, or Indian, or . . .?' This is curious since – at least in Singapore – there are absolutely no socio-economic or status implications in such questions. And yet, there is a residual sense of ethnicity that coexists with the sense of nationhood, which is a separate kind of identity. There is no reason why this dual sense of identity should not continue. For the present, one of the truly distinctive traits of being a Singaporean is the use of SME – a trait that is distinctive of nationhood and social class, but neutral as far as ethnic origin is concerned. (The situation in Malaysia, as explained above, is rather different.) Will there come a time when the SME speaker, even at the basilectal end, will openly and spontaneously use this variety in a British context without embarrassment, but – like more and more Yorkshire speakers, or speakers of WIC or Liverpudlian – with pride?[9]

Acknowledgements

The author wishes gratefully to acknowledge the assistance given by the two High Commissions in the preparation of this paper.

Notes

1. The distinction made by some writers (*eg* Todd 1984) should be kept in mind, between an *official* language and a widely spoken one. The former is the language of government, the law courts and of administrations. It is not necessarily the one most widely spoken.
2. By 'standard British English' I mean some kind of spoken approximation of Received Pronunciation (RP), in the sense of RP used by Quirk and Greenbaum (1973) rather than something that (say) Daniel Jones might have recognized as RP.
3. This policy originated, if we go back far enough, from the Education Act of 1836 associated with William Bentinck and with Macaulay's famous/notorious Educational Minute of that some period, ridiculing vernacular education and myths in India.
4. Figures taken from the 1985 edition of *Statistics of Students from Abroad in the UK*, published by The British Council.
5. As far as I know, authorities such as Platt and Weber, who have written extensive and helpful accounts of SME, are unaware of the questions that might be raised by a comparison between SME and one particular typological feature of the Sino-Tibetan group of languages (*eg* Chinese) that is well known in studies of 'topicalization' and 'subjecthood'. Sino-Tibetan languages are so-called 'topic-prominent' languages (Li, 1978). Topic-prominent languages have clauses where syntactic relationships (*eg* anaphoric ones) between the topicalized noun phrase (NP) and the rest of the clause *override* relationships between grammatical subject and the rest of the clause. This never happens in subject-prominent languages (*eg* in English). A direct con-

sequence of this is that when ellipsis takes place, it is always the *grammatical subject* that is deleted, while 'topic' is retained, *eg* 'This man, (he is) very silly' → 'This man very silly'. The resultant deleted string looks very much like a case of copula deletion, but it may have been prompted by topicalization. The problem of course is that it is difficult to work back from the surface form to say whether it is one or the other, though knowing the context will help. (Intonation cannot help – unlike English, a tone boundary is not obligatory between topic and the rest of the clause.) Platt and Weber's remarks about 'pronoun copying' (1980: 74) may also be implicated in this process, though they do not seem aware of the possibility. The other point is that while topicalization is a *stylistic* feature in English, in Sino-Tibetan languages – and almost certainly in SME – it is a *grammatical* one.

6. Tay (1978) is undoubtedly correct in suggesting 'la' is derived from Hokkien. As far I know, however, no one has investigated the very likely possibility that 'la' (and 'man') have a role in the variation of the tonicity of the tone unit. Speakers of SME are aware of at least two distinct senses of 'la', depending on its pitch. A point not noted by Platt and Weber (1980) is that 'la' occurs elsewhere in South and South East Asia: *eg* it occurs in Sri Lankan English, though whether this is entirely coincidental is not known. See chapter 10 in this volume.

7. I have, for reasons of space, left out all discussion of lexico-semantic variables.

8. In saying all this, I have no wish to risk the wrath of the Ministries of Culture of both these countries by appearing to suggest there is not a distinctive Singaporean or Malaysian culture. A rich and vigorous post-independence culture has been developing for decades – but there are certain methodological problems in using this developing culture as a defining feature.

9. These sociolinguistic questions play a large part in the SME speaker's *institutionalized* attempts to understand his/her own identity. There is currently much discussion going on in Singapore among educationists about the variety of English to refer to as a model or as a prescriptive standard.

References

I have tried to select examples and allusions from books which are most readily obtainable in the UK, both in the following list and in my text above. This chapter – to my knowledge – is the first attempt to report on SME in the UK. All references below are therefore necessarily to works on SME as found in South East Asia, not Britain. As a general reference, the best place to look for publications on this variety is RELC (Regional English Language Centre, Singapore) and the RELC journal which reports on the use of 'new English' in South East Asia and Australasia. Work published in Singapore attests to a very vigorous and wide-ranging recent history of research on this subject, while there are only a handful of comparable British publications.

BICKERTON, D. (1973) 'On the nature of a creole continuum', *Language* **49**: 3.

LABOV, W. (1968) *Sociolinguistic Patterns*. Oxford: Blackwell.

LI, C. N. (1978) *Subject and Topic*. London: Academic Press.

LIM, C. (1978) *Little Ironies – Stories of Singapore*. Singapore Heinemann.

Ministry of Culture, Singapore (1980) *Singapore Handbook*, 1980.

PLATT, J. and WEBER, H. (1980) *English in Singapore and Malaysia*. Oxford and Kuala Lumpur: Oxford University Press.

PLATT, J., WEBER, H. and HÓ, M L. (1984) *The New Englishes*. London: Routledge & Kegan Paul.

QUIRK, R. and GREENBAUM, S. (1973) *A Concise Grammar of Contemporary English*. London: Harcourt Brace Jovanovich.

TAY, M. W. J. (1978) *The Uses, Users and Features of English in Singapore. A Test Case of the EIAL Question*. Proceedings of the Conference of English as an International Auxiliary Language, East-West Culture Learning Institute, Hawaii, April 1978.

TODD, L. (1984) *Modern Englishes*. Oxford: Blackwell (Language Library, with André Deutsch).

WELLS, J. C. (1982) *Accents of English*, vol. 3. Cambridge: Cambridge University Press.

Chapter 15

The Vietnamese Chinese speech community

Lornita Yuen-Fan Wong

Môt kho vang không môt nang chu.
A house full of gold is not worth a small bag of learning.

TE (1962: 146)

The majority of the Chinese community in Britain are from Hong Kong, with a small proportion from China, Singapore and Malaysia. Since the arrival of the Vietnamese refugees in the mid-1970s, however, the Chinese community has become more heterogenous in terms of composition and language. Based on fieldwork on the Chinese Vietnamese community in London (Wong 1988), this chapter attempts to explore the sociolinguistic background of the Vietnamese Chinese in order to see to what extent their needs in terms of language education are different from, or similar to, those of the Chinese from Hong Kong.

The sociolinguistic situation in Vietnam

The great majority of the population of North and South Vietnam speaks Vietnamese, a language known also as Quoc Ngu. There is some speculation about its linguistic affiliation, though it is sometimes thought to be distantly related to the Sino-Tibetan family. Certainly there is a strong Chinese influence on vocabulary and Nguyen Dinh Hoa (1961) estimates that about 60 per cent of the vocabulary in formal writing may be of Chinese origin.

Vietnamese orthography is based on an alphabetic system devised by seventeenth-century Catholic missionaries (Katzner 1977). It contains a wide range of diacritics, some of which are used to distinguish between vowel sounds, while others indicate tone.

Vietnam is an extremely linguistically diverse country. Besides Vietnamese, Thai is spoken by more than 800,000 in the north and Khamer by some 400,000 near the border with Cambodia. There is also a wide range of other languages (Katzner 1977). Muong, Nung, Miao and Yeo are spoken in the north, Jarai, Rhade, Bahnar, Sedang and various other languages are spoken in the south. In addition, many educated people also speak French, which was introduced into Vietnam during the French colonial period, 1861–1945.

However, the largest minority within Vietnam are the Chinese and, since by far the biggest group of Vietnamese in Britain are ethnic Chinese, this is the group which will form the focus for this chapter. The Vietnamese Chinese are not, of course, a linguistically homogenous community (*cf* also the description of Hong Kong Chinese and Malaysian and Singapore Chinese in this volume), speaking, for instance, Cantonese, Putonghua, Hokkien (Fukien), Chiuchow (Teochiu), Hakka and Hainanese. However, Cantonese is the lingua franca of the Chinese community.

Following the French withdrawal from Vietnam, the country was divided into North Vietnam (communist) and South Vietnam. In North Vietnam, Vietnamese has been the medium of instruction at all levels in education (DeFrancis 1977). Despite the fact that the Vietnamese language, especially its writing system, had been very much influenced by Chinese during the Chinese colonialism (111 BC to AD 939), Chinese was not promoted at school. As a result, most schoolchildren in North Vietnam are monolingual in Vietnamese. If they can speak Chinese, they will have learned the spoken form either from their parents or friends and, in most cases, will not be literate in Chinese.

In South Vietnam, both the socio-economic environment and educational policy have been completely different. According to Chan (1983), the south had better educational facilities than the north. In terms of language policies at school, Vietnamese, the national language, together with Chinese and French, the colonial languages, were used as language(s) of instruction by schools, depending on whether the school was single-medium or dual-medium. English was taught as a subject for one or two lessons per week only. There is evidence that Chinese literacy was high in South Vietnam. Adults consulted during the course of fieldwork, for instance, indicated that the ability to read Chinese novels and newspapers was not unusual.

When war broke out in Vietnam, many of the Vietnamese Chinese fled to Hong Kong as 'boat people'. They were placed for a period of between one and two years in refugee camps to wait for acceptance by other countries. Though they seemed to have been cut off from the majority society, visits paid by Cantonese-speaking friends and relatives in Hong Kong, workers from the welfare and voluntary organizations, camp guards and the Chinese mass media created a Cantonese-speaking environment where Vietnamese children could acquire or further develop their knowledge of Cantonese. In contrast, there was no way that Vietnamese children could learn English at school since they received no formal education in Hong Kong.

The Vietnamese community in Britain

According to the statistics given in the *Report of the Fourth National Conference on the Chinese Community in Britain* (National Children's Centre 1984) and in the *Sunday Times*, 3 April 1988 (Anon. 1988), between 13,000 and 16,000 Vietnamese refugees have been accepted by Britain since 1975. However, other unofficial estimates of the present Vietnamese population place this figure in the region of 22,000.

Unlike other Chinese in Britain, Vietnamese people were admitted to Britain as refugees. Their distribution seems to have been governed by the social welfare services or refugee organizations responsible for the settlement of refugees. In the course of my fieldwork, the resettlement camps have been described to me as 'concentration camps'. Vietnamese people were offered no choice as to where they could live and had to accept offers made to them by the organization concerned, irrespective of their personal preferences. For this reason, the Vietnamese are distributed all over the country.

With the passage of time, however, the Vietnamese have apprised themselves of information on employment opportunities, and there would seem to be a shift towards the south. Community sources estimate that about half of the total Vietnamese population (10,000) live in London, and ILEA (1981–87) statistics provide confirmation of this population movement. The Vietnamese community is concentrated in Southwark, Tower Hamlets, Hackney and Lambeth and, in 1987, the numbers of Vietnamese children exceeded 1,000 for the first time. (Table 15.1).

Changing patterns of language use

Since English was not promoted in Vietnam and Vietnamese

TABLE 15.1   Data on Vietnamese children from the ILEA *Language Census*, 1981-87

Year	Number	% PHLOE*
1981	157	0.3
1983	371	0.7
1985	774	1.3
1987	1,028	1.6

*PHLOE=Pupils with a home language other than or in addition to English.

TABLE 15.2   Percentage of fluent English speakers among Vietnamese children in London (extrapolated from ILEA 1981-87)

1981	8.9
1983	14.3
1985	14.7
1987	20.2

refugees had no opportunities to go to school in Hong Kong, the major problem encountered by the Vietnamese Chinese in Britain is in the acquisition of English. The ILEA language censuses (see Table 15.2) indicate that the proportion of fluent English speakers among Vietnamese children was the lowest of all linguistic minority groups with the exception of Bengalis. Many children report considerable difficulties in adjusting to schools in Britain (*cf* Wong 1988). There are some signs, however, that the level of English proficiency in the group as a whole has increased during the 1980s.

In spite of the present low levels of proficiency in English, language shift would seem to be inevitable after the initial period in Britain, and there are already reports of tension within families on this question. There are many cases, for instance, of families where the parents and older children use only Chinese in the home situation but where the younger British-born children are showing increasing dominance in English. In the course of my fieldwork, the language of communication among the young people at the Vietnamese community centre seemed to be mainly English with some Cantonese. Vietnamese, however, was rarely used.

Considerable emphasis is placed within the community on Chinese-language maintenance. In addition to ensuring good communication within the family, Cantonese is important for other extremely utilitarian reasons. Since many Vietnamese do not know English, it is difficult for them to get employment in the majority society. On the other hand, there are many job opportunities for Cantonese speakers in Chinese restaurants in Chinatown in central London. At present it seems that working in Chinese restaurants has become the major occupation of the Vietnamese Chinese in Britain, even though their number is not as high as that of the Hong Kong Chinese. As well as the Chinese restaurants, there is a small number of Vietnamese restaurants in Chinatown which also provide job opportunities for Vietnamese people, and here, too, the staff are required to know Cantonese. The learning of Chinese by Vietnamese children in Britain is thus not simply a matter of cultural maintenance: to some of the Vietnamese, Cantonese appears to have become a language for survival.

Language, culture and community

Since the majority of the Vietnamese in Britain are Chinese in origin, they have access to the same range of linguistic and cultural activities as other Chinese groups in the UK. They can go, for instance, to the various Chinese community centres to watch Chinese videos and borrow Chinese books. They can also participate in parties organized by the centres for the celebration of some major Chinese festivals such as the Lunar New Year and the Mid-autumn Festival.

Recently, some Vietnamese community centres have also been set up. The Club Vietnam in central London, for instance, is partly funded by the ILEA. It also organized various activities similar to those of the Chinese community centres for Vietnamese people. Owing to limited finance, the centre is only open on Sunday afternoon. Many teenagers regard the club as a drop-in centre where they can socialize with other Vietnamese people.

Education and language reproduction

The Vietnamese Chinese, like other refugee groups in Britain (see, for instance, Vol. 1, Chs 8 and 10) support their own ethnic language rather than the national language of the country which they have left. In Britain, the Vietnamese Chinese are particularly anxious that their children should maintain their competence in Cantonese for both cultural and utilitarian purposes but, for obvious political reasons, do not wish to promote Vietnamese.

While Chinese is not commonly taught in state schools, many

of the Vietnamese Chinese simply take advantage of the Chinese community schools set up mainly by the Chinese from Hong Kong and study with children of Hong Kong Chinese origin (see Vol. 2, Ch. 13 for a description of the organization and content of Chinese community-run classes). Vietnamese Chinese constitute the second largest group, about 24 per cent of the pupils in community schools (Wong 1988).

Whereas Hong Kong and Vietnamese Chinese clearly have a great deal in common, the different sociolinguistic background of the Vietnamese Chinese may also have implications for the teaching of Cantonese. Any children educated through the medium of Vietnamese, for instance, will have learned the skills associated with a Romanized orthography. When they learn the pronunciation of the Chinese characters, Vietnamese children possibly have an advantage over their Hong Kong Chinese peers who simply have to rely on their limited knowledge of English to help them to memorize the pronunciation of the Chinese characters. At present many Chinese teachers are experimenting with various methods in order to make Chinese teaching more effective.

As in the case of the Chinese from Hong Kong, the Vietnamese Chinese seem to have no alternative other than to treat Britain as their permanent home. Ethnically they are Chinese and many of them speak Chinese. Their needs are sometimes assumed to be the same as those of the Hong Kong Chinese, though this view can, in many ways, be shown to be short-sighted. A relatively high proportion of Hong Kong Chinese children have been born in Britain and are fluent in English; a major concern for their parents is, therefore, that they should be helped to maintain the mother tongue. The position of Vietnamese children is quite different. A high proportion are still at the stage of acquiring English to help them to adjust to the British education system. In other words, many of the Vietnamese pupils in British state schools are in need of language support.

At the moment, language support in British state schools is provided either by English speakers or, in a small number of cases, by Chinese bilingual teachers (ILEA 1986) but there seems to be an absence of Vietnamese bilingual teachers. No research has been done in the UK to compare the two linguistic competencies, Vietnamese and Chinese, of the Vietnamese Chinese children. To what extent will support in Chinese help Vietnamese Chinese children to succeed in the mainstream curriculum? The presence of Vietnamese Chinese in Britain is a relatively recent phenomenon. There can be no doubt as to the urgency – or the usefulness – of further detailed study on the sociolinguistic situation of this community.

References

ANON. (1988) 'Howe spurns boat people,' *Sunday Times*, 3 April 1988.

CHAN, E. (1983) *Needs of the Chinese Community in Lothian*. Lothian: Lothian Community Relations.

DEFRANCIS, J. (1977) *Colonialism and Language Policy in Viet Nam*. The Hague, The Netherlands: Mouton Publishers.

Inner London Education Authority (1981, 1983, 1985, 1987) *Language Census*. London: ILEA Research and Statistics.

Inner London Education Authority (1986) *Review of Language Education*. London: ILEA.

KATZNER, K. (1977) *The Languages of the World*. London: Routledge & Kegan Paul.

National Children's Centre (1984) *The Report of the Fourth National Conference on the Chinese Community in Great Britain, November 1932*. Huddersfield: National Children's Centre.

NGUYEN, D. H. (1961) *The Vietnamese Language*. Saigon.

TE, H. D. (1962) 'Vietnamese cultural patterns and values as expressed in proverbs.' Unpublished Ph.D. thesis, Columbia University, New York.

WONG, L. (1988) 'Education of Chinese children in Britain: a comparative study with the United States of America. Unpublished Ph.D. thesis, Institute of Education, University of London.

Part eight

The Middle East

For purely historical reasons, there is no well-established tradition of migration from the Middle East. With the exception of Israelis who, for a short period of time following the Second World War, were issued with British passports, there are no formal colonial links with this area of the world. There are, of course, various different communities of Middle Eastern students studying in British universities, some of whom have chosen to settle permanently. There are also what some writers have labelled 'annual migrants' from a wide range of Arab countries who live for part of the year in the more expensive areas of London.

For the purposes of the present volumes, however, Arabic has been treated as a Mediterranean rather than a Middle Eastern language. Although this classification may at first sight appear to oversimplify the geolinguistic reality, the decision was based on the fact that the most significant Arab settlement in Britain is Moroccan. Since Morocco is physically a western Mediterranean country, and since the pattern of Moroccan migration to Britain is very similar to that of other western Mediterranean countries like Portugal and Spain, this seems to us to be a logical classification.

This present brief part on the Middle East draws thus on just two communities: Hebrew and Farsi (or Persian). In both cases, we are dealing with communities which contain a high proportion of middle-class, well-educated speakers, though here, perhaps, the similarities end. Hebrew is of interest in a British situation not only because of the 30,000 Israelis currently resident in the UK, but because of the long and unbroken tradition of Hebrew as the language of religion in Jewish communities all over the world. The foundation of the state of Israel and the development of

Modern Hebrew as the national language has implications not
only for Jews in Israel but also for the Diaspora communities. In
addition to the traditional study of Classical Hebrew, many –
though by no means all – Jews now wish to study Modern
Hebrew. Language priorities and preferences within the Jewish
community will depend on a wide range of factors, including degree of commitment to Zionism and religious belief (see also Vol.
1, Ch. 11).

Farsi, too, has a long history and has exerted influence over
large numbers of people. It played a significant role, for instance,
in the development of Urdu, the national language of Pakistan
(see Ch. 9). In a British context, it is the language of a small
group who decided to settle permanently in Britain in the 1960s
and 1970s and whose numbers have swelled considerably in recent
years as a result of the political turmoil in Iran. As a recent
émigré community, it is possible to see in embryonic form many
of the developments which have been documented for longer-
established communities. Of particular interest is the shift
from a laissez-faire to a more committed attitude towards mother
tongue maintenance.

Chapter 16

The Farsi (Persian) speech community

Shahla Taheri White

نه ترسا نه یهودم من نه گبرم نه مسلمانم

نه شرقیم نه غربی ام نه بریم نه بحریم

دوئی از خود بدر کردم یکی دیدم دو عالم را

یکی جویم یکی دانم یکی بینم یکی خوانم

na tarsaa, na yahudam, man na gabram, na mosalmaanam
na sharghiam, na gharbiam, na barriam, na bahriam
doee as khod bedar kardam, yeki deedam doe aalamra,
yeki jooyam, yeki daanam yeki beenam, yeki khanam.

I am neither Christian, nor Jew, nor Zoroastrian, nor Moslem
I am not of East nor West; land nor sea
I have put duality away, I have seen that the two worlds are one
One I seek, One I know, One I see, One I call.

JALALUDDIN RUMI (THIRTEENTH CENTURY)

Persian, or Farsi as we call it today, dates back to pre-Islamic days. Historians report that before Islam there were three languages which were spoken in Iran in a triglossic situation (Khanlari 1365 AH Solar[1]). These languages were Pahlavi, Farsi and Darri. Pahlavi was used among royalty for social purposes. Farsi was used by the Zoroastrian priests as the language of religion, as well as being the language of the Fars province. Darri was the official language of the royal court and the north-eastern parts of the country.

Over the years, beginning from pre-Islamic days and extending through the Islamic invasion (AD 642–1037) and beyond, the terms Farsi and Darri gradually became more closely associated with each other until they finally became synonymous (Stevens 1962). The term Darri lost its grammatical function as a noun and came to be used as an adjective to describe Farsi, meaning 'fluent and clear'. Writers who have used 'Farsi-e-Darri' in this way include Ferdowsi, the author of the *Shahnameh* ('The Epic of Kings') and the poet, Moghaddassi. After the Arab invasion Farsi-e-Darri remained as the official, academic, technical and literary language of Iran.

It may be of interest to the reader to mention at this point a word about the possible origin of the English term 'Persian' used to denote the language of Iran. For many years the terms Pahlavi and Parsi were used interchangeably by scholars of India and other countries when referring to Zoroastrian texts from pre-Islamic periods (the two varieties were very similar). Could this association and the eventual survival of the term Parsi, and also the Greek equivalent 'Persis' (Lambton 1963), be the origin of the Anglicized term 'Persian' which in English denotes Farsi?

Written literature in Classical Farsi can be traced back to the first millenium BC (Khanlari 1365AH Solar[1]), though the script has evolved in this period from the iconic through cuneiform to Arabic. In addition to the vast literary tradition of Farsi, there is a wealth of poetry and prose written in the non-standardized languages and dialects of Iran.

A brief glance at the history of Farsi shows the tenacity of the language in surviving over centuries through the Arab, Mongolian and Turkish invasions of Iran. During these periods, Farsi has always been used as an instrument of defence against total submission, as a weapon against both colonial forces and invading powers. True there have been many semantic and some syntactic changes but the language has adapted and grown, expanded and extended rather than disappeared.

The contemporary position of Farsi is no different. Today the official standardized language of Iran is New Farsi (Khanlari 1365 AH Solar). This is the term used to describe the form of Farsi in use since the end of the Qajar and beginning of the Pahlavi dynasties in the early 1900s. During this period Farsi went through a process of 'purification'. Reza Shah Pahlavi founded the Farhangestan-e-Zabon (Language Academy) to create new terminology to replace terminology borrowed from European languages which related mainly to the military and civil service. For example, *artesh* (army) became *padaahand* (national defence). There was also an attempt to replace Arabic nomenclature with Farsi. Thus *Darrai* was used instead of *Maalyeh* for 'Finance Ministry' and *Marzbani* was used instead of *Amnyeh* for 'Gendarmerie'. Some of these changes were accepted by the public as part of the oral tradition of Farsi, while others remained only in the written form and a number failed to become established at all. Of those phrases that remain in literary usage, but are not widely used in everyday spoken language, *sepideh* for *sahar* (dawn), *baamdaad* for *sobh* (morning) and *dorood* for *salaam* (greetings) are some examples.

This new shift in Farsi had greatest impact on the language of academics and scholars. Also government officials and civil servants were consciously using the new terminology to demonstrate their loyalties and political alliances. However, the majority of the population, most of whom were illiterate, were unaware of such developments and uninterested in their outcome.

Since the Revolution in 1978, Farsi has once more been subject to attempts to mould its vocabulary. The popular religious surge in Islamic fundamentalism has had an important influence on Farsi, and the language has become once more a tool for social and political reform. The language has taken on a very marked Arabic tone. Many Arabic words such as *ommat* for *mellat* (nation) and *issargar* for *nikookar* (benevolent), for instance, are now in daily use in the language of journalism. Even names of some new government organizations, such as Ensar-al-Mojahedin (Friends of Mojahedin), are borrowed from Arabic. There has also been a shift of meaning in some everyday Farsi words. 'Brother' and 'sister' are no longer merely references to one's siblings, but are used by total strangers to show politico-religious solidarity as well as purity of thought and intent. And *Haji* is not necessarily a person who has been on a pilgrimage to Mecca, but a title awarded to any respectable compatriot.

New Farsi is now the official language of Iran and is also spoken in some neighbouring territories. In Afghanistan, Tadjikistan, Gorjestan, north-east Iraq, Caucasia and Azerbaijan different varieties of Farsi are in daily use by some 25 million people. However, Farsi is only one of the languages spoken in Iran. The country is extensive in terms of its area (the size of Western Europe) and sparse in population. Various significant events in its history and mass movements of its population as well as other geolinguistic factors have brought about many languages and dialects. Other languages spoken within its borders are Baluchi, Hebrew, Kurdish, Turkish, Arabic, Armenian, Assyrian and Azeri. In spite of this linguistic diversity, it would perhaps be true to say that 90 per cent of the 45–50 million population of Iran use standard Farsi for official purposes and as the language of literacy. Children from linguistic minority communities entering school learn Farsi as a second language.

Farsi in Britain

The Iranian population in the UK is estimated to number around 131,000 of whom 100,000 live in London. The London group are now mostly concentrated around Ealing. Provincial concentrations of Iranians are in Brighton, Manchester, Birmingham, Newcastle and Cardiff.

A significant number of Iranian students of secondary school and university age began to arrive in the UK from 1960 onwards. This influx lasted till the mid to late 1970s, coinciding with the economic boom of the late Pahlavi period. In contrast, the influx of an adult Iranian population to the UK began around 1977–78, prior to the Revolution, and continued until the outbreak of the Iran – Iraq War in 1980 (White 1982). Since then there has been a steady increase in the Iranian population, which has inevitably led to an increase in the number of children at the primary age level. This is indicated, for instance, in the findings of the various ILEA language censuses set out in Table 16.1.

Iranians in the UK have entered a wide variety of professions. Those who have completed their higher education here have

TABLE 16.1 Data on Farsi-speaking pupils from the ILEA *Language Census* (1981–87)

Year	Number
1981	298
1983	328
1985	429
1987	582

entered law, medicine, architecture, education and the media. Many others have provided their own employment, having set up import–export companies, clothing and food shops, supermarkets and restaurants. Casual labour and other domestic services are also part of their employment opportunities. At this early stage in the history of the Iranian émigré community, no particular recognizable job pattern has emerged. It is noticeable, however, that whereas settlement during the period (say) 1977–82 was composed almost exclusively of middle-class professionals, new arrivals now come from a broader range of backgrounds, though there are hardly any illiterate Iranians in the UK community.

Changing patterns of language use

The new Iranian arrivals often come with a basic knowledge of book English, having learned it as a foreign language. The older generation seem to stay within the community and, apart from brief encounters in language classes, have little contact with the wider English-speaking community. But the younger groups are in touch with the English language daily. In either case, intercultural communication, be it through the media, English classes, schooling, shopping or work situations, has brought the two languages into close contact. Many English words, for stylistic reasons as well as a show of knowledge and perhaps belonging, enter daily conversation. 'OK', 'Underground', 'station', 'ticket' are a few of such words. But then the same phenomenon happened in Iran in reverse. The British in Iran borrowed from Farsi, and still use, words such as *jube* (stream/gutter), *kebab* and *kucheh* (alley).

It would seem that the influence of Arabic on Farsi in Iran is being consciously resisted by many Iranians living abroad, almost as an act of political defiance. Opposition newspapers outside Iran, such as the London-based *Kayhan*, seem consciously to avoid using the new terminology which has been introduced within the country. In a similar vein, Iranians abroad, who are mainly of the literate minority, have become highly aware of their own language choice, be it in everyday face-to-face communication or in the poetry or prose that is being created abroad. Another interpretation of this pattern of language choice is, of course, that Iranians abroad have not yet adapted to the 'new' vocabulary because they are not constantly exposed to it in their new environment. Alternatively considerations of both exposure and political commitment may be impeding the complete assimilation of such shifts.

There can be little doubt, however, that maintenance of language and culture has become a priority issue for families. Where it used to be fashionable to use a great deal of code-switching between English and Farsi, more and more Iranians are making a conscious effort to speak 'pure' Farsi. Nationalism has become a very strong force outside the country and is evident in the language choices made by members of the Farsi speech community.

The situation of British-born children is clearly very different from that of their Iranian-born parents. Many children whose parents were of the original student group of the 1960s are struggling to maintain their community language. Consciousness of cultural ties has only recently become an issue, and the all-pervasive use of English as the language of the wider community means that there has to be a sustained effort to use Farsi for family communication. In such a situation, language use can become artificial, structured and superficial rather than natural and spontaneous. Many of the phrases that do not have their equivalent in English, those to do with emotions and abstract concepts, are missing from their children's Farsi repertoire. This situation is changing, however, as children are starting to take advantage of community provision for mother tongue teaching. One parent, whose two children attended an Iranian community school remarked, for instance, that when he is looking at beautiful scenery while on a family outing and mentions how *Ba Safa* the view is, his children understand what he means even though there is no direct English equivalent of this sentiment.

Language, culture and community

The cultural activities of the Iranian community are gradually increasing. Concerts, plays, films, videos, audio cassettes, occasional issues of a variety of magazines, a bookshop in Kensington and a well-established Farsi newspaper (*Kayhan*) printed in London contribute not only to cultural maintenance but also to its extension, shift and adaptation. Many families who support community functions and organizations include their children in their outings and in this way maintain cultural ties with Iran.

Contact with Iran has an interesting and yet shifting pattern. As political exiles start gaining re-entry rights, families begin to travel back to 'base' after several years of exile. These visits have led to the import of story- and textbooks, magazines and brochures in Farsi, and many foodstuffs packaged in Iran with Farsi labels. Children from families who are now regularly visiting Iran are experiencing a sudden language explosion within their

homes and finding a more viable and worthwhile reason for their
own language maintenance.

Education and language reproduction

There is no provision for teaching Farsi in mainstream state
education in the UK. Only one London secondary school (Holland Park) provides tuition in Farsi in the evenings. The task of
maintaining and extending the children's language is therefore
left entirely to the community itself. In London, there is a variety
of such provision: the Embassy sponsors primary-level classes;
Kanoon-e-Iranian teaches children at the primary level; Kanoon-
e-Iran classes offer tuition up to O level; and the Rustam Iranian
School prepares students up to A level and the International Bac-
calaureate. The only known Farsi class provided outside of
London is in Brighton. While the number of children studying,
learning and extending their community language is very small,
the existing provision has raised consciousness of the issue, however, and seems to have created a demand.

In most cases, mother tongue teaching follows the methodology
used in Iran and makes use of the Iranian government's centrally
published textbooks. In other words the teaching is based on
mother tongue teaching within its own majority base, where the
target language is used both inside and outside the home and
school. Only in one community school (Rustam Iranian School)
have attempts been made to introduce modern communicative
methods of language teaching aimed at developing and extending
the children's language and producing a culture-related language-
learning experience. Teaching materials are scarce and mostly
teacher-made. All teachers are qualified and most have also
gained the RSA Diploma in the Teaching of Community Languages.

Although there is no provision for the teaching of Farsi in the
mainstream, both Persian and Classical Persian are available as
examination subjects. In June 1987, for instance 120 candidates
presented themselves for the University of London Examinations
Board O level in Persian, while there were 13 candidates for the
A level in Classical Persian. The current situation regarding examinations is in flux, but it is likely that Farsi GCSE will be
offered by the London and East Anglian Group by 1990.

Summing up the situation of Farsi in the UK, the community
is new and its future as a minority group in UK is presumably
dependent on political factors. The pattern of resettlement is unique and cannot be compared with that of any other community.

Attitudes of the first- and second-wave arrivals are different and it is difficult to make any confident predictions in terms of the future of this community. What is clear, however, is the growing importance of mother tongue maintenance within the community and the need for greater support for community efforts. The marked increase in the number of 5-year-olds who are brought to community schools for developing their literacy skills in Farsi, as well as a greater number of GCSE and A level candidates, demonstrates that we need institutional support at both ends of the literacy scale. This support must be in terms of materials, resources, teacher power and venues.

Note

1. The Iranian solar calendar is computed from the time of the prophet Muhammad's *hajira* or migration (AH signifies' after *hajira*) from Mecca to Medina.

References

ILEA (1987) *Language Census*. London: ILEA Research and Statistics.
*KHANLARI, P. N. (1365 AH Solar) *History of Farsi Language*. Tehran: Nashr-e-Noe.
LAMBTON, A. K. S. (1963) *Persian Grammar*. Cambridge: Cambridge University Press.
STEVENS, R. (1962) *The Land of the Great Sophy*. London: Methuen.
WHITE, D. V. (1982) 'Mother-tongue teaching with specific reference to Farsi.' Unpublished thesis, Education Department, Goldsmith College, University of London.

Further reading

*Bahman Press (1364 AH Solar) *Ketab-e-sokhan*. Iran (An anthology of prose).
BOCHNER, S. (ed.) (1982) *Cultures in Contact*. Oxford: Pergamon Press.
BOYLE, J. A. (1987) *Persia: History and Heritage*. London: Henry Melland.
LEVI, R. (1969) *An Introduction to Persian Literature*. New York: Columbia Univ. Press.
MATHESON, S. A. (1972) *Persia: An Archaeological Guide*. London: Faber & Faber.
SAFFAARI, K. (1357 AH Solar) *Persian Mythology and Stories in English Literature*. Tehran: Tehran University Press. (Bilingual text.)

*Books written in Farsi.

Chapter 17

The Hebrew speech community

Judy Keiner

וְעַד־אַרְגִּיעָה לְשׁוֹן שָׁקֶר׃   שְׂפַת־אֱמֶת תִּכּוֹן לָעַד

Sfas Emes tikun lo'ad, ve'ad argiyoh lashon shoker (Ashkenazi pronunciation)[1]
Sfat Emet tikun la'ad, ve'ad argiyah lashon shaker (Modern Hebrew/Sephardi pronunciation)

The language of truth endures forever, but the lying tongue is but for a moment   (PROVERBS 12:19)

Hebrew has a unique history. It can be looked on as both the oldest and the newest language in the world. In Jewish religious tradition, Hebrew is the divine language, through which the Creator brought the world into being and dictated the words of the Torah to Moses. In the tradition, it was also the language that all the people of the world spoke before the building of the Tower of Babel, and its subsequent destruction, created our present multilingual world.

Hebrew is perhaps unique in the modern world in having been successfully re-created as a modern state/ethnic vernacular and official language as the result of a conscious commitment having been made by several generations of pioneers to its renewal.

The present chapter looks at the use of Hebrew in the UK by two different groups of speakers; those Jews who use the language for religious purposes alone, and speakers of Modern Hebrew, who, for various reasons, have migrated from the state of Israel, or who use Modern Hebrew as an expression of their relationship to Zionism.

The historical development of Hebrew

Linguistically, Hebrew is classified as a Semitic language. Linguistic classification alone, however, obscures those historical and ideological features of languages which make them remarkable. Hebrew was first spoken by the Jews of the historical land of Israel, which includes modern Israel and wider areas of present-day Syria, Jordan and Egypt. Well before the final destruction of the last Jewish kingdom of Judah by the Romans, it had been replaced as the main vernacular by Aramaic. None the less, it continued to be in daily use by Jews for over 2,000 years. All prayers were said in Hebrew and it was regarded as important from the earliest days of the exile to the present that children should be taught at least to read Hebrew for the purposes of prayer. Hebrew was also used as the language of communication between the rabbis of Jewish communities in the Diaspora, for both religious and academic and legal purposes.

Historically, the Jewish tradition was very supportive towards a bilingual approach to the use of Hebrew. Bilingual texts of prayers were produced because it was felt important that Jews who had no extended education in Hebrew, including women, should be able to understand what they were saying, as well as understand the meaning of the Scripture passages, readings of which are central to synagogue services.

It was perhaps only because the broad mass of Jews already had this background of familiarity with the Hebrew language, if only at the level of reading with bilingual texts, that the Zionist project of reclaiming the language was able to be made a reality.

There are four main classes of Hebrew users today. The first are mother tongue Hebrew speakers from birth, for whom Israel is the country of origin. It must be remembered, however, that Israel itself is only just over 40 years old, and that the majority of the present population were not born in Israel, having immigrated after the founding of the state in 1948.

The second are speakers for whom Hebrew is either today their first or second language, but whose mother tongue was another language: native speakers have only recently become the majority in Israel. A very substantial section of Israel's Jewish population are the Mizrachi Sephardi Jews[1] whose countries of origin are the Mediterranean and Arab countries, and their Israeli-born children. Their mother tongue languages are Arabic and other oriental languages. Many of the Israeli Hebrew speakers resident in Britain are Mizrachi Sephardis.

The third are Orthodox religious Jews, and particularly those from the small but growing minority of fundamentalist Jewish communities. They are users whose command of Hebrew is extensive, but who regard Hebrew, as the Divine language, as being appropriate only for the sacred purposes of prayer and study. Some of these communities explicitly forbid the use of Hebrew for other than sacred purposes. Their main vernacular is likely to be Yiddish, as for the most part they are the descendants of Eastern European Ashkenazi Jews (see Vol. 1, Ch. 11). However, in Israel, such Jews may nevertheless use Modern spoken Hebrew as a vernacular when they are obliged to do so by the needs of official exchanges with the state and with the secular Jews who form the majority of the Jewish population.

The fourth class of Hebrew users are the majority of community-identified Diaspora Jews who continue to use Hebrew for prayer, as their ancestors did, reading but usually not having reading comprehension without the help of bilingual texts. An increasing number of Jews in the Diaspora, however, have no current involvement in religious practice, and their children will not be learning Hebrew even at the level of reading capability. Some have, however, developed a commitment to learning Modern Hebrew as a mark of their commitment to Zionism, and as a substitute for the religious commitments of their parents' or grandparents' generation.

Hebrew is one of three national languages of Israel. The other two are Arabic and French. As a Jewish state, it is Israel's principal language, used in Knesset (parliamentary) and court proceedings. However, the position of the substantial Arab minority within the 1948 borders is recognized by according Arabic the status of a national language, and schools for Arab Israelis are conducted in Arabic. There is, however, an asymmetrical position, reflecting the political dominance of the Jewish majority: Arabic-medium schools are required to teach their pupils Hebrew, whereas Arabic is an optional language for Jewish Israeli schoolchildren in spite of the fact that it is the mother tongue of a very substantial proportion of Israeli Jewish families.

The successful re-creation of Hebrew as mother tongue and principal vernacular did not come about simply through the acts of will and commitment of the pioneers of modern Israel. During the pre-Second World War years of Jewish settlement in Israel, Zionist groups pursued a militant *Rak Ivrit* (only Hebrew) campaign, particularly directed against the use of Yiddish, which was the main language of immigrants to Palestine. The campaigners followed the extraordinary example of the pioneer of Modern Hebrew, Eliezer Ben-Yehuda, who adopted the language as his sole means of communication in 1882 when there were no other vernacular speakers, and insisted on using only Hebrew, regardless of whether listeners had any understanding or not. Pressure was also applied to other Jewish settlers who did not adopt this course, including threats to newspaper kiosk owners, attacks on Yiddish presses, as well as open opposition to Jews in public places seen to be using languages other than Hebrew.

As children either arrived in Israel as immigrants and refugees, or were born there, the education system insisted on use of Hebrew alone, with strong pressure being put on parents to abandon the use of their own mother tongues in favour of the language of what was seen as secular Jewish redemption. Since the days of the state, compulsory army service for both men and women, with long periods of continuing reserve call-ups for men, has equally served to reinforce Hebraization, by involving the participants in extended total immersion in Hebrew. Since the foundation of the state, all new Jewish immigrants now spend a period of up to six months in an *Ulpan*, an immersion course in Hebrew which aims to give them enough Hebrew for most purposes of daily life.

Modern Hebrew was standardized by the work of Eliezer Ben-Yehuda and others from the 1880s. The forms of Hebrew from the earliest known texts, through to that used by rabbis and the first Modern secular Hebrew writers in the Diaspora in the eighteenth and nineteenth centuries, have evolved as extensively as has English in a much shorter period of history. A Hebrew academy exists, whose functions include guardianship of the language, analogous to the role of the Académic Française. This issues new Hebrew words required by changes in technology, etc. However, because of the very extensive involvement of Israelis, including leading technologists and professionals, with the United States, the adoption of English loan words and phrases is extensive.

The Zionists' adoption of Hebrew marked a commitment to follow the Sephardi rather than the Ashkenazi pronunciation system, which was the traditional one of European Jewry. This choice was based on their belief that the Sephardi pronunciation was closer to that used by the Jews in the pre-exilic period than the Ashkenazi.

From the start, however, there has been considerable opposition to this by fundamentalist Jews, who reject in principle the appropriation of one Jewish community's historico-linguistic inheritance by another. Moreover, by their commitment to retaining Ashkenazi Hebrew, they help to demonstrate their rejection of any activities which might constitute secularization of Hebrew. They use Hebrew for all prayers, and for purposes of study.

Hebrew is written from right to left and uses two scripts: the 'square' block script for print, and a cursive for writing. Vowels are indicated in school-books, prayer books and textbooks for learners with a system of diacritics above and below the consonants, but are omitted in newspapers, magazines and books for general use.

Hebrew in Britain

The Cultural Attaché of the Israeli Embassy estimated in late 1988 that 30,000 Israelis are now settled in Britain. Thus Israelis form almost 10 per cent of the total UK Jewish population. However, as we have already seen, there is not necessarily a straightforward relationship between bearing Israeli nationality and speaking Hebrew.

There is a wide variety in patterns of settlement by Israelis in Britain. Significant numbers live in university towns, as coming to Britain to study was in the past a frequent reason for subsequently settling in the country. However, most Israelis are to be found in London where the community consists of two main groups. The first tends to be more prosperous, and is often professionals who are either first- or second-generation Israelis-born of Ashkenazi descent. They tend to live in and around the London borough of Camden, and will frequently define themselves as secular Jews. More religiously committed expatriate Israelis of this type would tend to settle in the main Jewish community centres in the north-west of the city, such as the London boroughs of Barnet and Brent.

The second grouping is of largely blue-collar and self-employed Israelis of Sephardi origin. The adults are frequently second-time immigrants, having left one of the Arab countries, Persia or India to settle in Israel, and subsequently moving on to Britain by reason of having a British passport from colonial days. The children of this group are almost invariably Israeli-born. They tend to retain strong links with their own community, being generally highly religiously committed, and founding their own synagogues or prayer groups.

Another large group of Hebrew users, only a few of whom may have been born in Israel, are the fundamentalist Jews who live in separate communities, mainly based in the Stamford Hill area of the London borough of Brent. They use Hebrew every day,

TABLE 17.1   Data on Hebrew speakers from ILEA *Language Census*
(1981–87)

Year	Number
1981	356
1983	325
1985	363
1987	968

but almost exclusively for purposes of prayer. This Hebrew will
be spoken or read in the Ashkenazi pronunciation.

ILEA *Language Census* data, set out in Table 17.1, point to
steady numbers of children reporting themselves as speakers of
Hebrew.

According to the last survey of the Board of Deputies published in 1985, there are some 330,000 Jews in Britain. Almost
all British Jews over the age of 40 are likely to be able to read
Hebrew, but this knowledge cannot be assumed of young adults
and children. Their degree of familiarity with Hebrew and
methods of acquiring the language will be discussed below in the
sections on language, culture and community and education and
language reproduction.

Changing patterns of language use

Among the Israeli-born Modern Hebrew speakers referred to
above, Hebrew will usually be used in the family, but only in
those cases where both parents are Hebrew speakers; many Israelis who settle marry British Jews or Gentiles. Of the children
who have both parents as Hebrew speakers, very few will use the
language outside the home, even if they are in a Jewish school
with large numbers of other Hebrew speakers. During a three-
month period the writer spent teaching in a Jewish primary school
in north London, only one pair of first-language Hebrew-speaking
siblings was observed spontaneously using Hebrew to communicate with each other, although the school strongly supports,
indeed prizes, the use of Hebrew.

It might be expected that there would be a significant difference between those Israeli settlers in the UK who are
permanent settlers, and those who are temporary, in terms of
commitment to maintaining their language. However, attitudes
towards settlement outside Israel carry particularly strong
ideological overtones among both the Israeli and the wider Jewish

community. Since Israel's very foundation rests on the Zionist project of promoting universal Jewish *Aliyah* – or emigration to Israel, the very idea of Jews voluntarily emigrating from Israel to the Diaspora is anathema. Official Israeli and British Jewish attitudes have been until recently to downplay or ignore continuing Israeli Jewish emigration. The Hebrew words for emigration and emigrants *Yeridah* and *Yordim* carry overtones of shame, and few emigrants would voluntarily apply this label to themselves. Thus, most settlers would tend to describe themselves as temporary, however permanent their settlement might be in practice.

There is a significant number of 'professional Israelis' who are here either as temporary officials with the role of promoting Israel in the Jewish community, or who may be settled here as teachers and community workers for Jewish schools and communal organizations. These Hebrew speakers do usually use Hebrew among themselves in their professional environment, but, as observed by the writer, its use varies according to the sensitivity of the subject-matter concerned and the relationship between the speakers. Thus, in the primary school referred to above, two teachers who were not mother tongue Hebrew speakers regularly conversed in Hebrew where the situation appeared to be one which required some demonstration of solidarity between them.

Another important issue in the area of language change is associated with the adoption by Ashkenazi British Jewish communities of the Sephardi pronunciation. The situation familiar to generations of immigrants now exists, where children rather than parents are the users of the new prestige form. Children can be heard correcting their parents when the latter refer to *Shabbes* rather than the Sephardi *Shabbat*. In synagogues, congregations hover uneasily between Ashkenazi and Sephardi usage, particularly among the under-40 age-range. Many individuals are now unable to sustain either usage consistently and slide between the two. There are also instances of hypercorrection among former Ashkenazi readers who have subsequently either learnt Modern Hebrew or to read with Sephardi pronunciation.

The Jewish community in Britain may therefore be bidding farewell to a great historic variety of Hebrew pronunciation which was shared with Jews all over Europe over hundreds of years, with as little thought as it formerly took to discarding Yiddish. It remains the case, however, that the fundamentalist community continues to retain and prize the Ashkenazi usage, and is becoming more militant about it, seeing this as an important marker differentiating them from the secular state and Jewish idol-worshipping, as they would put it. It may come about that those non-fundamentalist Jews who are increasingly disillusioned with Israel and with the Zionist project will seek to preserve Ashkenazi Hebrew in the wider Jewish community, in the same way that they have begun to support the revival of Yiddish.

Language, culture and community

There has traditionally been a strong degree of communal support among British Jews for fund-raising and cultural activities concerned with Israel, and admiration for the use of Modern Hebrew. However, particularly since the Israeli invasion of Lebanon and the more recent Palestinian uprising, that support has become more muted, or rather, the community has tended to polarize between those who continue to support Israel unreservedly and those who feel either mildly or more strongly critical.

For the most part, Israelis tend to retain strong contacts with their home country, visiting family at least once a year, and those from the Sephardi communities tend to have the strongest and most regular contacts, with large extended families. Among the religiously committed, any opportunity to spend major festivals in Israel, particularly Passover, and the high holidays in the early autumn, is much welcomed.

There is, however, a very small minority of Israelis who have settled here because they wish to dissociate themselves either from the current situation of the Israeli occupation of the West Bank and Gaza, or because they have fundamental political objections to the existence of a Zionist state *per se*. Their main contacts are with like-minded Israeli oppositionists in Israel and in other countries, but some feel unable to visit Israel either because they fear arrest, or because they cannot bear to return to Israel in its current state.

There is a significant number of Sephardi Israeli settlers who work entirely in businesses run by other Israelis, such as bakeries and restaurants. In this environment, almost all language use is Hebrew, and there are some speakers who can only speak a very little English, although they may be Arabic as well as Hebrew speakers.

There tends to be relatively little contact between Israeli secular Jews and the mainstream British Jewish community, except where the former have a specific role in Zionist organizations. Until very recently, there were no organized institutions specifically for Israeli Hebrew speakers in England. Although there are a number of Hebrew booksellers in London, these cater for the religious market, and stock few modern secular texts in Hebrew. A selection of the most popular Hebrew newspapers such as *Yediot Achronot* (Latest News) and *Maariv* (Evening) can, however, readily be obtained from those newsagents in central and north-west London who carry a range of foreign-language newspapers. Recently, the Israeli Embassy has promoted the foundation of a Hebrew-language speaking club in London for Israeli settlers in Britain; it has an underlying aim of fostering a return to Israel, and, for this reason, may have relatively limited success.

The Israeli state, through the Zionist Federation, has developed an extensive array of schemes to promote Hebrew and contact with Israel for British Jewish adults and youth. These include kibbutz volunteer work, and courses for those involved in youth work and leadership roles in various professions related to Jewish communal organizations. In addition, all children at Jewish day schools are now being given an opportunity to spend at least a two-week period in Israel at some point in their school careers. The only Jewish comprehensive school in London, the JFS comprehensive, offers an opportunity for a one-term exchange with a school in Israel.

For those who have not acquired Hebrew as a mother tongue, and who do not attend a Jewish school, the main and often sole exposure to the language is in a religious context.

It has been since the earliest days of the Jewish Diaspora a standard requirement for a boy reaching the age of 13 to memorize and chant extended passages of the Torah and an associated reading from the Scriptures for the bar mitzvah ceremony that marks his assuming the religious obligations of the adult male. In the Reform and Liberal congregations to which up to 20 per cent of British Jews belong, the same requirements are made of girls.

Prayers in Hebrew are also a constant accompaniment of the Orthodox Jewish home; blessings for all manner of foods, for the completion of religious duties, such as lighting of sabbath candles, and in celebration of festivals, and a wide range of natural phenomena, such as witnessing a rainbow. Women and children have traditionally had as much involvement in using Hebrew for such purposes in daily life in the home as men.

Hebrew speakers have access to a very wide range of literature. First and foremost, of course, come the Scriptures. For Orthodox and fundamentalist Jews, the words of the Torah (the Pentateuch) are the literal words which the Almighty dictated to Moses. Portions of the remaining sections of the Tanach (Old Testament) are also read as part of the synagogue service readings of the Law, and the prayers of services and private prayer alike are for the most part compiled from extracts from the various books of the Tanach, particularly from the Psalms.

In post-exilic times, poetry, philosophical, mystical and other devotional works were written in Hebrew, although it was no longer the mother tongue of the speakers (*cf Penguin Book of Hebrew Verse*, Carmi 1987). Many of the poems in particular came to be incorporated in the services and prayers for the major holy days, particularly the New Year and the Day of Atonement.

Modern Hebrew built an extraordinary range of literature from the early days of its revival. One of the decisions of the First Zionist Congress, in 1897, was to set up a committee for literature (Vital 1975). The stories and poems of such writers as Achad Ha'am and Chaim Nachman Bialik were demonstrations that, although they were fervent and committed Zionists, what they produced was not Zionism-as-literature but outstanding literature which was imbued with Zionist perspectives. In the last forty years, there has been a great flowering of literature, poetry and drama. Among those who have acquired international reputations are the late Nelly Sachs, and Amos Oz, A. B. Yehoshua, Aharon Apelfeld and Yehuda Amichai. The themes of the Holocaust and the Arab–Israeli conflict are central to the work of these writers.

There is another vast literature in Hebrew, originating from early exilic days, which continues to be produced today, and that is religious textual commentary and ethical works, particularly that originating in the fundamentalist communities. This literature is just as likely to be produced in New York, or one of the other main contemporary centres of fundamentalist community life, as in Israel.

Education and language reproduction

It is estimated that 25 per cent of Jewish children in the UK are being educated in Jewish day and boarding schools. A further 28 per cent are estimated to attend community-organized religious supplementary classes, but it is not clear what degree of overlap there is between these categories of children.

Although Hebrew is not taught in mainstream state schools, the University of London Examinations Board (ULEB) offers GCE O level and A level examinations in Modern and Classical

TABLE 17.2 Examination entries for Classical and Modern Hebrew

Examination Board	Date	Examination	Subject	No. of candidates
NEA	June 1988	GCSE	Modern Hebrew	249
ULEB	June 1987	O level	Classical Hebrew	226
ULEB	June 1987	O level	Modern Hebrew	61
ULEB	June 1987	A level	Modern Hebrew	37
ULEB	June 1987	A level	Classical Hebrew	43
ULEB	June 1988	A level	Modern Hebrew	30
ULEB	June 1988	A level	Classical Hebrew	34

Hebrew while the Northern Examining Association (NEA) offers a GCSE in Modern Hebrew (see Table 17.2).

Through the Zionist Federation, Israel is able to play a key role in determining the nature of Hebrew taught in Jewish schools and supplementary classes. Almost without exception, all such schools outside the 15,000 strong fundamentalist community have adopted the Sephardi pronunciation for their teaching. All children in Jewish schools, including primary schools, learn Hebrew as a modern language; Hebrew for religious purposes is additionally taught through a Jewish studies curriculum. Classes in conversational Modern Hebrew are also offered through adult education institutes, and extensively through synagogues and other Jewish community organizations. In such classes, the emphasis is on promotion of and support for Israel.

However, there has also been a recent resurgence in the British Jewish community of religious commitment, and there are increasing numbers of evening and short-course classes for adults which involve studies of biblical and rabbinic Hebrew. The supplementary schools which are attended by Jewish children are organized through synagogues, and Hebrew for religious purposes is taught, usually at the level of reading, and following a dual text. More advanced pupils may learn translation. It remains an important aim for boys of even moderately religiously committed families to acquire the not inconsiderable command of reading, memorizing and chanting Hebrew required for the bar mitzvah ceremony. Increasingly, parallel ceremonies for girls are being developed, known as the bat mitzvah or eshet chayil (woman of worth) ceremonies. In the Reform and Liberal religious communities, girls undertake exactly the same part as boys in their bar mitzvah. In the Orthodox communities, girls follow a programme which includes Hebrew studies and a special service, but do not read from the Law in synagogue.

The fundamentalist communities regard studies in Hebrew as central to their educational programmes. Under Jewish law, all Jews, including women, are required to study, and this study should include knowledge of prayers and the Tanach. The Hebrew taught is the Ashkenazi pronunciation.

The Zionist Federation has sponsored the development of a range of teaching materials for Modern Hebrew, and, in London, the London Board for Jewish Religious Education has played a leading part in developing materials for religious use of Hebrew for children. For adult education classes, use is frequently made of videos of Israeli television series designed to teach Hebrew to newly arrived immigrants. These feature families finding their way in Israel in the period following their arrival.

The materials produced for children unfortunately retain many of the worst features of traditional grammar books and graded reading schemes. They are usually monochrome print, consisting of simple narratives and series of repetitive exercises. The content usually features life in Israel or in the Jewish family, although some include fairy-tale narratives.

Many people have begun to question the quality and efficacy of the Modern and religious Hebrew teaching currently being delivered to children in Jewish schools and supplementary schools. It is commonly believed in the community that the teaching, although often carried out by devoted individuals, is remarkably unsuccessful. Many children who have had some years of daily Modern Hebrew lessons are unable to speak it spontaneously, and do not find it easy to recite or follow prayers. Some part of this situation may well be related to the unimaginative materials and approaches used.

In a situation where most Jewish primary schools are now using 'real books' – first-class picture books with simple texts – for teaching reading in English, the same children are expected to learn to read Hebrew from primers which have little or no attraction for them. It would be an interesting research project to seek to produce a 'real books' approach to teaching Hebrew, using Hebrew translations of internationally famous children's authors, such as Sendak and others, and compare its success.

A deeper problem may arise from the paradox of teaching Hebrew to children as a modern language when very few of them are likely to use it to any extent in the short term. It is of course a problem which led to the failure of the early 1960s attempts to promote the teaching of French in British primary schools. The main opportunity most British Jewish children have to use Hebrew is for religious purposes – and this only if they come from families that have a significant degree of religious involvement. For most British Jewish families today, this is increasingly unlikely, ironically, because for many of them identification with Israel has long since replaced religious involvement as the main manifestation of Jewish ethnic identity.

It may be that more attention is needed to match Hebrew teaching to the purposes for which children either enjoy using it or are successfully engaged in using it. This may imply a reconsideration of the separation between language and religious studies, and a greater integration, in Jewish schools, of the Hebrew/religious studies curriculum into the secular curriculum.

It is likely that the number of Israelis settling in this country will continue to increase, notwithstanding the ferocity of British immigration laws, though not in numbers that would sound alarm bells with the anti-immigration lobbies. At present, there is little support for this group of Hebrew speakers, paradoxically because so much is being devoted by the Israeli government and by the Jewish community to promoting Hebrew for British Jews. Many of these speakers in any case would feel alienated from any Israeli government venture. While sending their children to Jewish schools does provide a way of sustaining their children's knowledge of Hebrew, it is unlikely to provide for future linguistic vitality.

Whatever the outcome of these issues, it remains the case that, 2,000 years after the apparent demise of Ancient Hebrew as a living language, the vibrant state of Modern Hebrew, and the equally fervent continuing promotion of traditional religious Hebrew in Orthodox Jewish communities, serve as an inspiration to those who struggle against the idea that minority languages are dying or redundant.

Notes

1. Stephardi Jews are those who settled in Spain and Portugal following dispersal from Palestine. Following persecution under the Inquisition and subsequent expulsion from Spain at the end of the fifteenth century, the major Sephardi communities were re-established in the predominantly Arab countries bordering the Mediterranean and Persian gulf.
2. The term Ashkenazi applies to the Jews who following dispersal from Palestine by the Romans came to settle in Germany but, following widespread persecution, remigrated to Poland, the Ukraine and other Eastern European countries.

References

CARMI, T. (1987) *The Penguin Book of Hebrew Verse*. Harmondsworth: Penguin.
VITAL, D. (1975) *The Origins of Zionism*. Oxford University Press.

Further reading

BEN-YEHUDA, E. and WEINSTEIN, D. (eds) (1961) *Ben-Yehuda's Pocket English–Hebrew/Hebrew–English Dictionary*. New York: Washington Square Press.
BLANCH, H. (1988) 'The Israeli koine as an emergent national standard'. In Fishman, Ferguson and Das Gupta, op. cit., pp. 236–51.
BLAU, Y. (1976) *A Grammar of Biblical Hebrew*. Wiesbaden: Harrassowitz.
Centre for Information on Language Teaching Research (1984) *Modern Hebrew: Language and Culture* Guide 12. London: CILT.
CHOMSKY, W. (1957) *Hebrew – the Eternal Language*. Philadephia: Gitelson.
FELLMAN, J. (1974) 'The Academy of the Hebrew Language', *International Journal of the Sociology of Language* 1
FISHMAN, J. (1974) 'The sociology of language in Israel', *International Journal of the Sociology of Language* 1: 1–19
FISHMAN, J., FERGUSON, C. and DAS GUPTA, J. (eds) (1968) *Language Problems of Developing Nations*. New York: John Wiley.
ROSEN, H. B. (1977) *Contemporary Hebrew*. The Hague: Mouton.
SHOKEID, M. (1988) *Children of Circumstances: Israeli Emigrants in New York*. Cornell University.

Notes on the Contributors

SAFDER ALLADINA was born in Tanzania. His paternal grandparents went from Gujarat to what was then the German colony of Tanzania at the turn of the last century. His maternal grandparents were Kachchi speakers whose family was settled in Zanzibar from the early part of the last century. He has fifteen years of teaching experience in a variety of primary, secondary and adult institutions and worked as Director of the Berkshire Support Service for Intercultural Education before moving to his present post as Principal Lecturer at the Polytechnic of North London. There he has been responsible for developing the PGCE in Multilingual Primary Education, unique to teacher education institutions in Britain, which prepares teachers for multilingual inner city primary schools. In 1983 he won the ILEA Teacher Fellowship to the Centre for Multicultural Education at the University of London Institute of Education. His publications are in the area of South Asian languages and multicultural education. His research interests include patterns of language maintenance and shift among children of South Asian origin in Britain.

RONALD CHAN was born in Singapore in 1943. He was a pupil at St. Andrew's School, Singapore and took his degree at Singapore University in 1965. After some years as a teacher of English in Singapore, he entered the University of Reading (England) where he took an MA in Linguistics in 1970 and a Ph.D. in Linguistics in 1975. He has been a lecturer in the Department of English and Drama at Loughborough University since 1977. Among his publications are 'Formality in English', York Journal of Linguistics, vol. 6, 1976; and 'The Non-Uniqueness of Stylistic Descriptions' in the Nottingham Linguistic

Circular, 1981. He has abstracted for Language and Language Behaviour Abstracts since 1982. His current research interests are in the linguistic structures of both personal and fictional narrative, the language of dramatic discourse and cognitive approaches to symbolism in language.

MORGAN DALPHINIS was born in Saint Lucia and came to Britain at the age of 11. He did a first degree in Hausa and Linguistics as a preliminary to his doctorate on African influences on creole languages at the School of Oriental and African Studies, University of London. He has a PGCE in English as a Second Language and has taught in a variety of settings, including the Marcus Garvey and Kwame Nkrumah Black Supplementary Schools in London, the University of Maiduguri in Nigeria where he lectured in Hausa and linguistics, Norlington High School, London, where he taught French and English and Hackney College, London where he was Senior Lecturer in Multi-ethnic Education. Since 1986 he has worked as Languages Inspector for the Borough on Haringey. In addition to his work with Black supplementary schools he has been actively involved in community projects and adult education. He has presented many papers at international conferences, given many radio and TV interviews and lectured to teachers on Creole and African languages and cultures. His publications include *Caribbean and African Languages* (Karia, 1985) *For Those Who Will Come After* (Karia, 1985), *Hausa Game-Songs and Education* (Karia, 1990) and a collection of papers on *Superliterates and the Struggle for Multilingualism*, co-edited with Thomas Acton (Karia, 1990).

JAGDISH DAVE was born in India. He holds a BA and MA in Gujarati and Sanskrit from the University of Bombay and Gujarat University respectively, and a Ph.D. on 'A Comparative Study of Gujarati and Marathi Drama' from Saurashtra University. He taught Gujarati and Sanskrit at various colleges in India, first as a lecturer and then as professor, between 1950 and 1984, when he came to the UK. He is academic director of the Academy of Vedic Heritage in London where he is also editor-in-chief of academic publications and chief examiner. He is a fellow of the Gujarati Literary Academy and the Institute of Linguists, UK; a member of the executive committees of the South Asian Literature Society UK and the Gujarati Shikshan Sangh UK and a member of the drama, education and projects committees of the London Bharatiya Vidya Bhavan. He is a tutor for the Community Languages option of the University of London

Institute of Education's PGCE course and a consultant for the
INSET course on Multilingualism in Schools, also at the Institute.
His publications include a series of 6 books on learning Gujarati.

VIV EDWARDS was born in the Rhondda, South Wales. Experience of bilingualism within the family and the wider
community acted as a catalyst for her interest in language as a
whole and she went on to do first a BA and later a Ph.D. in
Linguistics at the University of Reading. She is currently lecturer
in Applied Linguistics at Birkbeck College, University of London. Her research interests are in oral culture and language in
education and publications include *The West Indian Language
Issue in British Schools* (Routledge & Kegan Paul, 1979), *Language in Multicultural Classrooms* (Batsford, 1983), *Language in
a Black Community* (Multilingual Matters, 1986) and *At Home
in School: Parent Participation in Primary Education* (with An-
gela Redfern, Routledge, 1988). She is a parent governor in a
primary school where the children speak some 32 different languages between them.

JYOTI HUSAIN was born in Panjab, India but was brought up
and educated in Britain. She is married to a Bangladeshi and,
after obtaining an MSc from King's College, University of London.
she went to Bangladesh where she travelled extensively, including
to Sylhet. She speaks Bengali fluently. Her personal experiences
and close associations with ethnic minorities, especially
Bangladeshis, led to a change in career. After a period of voluntary work, she went on to become a qualified teacher of English
as a second language for Adult and Further Education. She is
currently Deputy Head of Department for Access and Communications in the Islington Adult Education Institute, London.
She is also working for a Ph.D. on language policy in adult education. As part of this work, she has spoken at various
conferences. She has also acted as adviser to various professional
and academic bodies and been interviewed on television on this
subject.

JUDY KEINER was born in 1944, the daughter of Polish Jews
who escaped to Britain from Berlin in the nick of time. She grew
up in the Jewish East End of London, in a home where Yiddish
was an everyday language and Hebrew was the language of blessings and ceremonies. She is Senior Lecturer in Education at the
University of Reading Department of Educational Studies and
Management. Her commitment to Yiddish and Ashkenazi

Hebrew has been strengthened by the desire to teach both to her daughter, who was born in 1986.

FARHAT KHAN was born and educated in Rajasthan, India. She completed an MA and M.Phil in English at Aligrah University, India and taught English for ten years at the Women's Polytechnic which forms part of the same university. She came to England in 1975 on a British Council scholarship and did an MA in Applied Linguistics at the University of Lancaster. More recently she has completed a Ph.D. on the subject of variation in Indian English at the University of Reading. Her publications include 'Phonological Development in Urdu-speaking Children' (*International Review of Applied Linguistics*, XXII/4) and 'A Sociolinguistic Analysis of Consonant Cluster Deletion in Indian English' (in J. Cheshire (ed.) *English Around the World*, CUP, in press). Currently she is ESL co-ordinator for the Youth Training Scheme in the London Borough of Barking and Dagenham. She has also worked for a number of years as a part-time lecturer in ESL at Newham Community College, London.

VASANT MAHANDRU was born in Nairobi, Kenya in 1938 and was educated partly in Kenya and partly in India, where he also obtained a BA degree in North Indian languages and an MA in English. He went back to Kenya to teach first in a high school and then at Kenyatta University Teacher Training College. He came to England in 1974 and did an MA in Linguistics at the University of Reading. Since 1975 he has been teaching English as a second language in East London.

YOSHIKO NAMIE recently obtained her Ph.D. from the University of London on 'The Role of the University of London Colonial Examinations between 1900 and 1939, with special reference to Mauritius, Ceylon and the Gold Coast (1989).'

HUBISI NWENMELY was born in St. Lucia and came to Britain at the age of 9. She did her first degree in Sociology and General Management Studies at the North East London Polytechnic. Her abiding interest in language, which derives both from her own bilingualism and from her work as a Kwéyòl teacher led her to go on to do an MA course in Second Language Learning at Birkbeck College, University of London. For a number of years she has been involved in the teaching of Kwéyòl and Black Studies in adult education and she is a founder member of the London-based *Mouvan Kwéyòl*. She has worked in a variety of settings as researcher, outreach and community worker and is currently training officer for Waltham Forest Social Services. She is also active in community affairs and is on the management committee of the Hackney Black People's Organisation, the Saxon Youth Club, the Uhuru Project, Tower Hamlets Afro-Caribbean Association, the Zuriya Theatre/Education project and East London Black Women's Organisation.

GNANI PERINPANAYAGAM joined the staff of Trinity College, Ceylon after graduation from Madras Christian College, India, where he was a double gold medalist in English and an Indian Christian scholar. During his fifteen years at Trinity College, he did his Diploma in Education. He was then awarded a Fulbright Scholarship to do an MA at the University of Indiana, USA, and went on to do a Ph.D. at the University of New Mexico on Language Acquisition and Bilingualism among Navajo children. Since that time he has been Assistant Professor at Riyad University, Saudi Arabia; Senior Lecturer in Applied Linguistics in the School of Australian Linguistics; Principal Lecturer in Educational Psychology at an Advanced Teachers' College in Nigeria; and Senior Staff Development Officer in the World Bank Teacher Education Project in Papua New Guinea. Currently he is Educational Assessor in the London Borough of Ealing where he is also Co-ordinator for the Pilot Project on Bilingualism. His research interests are in the Socio-Psycholinguistics of learning and teaching languages and their assessment.

AMY THOMPSON was born in Hong Kong and is a native speaker of Chinese. She was educated in Britain and graduated from Durham University in Russian with French. She also has an MA in Second Language Learning and Teaching from Birkbeck College, University of London. She taught French and Music for two years before specializing in English as a Second Language. She has also taught for a number of years as a teacher in Chinese community schools. She is currently Head of the Language Support Service at her school. As a teacher she has worked closely with Filipino pupils and parents.

MAHENDRA K. VERMA was born in India in 1937 in a Hindi-English bilingual family. After studying Hindi and English at graduate and postgraduate levels, he lectured at various Indian universities. Later he studied Linguistics at the Central Institute of English and Foreign Languages in Hyderabad, where he wrote a dissertation on sentence and clause patterns in Hindi. He has been teaching Linguistics and Hindi since 1971 at the University of York. His field of interests include Multilingualism and Second Language Acquisition and Learning. His publications include: *Colloquial Hindi-Urdu* (University of York, 1980); *Papers in Bilingualism and Biliteracy* (NCMTT, 1985) and *Community Languages and Broadcasting* (NCMTT, 1987). In addition, he has written on issues in mother tongue maintenance; language attitudes; literacy and Hindi. He is a former chairman of the National Council for Mother Tongue Teaching and is currently a member of the steering committee of the National Congress for Languages in Education and the Committee for Linguistics in Education.

SHAHLA TAHERI WHITE was born and educated in Iran. She came to Britain at the age of 18 to train as a teacher and stayed in the country for five years before returning to Iran where she taught English and science in schools and also at a teacher training college. In 1973, she, her husband and other colleagues set up a dual language school in Iran which, along with other private institutions, was nationalized some 7 years later after the revolution. At that point, she came back to England to set up a language school and tutorial college in central London. She also set up a community school, also in central London. She worked with ILEA for three years at the Centre for Urban Educational Studies as an advisory teacher and tutor on the RSA Diploma course in the teaching of Community Languages. She is now chief assessor for the RSA course. Currently she works for Hertfordshire LEA as county advisory teacher for multicultural education, bilingualism and community languages.

LORNITA YUEN-FAN WONG was born and had her basic and university education in Hong Kong. After graduating from the Chinese University of Hong Kong, she was a secondary teacher in Hong Kong for three years. She then lived in England from 1983 to 1989. During this time in England, she taught Chinese at a Chinese community school at weekends and, in order to collect data for her Ph.D. from the University of London School of Education, did additional voluntary/part-time work as a Chinese teacher at two ILEA secondary schools, as a translator and as a community worker at a Chinese Centre in London. The articles which appear in this volume on the Hong Kong Chinese and Vietnamese speech communities are based mainly on the fieldwork for her Ph.D., which she successfully completed in 1988. She is now a Research Fellow in the Department of Applied Social Studies at the City Polytechnic of Hong Kong.

LAKSHMI DE ZOYSA was born in Sri Lanka and educated first in Sri Lanka and later in the USA, where she did an MA in Applied Linguistics at the University of Indiana, and in Britain where she did an MA in Language and Literature at the University of London Institute of Education. She worked first in Sri Lanka training teachers at the Government Specialist Teachers College. Part of her job was to set up the first language laboratory in Sri Lanka and she travelled extensively to study provision in this area overseas. She also worked as language consultant to the American Embassy, helping to develop Sinhala teaching for Peace Corps volunteers. She came to England in 1973, joining the Brent Language Service where she was responsible for the RSA Diploma in ESL. Later she set up the same RSA course in Harrow before going on to become Director of the language division of the ILEA Centre for Urban Educational Studies. Currently she is Head of the Language Service for Brent.

Community Addresses

Africa
Africa Centre, 38 King Street, London WC2
Hackney African Association, 4 Dalston Lane, London E8.

Afro-Caribbean
Grassroots Community Bookshop, 71 Golbourne Road, London W10
Headstart Bookshop, 25 West Green Road, London N15
Race Today Collective, 165 Railton Road, London SE24

Bengali
Bangladesh Educational and Cultural Centre, Highbury Hill, London N5
Bangladesh High Commission, 28 Queen's Gate, London SW7
Bangladesh Institute, 85 York Street, London W1
Bangladesh Welfare Association, 39 Fournier Street, London E1
Bangladesh Women's Group, Calshot Neighbourhood Centre, Calshot Street, London N1
Bangladesh Youth Approach, Community Centre, Duckett Street, London E1
Bangladesh Youth Movement for Equal Rights, 21/3 Henriquest Street, London E1
Bengali Cultural Association, Dryburgh Hall, Alderney Street, London SW1

Farsi
Iranian Community Association, 17 Ditchling Rise, Brighton, East Sussex
West London Iranian Association, Project Enterprise, 16 Askew Crescent, London W12.

Iranian Community Centre, 465 Green Lanes, London N4 1HE
Kanoon-e-Ketab (Persian Book Centre), 2a Kensington Church
Walk, London W8 9BL
Rustam West Ltd., 5 Wayside, Saint Paul's Cray Road, Chis-
lehurst BR7 6QQ (sponsors community school in Central
London)

Filipino
The Embassy of the Philippines, Consular Section, 1 Cumberland
House, Kensington Road, London W8.
The British Philippine Society, 7 Kingly Street, London W1R
5LF
Pahayagan (The Filipino Community Newspaper), 49 Connaught
Street, London W2 2BB
Commission for Filipino Migrant Workers, St. Francis of Assisi,
Pottery Lane, London W11 4NQ
Filipino Chaplaincy, 18 Gunnersbury Cresent, London W3 9AA

Gujarati
Gujarati Literary Academy, 'Cornerways', 2 Beechcroft Gardens,
Wembley, HA9 8EP
Academy of Vedic Heritage, 19 Spencer Road, Harrow
Wealdstone, HA3 7AN
South Asian Literature Society, 9 Chenies House, 43 Moscow
Road, London W2 4AH
Gujarati Shikshan Sangh (Association for the Teaching of
Gujarati), 50 June Avenue, Leicester
National Federation of Gujarati Associations, c/o 8–16 Coronet
Street, London N1 6HD

Hebrew
Israeli Embassy, 2 Palace Green, London W8.
Agudas Israel Organization, 97 Stamford Hill, London N16.
(Representative body for the largest group of fundamentalist
Jewish religious and communal organizations)
Board of Deputies of British Jews, Woburn House, Upper
Woburn Place, London WC1H (The representative body of
mainstream – but not fundamentalist – Jewish religious and cul-
tural organizations. Operates a general information service on
all aspects of Jewish communal life and culture in Britain)
Spiro Institute for the Study of Jewish History and Culture,
Westfield College, Kidderpore Avenue, London NW3 (Or-
ganizes a wide range of adult education courses, including
Modern Hebrew; also conducts research and organizes cultural
events and school level courses)

Zionist Federation of Great Britain and Northern Ireland, Manor
House, 80 East End Road, London N3. (General promotion
of educational and cultural activities related to Jewish life)

Hindi
Indian High Commission, India House, Aldwych WC2

Hong Kong Chinese
Hong Kong Government Office, 6 Grafton Street, London W1X
3LB
Chinese Information Centre Co-operative, First Floor, 16
Nicholas Street, Manchester M1 4EJ
Chinese Liaision Unit, (Patron: Council of Chinese Organis-
ations), c/o North West Chinese Association, Top Floor,
47 Faulkner Street, Manchester M1 4EE
The Chinese Community Centre, 44 Gerrard Street, London W1.
Camden Chinese Community Centre, 173 Arlington Road, Lon-
don NW1 7EY
Haringey Chinese Community Centre, 211 Langham Road, Lon-
don N15 3LH

Japanese
Japan Information Centre, 9 Grosvenor Square, London W1X
9LB
The Japan Society, Room 331, 162–168 Regent Street, London
W1X 9LB
Japan Foundation, 35 Dover Street, London W1

Kwéyòl
Dominican High Commission, 1 Collingham Gardens, London
W8
St. Lucia Association, 375A Hornsey Road, London N19 3HP
The Patwa/Kwéyòl Project, Tower Hamlets Adult Education In-
stitute, The Mile End Centre, English Street, Bow, London E3
Mouvman Kwéyòl, c/o The Education Shop, 75 Roman Road,
Bethnal Green, London E2.
Yaa Asantewa, 1 Chippenham Mews, London W9
Claudia Jones Organization, 103 Stoke Newington Road, London
N16
The Book Place, 13 Peckham High Street, Peckham, London
SE15

Panjabi
Sikh Cultural Society of Great Britain, 88 Mollinson Way, Edgeware, Middlesex.
The Sikh Missionary Society (UK), 27 Pier Road, Gravesend.

Sinhala
Sri Lanka High Commission, 13 Hyde Park Gardens, London W2
London Buddhist Vihara, 5 Heathfield Garden, Chiswick, London W4
Thames Buddhist Vihara, Dulverton Road, Selsdon, Surrey
Namel and Malini Arts, 302 High Road, Leyton, E10 5BW

Singapore and Malaysian Communities
Singapore High Commission, 2 Wilton Crescent, London SW1X 8ND
Malaysian High Commission, 45 Belgrave Square, London SW1X 8QT

Tamil
UK Tamil Refugees Organisation, 211 Katherine Road, London E6 1BU

Urdu
Urdu Markaz, 28 Sackville Street, London W1X 1DA
Academy of Urdu Studies, 104 Lexham Gardens, London W8 6LQ
The Education Division, Embassy of Pakistan, 35–36 Lowndes Square, London SW1X 9JN
Muslim Education Trust, 130 Stroud Green Road, London N4 3AZ
UK Islamic Mission, 202 North Gower Street, London NW1.

Vietnamese Chinese
Vietnamese Association of Services, Club Vietnam, 12 Adelaide Street, London WC2
Opening hours: Sunday afternoon only

Index